DEDICATED TO THE
HERO IN ALL OF US...

ISBN: 978-63140-998-1 First printing. June 2017. Printed in Korea.

COVER COLLAGE: An original illustration by Steven Chorney celebrates the top half-dozen comic book movies as ranked by this overview. 1st PAGE: Robert Downey Jr. as the invincible *Iron Man* (Marvel, 2008). ABOVE: The Dark Knight (Christian Bale) rescues Rachel (Katie Holmes) from deadly danger in *Batman Begins* (Warner Bros., 2005).

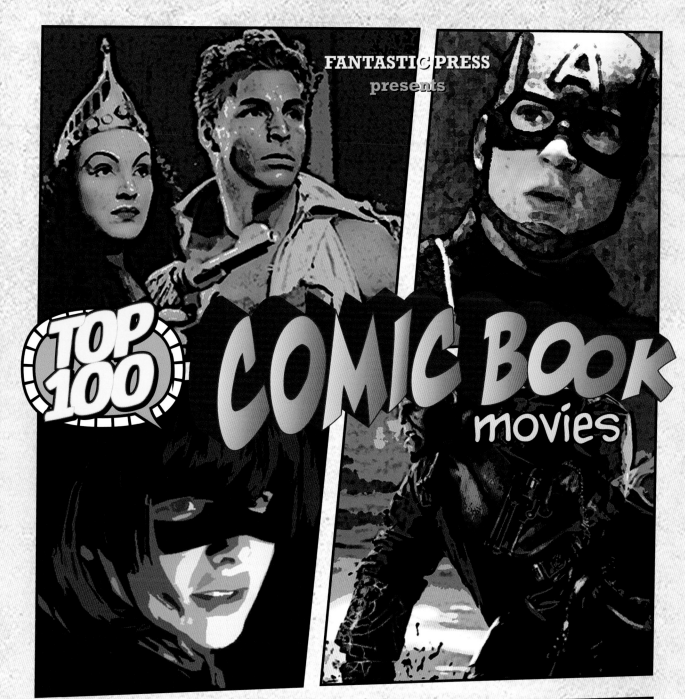

FANTASTIC PRESS
presents

TOP 100 COMIC BOOK movies

Written, Edited and Designed by
GARY GERANI

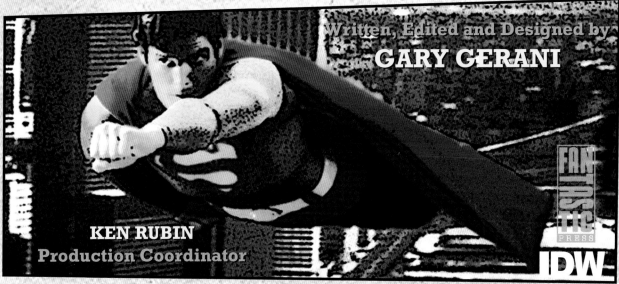

KEN RUBIN
Production Coordinator

FANTASTIC PRESS

IDW

POSTER/PHOTO CREDITS: Universal Studios (8-9, 10, 28, 30-32, 44, 45, 55, 68, 69, 81, 88, 93, 94-95, 138-140, 194-198, 201); Twentieth Century Fox (11, 22-23, 24-27, 42-43, 52, 64-65, 66-67, 73, 102-103, 131, 136-137, 150-151, 154-155, 162, 163, 172-173, 195, 197, 198) Columbia Pictures (12-15, 16, 37, 38, 46-48, 128-129, 160-161, 182-183, 194-198); Embassy (17); Warner Bros. (2, 3, 18-19, 29, 33-35, 36, 40-41, 66-67, 78-79, 100-101, 104-105, 108-111, 118-119, 123-125, 126-127, 130, 144-149, 152-153, 158-159, 184-185, 190-193, 194-198, 200, 201); New Regency (201); PolyGram/Gramercy (20); LionsGate Entertainment (21, 196, 197); King Features Syndicate (3, 28, 30-32, 45, 74-75, 116-117, 178-181); Paramount Pictures (4, 5, 39, 53, 58-59, 60-63, 87, 90-91, 194, 197, 198); Lonely Film Productions (54), New Line Cinema (56-57, 72, 82-84, 172, 194, 197, 201); Touchstone Pictures (70-71, 76-77, 198), Marvel (1, 3, 80, 85-86, 96-97, 98-99, 120-122, 134-135, 164-165, 166-169, 174-175, 176-177, 186-189, 198, 201), Summit Entertainment (89); First National (92); Relativity Studios (3, 106-107); Republic Pictures (112, 143, 195, 196, 198); Dredd Productions (113); Amicus Productions (114-115); KA Films (3, 132-133); Dimension Films (141-142, 197); Miramax Films (156); United Artists Films/Granada Films (157); PW Studios (163); Home Box Office (171), Sony Pictures Classics (195, 198)

PHOTO SOURCES: The Gary Gerani Photo and Poster collection, Photofest (Buddy Weiss), Jerry Ohlinger's Movie Material Store, Hollywood Movie Posters (Ronald V. Borst).

Table of Contents

LEFT: The sailor (Robin Williams) and his lady (Shelley Duvall) in *Popeye*. ABOVE, TOP: Durand-Durand's ultimate weapon from *Barbarella*. ABOVE, RIGHT: *Danger: Diabolik* (John Phillip Law).

INTRODUCTION
KENNETH JOHNSON

"Kenny, we've acquired the right to several Marvel Comics. I'm giving you the first choice of which you'd like to do." The person speaking was Frank Price, head of Universal TV, where I'd just had lovely success creating *The Bionic Woman* and spinning it off into a series apart from its parent *The Six Million Dollar Man*. I told Frank I was flattered, but not interested in doing any comic book series with spandex and primary colors. He implored me to think on it.

That night I was pondering how to politely say no. But I was in the midst of reading *Les Miserables* that my uber-literate wife Susie had given me. I had been deeply into the world of the fugitive Jean Valjean and his obsessed pursuer, Inspector Javert. And the idea occurred to take that cue from Victor Hugo, add a bit of Robert Louis Stevenson's *Dr. Jekyll and Mr. Hyde* and blend them into this ludicrous comic called *The Incredible Hulk* to create a series rooted in the classic Greek tragic tone of a hero undone by his own hubris. Frank loved the concept – and in return he agreed to let me make a four-hour miniseries I was eager to do based upon Sir Walter Scott's great romantic novel *Ivanhoe* set in the days of Robin Hood and King Richard.

We shook hands on the deal and in less than two weeks I had written the screenplay for *The Hulk* (initially I purposely omitted *Incredible*) which I'd produce and direct. It was vital to me from the beginning that it be a dark and seriously adult drama about a tortured man who'd brought down this horrible curse upon himself: he had liberated his enemy within. The series would be his search for a way "to control the raging spirit that dwells within him."

For the concept to work for me it had to take place in the real world, not some comic book universe. I wanted no alliterative names like Clark Kent, Lois Lane, etc. The great Stan Lee (who became my dear friend and compatriot), whose numerous creations have captured the imagination of millions over the years, was extremely generous in allowing me to change Bruce Banner to David Bruce Banner. I also pressed to change the color of Creature (whom I never called The Hulk – only tabloid journalist Jack McGee did that. And kudos to the late Jack Colvin for making his character work so well). I argued that the color of rage was not green. When flushed with anger people turn red. I lost that battle.

But I held my ground when Stan suggested that when the Creature had a fight with a bear it should be a robot bear. I convinced Stan that we were asking the audience to buy that Bill Bixby metamorphosed into Lou Ferrigno and that was a very big buy. This wasn't like the bionic shows, which lived in that alternate universe. Bless Stan's heart, he understood. And that real-world approach – brought to life by an exceptional crew, underscored by the sensitive and stirring music of Joe Harnell – made the pilot and resulting series a success.

The contributions of Bix and Jack were of course immeasurable, as were the performances of Susan Sullivan in the movie-pilot and, down the line, Mariette Hartley in our two-hour *Married* movie. Mariette was so good she wound up winning the Emmy for Best Actress in a Drama Series, and the film was released as a theatrical feature in Europe, as the pilot had been.

Looking back, it was a grand, amazing and humbling experience for me personally to have created a show that became so iconic, and that immortalized my line, "Don't make me angry…You wouldn't like me when I'm angry."

As for *Ivanhoe*, by the time I'd written the script and was ready to go Frank Price had left the studio. Universal said sorry, but the hand that had shaken mine on the deal was no longer around to write the check.

Ah, Hollywood.

Kenneth Johnson, 2017

OVERVIEW

GARY GERANI

Comics and the movies have a lot in common. Both employ sequential images to tell a story or drive home a message, often doing so with distinctive, memorable characters and quotable dialogue. Anything but subtle, comic books/strips were considered the perfect medium for exaggerated comedy, fantasy, and action melodrama… inexpensive fodder for kids who didn't have the patience or the attention span to read pulp novels. When these guilty pleasures were adapted into movies, the productions generally reflected this second-class status. For every *Skippy* or *Flash Gordon*, there were dozens of cheapjack adventure serials and low-budget "B" programs. Later, campy self-parody seemed the only way for this fanciful material to play as mainstream entertainment.

That all changed with the coming of the Baby Boomers, who fully embraced fantasy adventure in all entertainment media. The thrilling and imaginative movies of Steven Spielberg and George Lucas soon led to an acceptance of actual comic book properties as major motion pictures. Finally, in the 21st Century, the genre exploded beyond anyone's expectations. A fortuitous combination of savvy filmmakers and advanced special effects technology resulted in some of the most successful movies ever made, inspiring nothing less than a global phenomenon.

The comic book movie says a lot about who we are and the kind of world we're living in, all wrapped up in an exciting package of unapologetic imagination. After a shaky start, this oddest of all genres has more than earned its place in cinema history. And who knows? The best may be next to come...

Gary Gerani 2017

ABOUT THE BOOK
The 100 movies you're about to read about represent my choices for the cinema's most significant live-action comic book adaptations. Ranking is a subjective party game, of course. But all of the films showcased here are worth experiencing, from the popular classics to way-below-the-radar obscurities.

ABOUT THE AUTHOR
Gary Gerani is a screenwriter (*Pumpkinhead*), graphic novelist (*Bram Stoker's Death Ship*), children's product developer at Topps, film and TV historian (*Fantastic Television*), award-winning art director, photo editor, designer and publisher (the Fantastic Press trade paperback book series).

KEY TO UNDERSTANDING

 (100) 1.85 🎧 🎧

Clock: Running time
Monitor: Aspect ratio
Full headphone: Stereo soundtrack
Half headphone: Mono soundtrack

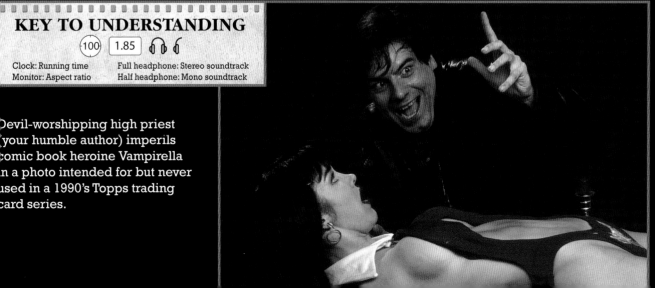

Devil-worshipping high priest (your humble author) imperils comic book heroine Vampirella in a photo intended for but never used in a 1990's Topps trading card series.

Unfunny sci-fi adventure is no feather in producer George Lucas' cap...

100 HOWARD THE DUCK 1986

(110) 1.85 🎧

Poster/photos: © 1986 Universal Studios/Marvel characters™

Trapped in a world he never made.

HOWARD THE DUCK

More adventure than humanly possible.

WHO MADE IT:

Universal Pictures/Lucasfilm (U.S.). Director: Willard Huyck. Producers: Ian Bryce, Gloria Katz, Robert Latham Brown, George Lucas. Writers: Willard Huyck, Gloria Katz, based on the comic book by Steve Gerber and Val Mayerik (Marvel). Cinematography (color): Richard H. Kline. Music: John Barry, Thomas Dolby. Starring Lea Thompson (Beverly Switzler), Tim Robbins (Phil Blumburtt), Jeffrey Jones (Dr. Walter Jenning), Chip Zien (Howard Duckowitz, voice), David Paymer (Larry), Paul Guilfoyle (Lt. Welker), Holly Robinson (K.C.).

WHAT IT'S ABOUT:

Hapless Howard from Duckworld is accidentally plucked from his universe and beamed to earth by a pair of well-meaning, eccentric physicists. After rescuing and befriending a pretty young rock star named Beverly, Howard connects with these scientists and is on the verge of being returned to his own planet when one of them is suddenly possessed by a malevolent life form. The plucky duck uses a neutron disintegrator to obliterate the beast, and, in the process, destroys the machine that brought both alien beings into our world to begin with. His hopes of returning home now dashed, a pragmatic Howard adjusts to life on Earth with his new friends.

WHY IT'S IMPORTANT:

Howard the Duck had been on producer George Lucas' radar since the late 1970s. As a comic book, Steve Gerber's oddball creation stood out among the more conventional mainstream superheroes of the day. Glib and irreverent, it offered a welcome, far-reaching sense of social satire, the character functioning in many ways like Marvel's web-footed equivalent of *Fritz the Cat*.

As a movie, *Howard the Duck* hedges its edgy bets and instead indulges in an explosive, special effects-laden comedy adventure. No longer a wry and pissed-off observer of society's moronic behavior, Howard is presented as a lovable nebbish just trying to get home after his accidental dimensional abduction. His relationship with sympathetic rock and roller Beverly Switzler (played fearlessly by Lea Thompson, who would fare much better in *Back to the Future* a few years later) is chaste enough for a family-friendly rating, although Howard's more personal needs are occasionally addressed (our hero's little condom usually gets a laugh).

Ultimately, everything comes down to an apocalyptic battle with a gross alien monster, also brought to Earth by the same infernal machine that grabbed Howard. With possessed scientists and super weapons part of the mix, this noisy climax plays like a nowhere-as-funny variation of the Ghostbusters' final stand against impossible odds.

Also key to the film's failure is the unsatisfying realization of Mr. Duckowitz himself. Although Lucas was the master of state-of-the-art special effects during this period, the combination of a stiff duck suit and Chip Zien's zany "in over his head" voice produced a Howard few viewers wanted to spend time with.

Howard famously makes a cameo appearance at the end of Marvel's 2014 *Guardians of the Galaxy*, suggesting that a future incarnation of the unstuck duck may yet transpire. This time more sophisticated CGI wizardry would obviously be employed under the guidance of a new generation of filmmakers who "get" Gerber's original vision and the Marvel tone in general. Unlike 1985's haplessly cute hero, Howard may yet emerge as a cynical observer of our troubled times, even while dealing with the inevitable cosmic threats audiences have come to demand from their comic book extravaganzas. And that would be just "ducky."

Howard (suit inhabited by Ed Gale and others), a self-fancied ladies' man, prepares for a night on the town. BELOW: The heroic duck takes flight with a most reluctant passenger (Tim Robbins as Phil).

Weapon-wielding Howard is eventually pressed into service as an extraterrestrial monster-buster.

Beverly Switzler (Lea Thompson) adds a fine feathered guitarist to her rock and roll band Cherry Bomb.

Unsuspecting Dr. Jenning (Jeffrey Jones) finds himself possessed by an evil alien with world-domination plans.

It's plucky duck vs. alien monstrosity!

Famed stop-motion animator Phil Tippet puts some finishing touches on Howard's third-act antagonist.

FIRST CONTACT. LAST STAND.

DANIEL CRAIG   HARRISON FORD   OLIVIA WILDE

COWBOYS & ALIENS

FROM THE DIRECTOR OF IRON MAN AND EXECUTIVE PRODUCER

IN THEATRES AND MAX
COMING SOON

WHO MADE IT:

Universal Pictures/DreamWorks SKG (U.S.). Director: Jon Favreau. Producers: Brian Grazer, Ron Howard, Alex Kurtzman, Roberto Oci, Scott Mitchell Rosenberg. Writers: Roberto Orci, Alex Kurtzman, Damon Lidelof, Mark Fergus, Hawk Ostby, based on the comic book by Scott Mitchell Rosenberg. Cinematography (color): Matthew Libatique. Music: Harry Gregson-Williams. Starring Daniel Craig (Jake Lonergan), Harrison Ford (Colonel Dolarhyde), Olivia Wilde (Ella Swenson), Sam Rockwell (Doc), Paul Dano (Percy Dolarhyde), Clancy Brown (Meacham), Keith Carradine (Sheriff John Taggart).

WHAT IT'S ABOUT:

In 1873 Arizona, a stranger with no memory, but with a mysterious shackle encircling one wrist, stumbles into the desert community of Absolution. There, he and no-nonsense town boss Colonel Dolarhyde form an uneasy alliance against a mutual enemy – alien marauders from the sky, who take many of the locals prisoner and threaten everyone in the territory with annihilation.

WHY IT'S IMPORTANT:

Cowboys & Aliens is more of a high concept packaged for Hollywood than an adaptation of a legitimate comic book, since the 2006 Platinum Studios graphic novel it's based on was created only after the original movie project went into turnaround. Regardless, what caught everyone's attention was the unusual mix of wild west heroics and outer space invasion, this combination more-or-less in keeping with audacious comic book sensibilities.

Not a dreadful movie, *Cowboys & Aliens* just isn't good enough to rise above its gimmick premise. Both male leads have star power and acquit themselves nicely, and director Favreau clearly knows how to stage effective action scenes. But while the mystery structure is serviceable (Craig's slowly lifting amnesia reveals how he received that weird gizmo on his arm, and what manner of enemy our unlikely heroes are up against), the emotional concerns of the characters are stretched pretty thin over 119 long minutes. Dark photography meant to evoke the period often seems gratuitous and unnecessarily dour. When they do arrive, the titular aliens are ambitious enough but repulsively familiar... although the notion that they're here to prospect for gold and lasso some two-footed livestock has ironic merit. Somewhat more interesting than the galloping "demons" themselves is their half-submerged space vessel, a mountainous tower that neatly blends in with the natural canyon formations around it.

Considered a significant critical and boxoffice failure given the talent involved (this was director Favreau's first project after *Iron Man*), *Cowboys & Aliens* has yet to develop a discernable cult following, although its odd flavors and watchable stars may eventually earn it one. After all, how many times have we seen both James Bond and Indiana Jones take on alien monsters?

98 MONKEYBONE 2001

 93 1.85

WHO MADE IT:

Twentieth Century Fox Film Corporation/1492 Productions (U.S.). Director: Henry Selick. Producers: Henry Selick, Mark Radcliffe, Michael Barnathan, Chris Columbus, Sam Hamm. Writer: Sam Hamm, based on the graphic novel by Kaja Blackley and Vanessa Chong (Mad Monkey Press). Cinematography (color): Andrew Dunn. Music: Ann Dudley. Starring Brendan Fraser (Stu Miley), Bridget Fonda (Dr. Julie McElroy), Chris Kattan (Organ Donor Stu), Whoopi Goldberg (Death), Rose McGowan (Miss Kitty), Giancarlo Esposito (Hypnos), John Turturro (Monkeybone, voice), Ted Rooney (Grim Reaper, voice), Dave Foley (Herb), Megan Mullally (Kimmy Miley), Lisa Kane (Medusa), Thomas Molloy (Arnold the Super Racer), Jon Bruno (Stephen King), Owen Masterson (Jack the Ripper), Shawnee Free Jones (Lizzie Borden), Doug Jones (Yeti), Ilia Volok (Rasputin), Edgar Allan Poe IV (Edgar Allan Poe).

WHAT IT'S ABOUT:

Stu Miley is a cartoonist who has created the comic strip character Monkeybone, a rascally simian prone to wisecracking and racy antics. Happy and in love with girlfriend Julie, Stu is suddenly struck down in a freak accident. His body lies comatose – Julie maintaining a constant bedside vigil – as his conscious spirit is transported to Down Town, a purgatory-like limbo existing between life and death. This place is a bizarre carnival landscape populated by mythical gods and creatures. Trapped, Stu must outwit Death herself in order to return to the world of the living before doctors pull the plug on his own body. Complicating these desperate escape plans is the troubling appearance of his alter-ego Monkeybone, who hatches a wild and wicked counterplot that could thwart his creator's efforts.

WHY IT'S IMPORTANT:

Hoping for a movie experience not unlike Tim Burton's *Beetlejuice* (with a detour into *Roger Rabbit* territory), the high-profile Hollywood producers of *Monkeybone* looked to a little-known published work for inspiration. Kaja Blackley's *Dark Town* is a self-consciously odd graphic novel with a compelling central idea. The protagonist is a man in a coma who must fight his way out of a mysterious limbo-universe before a loved one legally disengages his life support. As with Powell and Pressberger's classic *A Matter of Life and Death/Stairway to Heaven*, we wonder if all the arcane madness before us is real, or simply going on in the character's tortured mind.

Reworking *Dark Town* for lovable star Brandon Fraser meant changing the tone of the piece into a scary but fun fairy tale. Stu Miley (suggested by comedy writer/producer Stu Smiley?) is a broad smile away from original, married protagonist Jacques De Bergerac (another familiar name), and it's Jacques' wife, not a ditsy sister, who is looking to end his comatose life. Given this major change, elevating the Monkeybone character into Stu's horny, aggressive side gone amok makes some kind of psychological sense (in the original story, what the hero carries around in a red suitcase is his often-useful 'imagination,' not an untrustworthy, adversarial extraction of his id).

Although Fraser does everything he can to keep things interesting, he is no match for the avalanche of bizarre material that is hurled at the audience over the course of 93 minutes, punctuated by the irritating antics of a wisecracking monkey.

97

SHEENA 1984

117 2.35

She is an ancient prophecy fulfilled.
A golden God child possessed with a mystic gift.
A gift which grew in strength as she grew in years.
A gift about to be put to the ultimate test.
Innocence against evil.

S·H·E·E·N·A

She alone has the power to save paradise.

COLUMBIA PICTURES Presents A JOHN GUILLERMIN Film
SHEENA
TANYA ROBERTS · TED WASS · DONOVAN SCOTT
PASQUALINO DE SANTIS   YORAM BEN-AMI
DAVID NEWMAN and LORENZO SEMPLE, JR.
DAVID NEWMAN and LESLIE STEVENS   PAUL ARATOW
JOHN GUILLERMIN

WHO MADE IT:

Columbia Pictures Corporation (U.S.). Director: John Guillerman. Producers: Paul Aratow, Yoram Ben-Ami, Christian Ferry. Writers: Lorenzo Semple Jr., David Newman, based on the comic book by Will Eisner and S.M. Eiger (Fiction House). Cinematography (Metrocolor): Pasqualino De Santis. Music: Richard Hartley. Starring Tanya Roberts (Sheena), Ted Wass (Vic Casey), Donovan Scott (Fletcher), Elizabeth of Toro (Shaman), France Zobda (Countess Zanda), Trevor Thomas (Prince Otwani), Clifton Jones (King Jabalani), John Forgeham (Jorgensen), Errol John (Bolu).

WHAT IT'S ABOUT:

Raised in the African jungle after her scientist parents are killed in a cave-in, young Sheena grows into a beautiful and athletic woman blessed with extraordinary psychic powers that enable her to telepathically communicate with the wild animals in her midst and command their actions. Evil comes to Zambouli territory when ruthless Price Otwani of Tigora conspires with equally amoral Countess Zanda to murder King Jabalani and take control of the country. Visiting journalist Vic Casey stumbles onto the truth, along with a plot to blame Zambouli's Shaman for the crime, and becomes a hunted man himself. The imperious Jungle Queen leads both her Zambouli followers and a variety of local beasts to thwart Otwani's military forces. Along the way, she discovers first love, and eventually saves Vic's life with the mysterious healing powers of the land she so steadfastly protects.

WHY IT'S IMPORTANT:

Obviously inspired by *Tarzan*, but very much a groundbreaking comic book heroine in her own right, jungle queen Sheena was a feminist icon who just happened to be a pin-up sensation, or vice-versa. Her first live-action incarnation was a minor 1950s TV series starring the perfectly-cast Irish McCalla. But it wasn't until 1984 that Columbia Pictures unleashed a relatively big-budget movie adaptation, featuring former *Charlie's Angels* star Tanya Roberts as the scantily clad Protector of Paradise.

Producer Paul Aratow and director John Guillerman took a page or two from *Green Mansions* to redefine the character for '80s audiences, giving us less of a physical wildcat and more of a dignified goddess. She's Eve plunked in the middle of a war to wrest control of a modern African province, all the while defending local natives and a jungle full of animals whom she controls telepathically. An American TV journalist soon becomes her accidental ally and eventual lover.

Roberts gave her all for this part, mastering an African accent (which echoes the inflections of her adopted Shaman mother, nicely played by Elizabeth of Toro), and working out relentlessly until her sleek and amazingly sexy body took on more muscle. Sadly, most of Roberts' heartfelt readings play as melodramatic and earn unintentional laughs, although her pissed, no-nonsense tough chick commands ring true. Ted Wass is serviceable as nominal hero Vic Casey, while sultry France Zobda as Countess Zanda, Sheena's villainous opposite number, lives up to her self-proclaimed reputation as "the most wicked woman in Tigora."

On the plus side, *Sheena* offers some lush African photography and a plethora of wild animals trained to do interesting stunts... there is no CGI at work here, just real jungle creatures and very adept trainers.

Although the movie failed with viewers and critics big-time in '84, it managed to inspire a fervent cult following (not quite as big as another misfire, 1980's *Flash Gordon*, but sizeable). The groundbreaking degree of nudity offered in this PG-13 family offering may have something to do with it. Burdened or blessed with a star whose unique approach has almost single-handedly kept its memory alive, *Sheena* continues to amuse and entertain audiences, although not necessarily for the reasons originally intended by its makers.

FAR LEFT: Sheena (Tanya Roberts) demonstrates that chains are no obstacle to defeating militaristic invaders. LEFT: Youthful Sheena (Kathryn Gant) cuddles with a cold-blooded friend. BELOW: A chopper scatters defenseless Zamboulis. Can the Jungle Queen and visiting journalist Vic Casey (Ted Wass) thwart Prince Otwani's evil ambitions? They're certainly going to give it a shot, arming themselves with primitive weapons.

ABOVE: A tearful Sheena spends some heartfelt final moments with her dying Shaman mentor (Elisabeth of Toro). LEFT: Taking aim against the evil of Otwani!

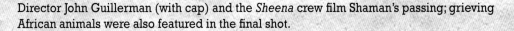

Director John Guillerman (with cap) and the *Sheena* crew film Shaman's passing; grieving African animals were also featured in the final shot.

Tanya Roberts hoped to achieve both feminist fame and pin-up glory with her emphatic performance as Sheena, freely offering nudity (of the Eve in Paradise variety) mixed with take-no-crap Girl Power defiance. RIGHT, MIDDLE: Already quite athletic, Roberts worked out extensively before filming began, with the character's signature 'summoning' gesture enhanced by her newly-broadened biceps. FAR RIGHT: Originally, Sheena's costume featured politically incorrect animal spots, suggesting a leopard pelt. Star Roberts posed in this version for press coverage shot in Disneyland about six months before actual production started.

WOMAN ON THE WILD SIDE

96

GHOST RIDER 2007

(114) | 2.35 |

LONG AGO

HE MADE A DEAL

TO SAVE SOMEONE

HE LOVED.

NICOLAS CAGE EVA MENDES

GHOST RIDER

MARVEL   FEBRUARY 16

WHO MADE IT:

Columbia Pictures Corporation/Crystal Sky Pictures/Relativity Media/Marvel Studios (U.S.). Director: Mark Steven Johnson. Producers: Avi Arad, Steven Paul, Michael De Luca, Gary Foster. Writers: Mark Steven Johnson, from the Marvel comic book. Cinematography (color): Russell Boyd. Music: Christopher Young. Starring Nicolas Cage (Johnny Blaze/Ghost Rider), Eva Mendes (Roxanne Simpson), Sam Elliott (Carter Slade/Caretaker), Wes Bentley (Blackheart/Legion), Donal Logue (Mack), Peter Fonda (Mephistopheles), Brett Cullen (Barton Blaze), Matt Long (young Johnny Blaze), Raquel Alessi (young Roxanne Simpson),David Roberts (Captain Jack Dolan), Rebel Wilson (Girl in alley).

WHAT IT'S ABOUT:

Young stunt cyclist Johnny Blaze is forced to make a fateful decision, selling his eternal soul to Mephistopheles in exchange for the life of his dying father. A number of years later, adult Blaze reconnects with his Satanic master, who offers to release the cyclist's still-captive soul if Johnny adopts a startling new identity: the fabled, fiery supernatural agent of vengeance/justice known as the Ghost Rider. This fearsome entity is charged with defeating Blackheart, Mephistopheles' ongoing nemesis and offspring, who intends to displace his father and create a new, even more terrible hell.

WHY IT'S IMPORTANT:

The universe of Marvel Comics encompasses all forms of imaginative fantasy, with supernatural subjects ranging from the Lovecraftian mythos of *Dr. Strange* to spins on more classical horror parables. *Ghost Rider* is a reasonably clever updating of *Faust*, offering up fearless cyclist Johnny Blaze (Nicolas Cage) as the self-damned protagonist, reborn as Mephistopheles' nocturnal, skull-headed, cycle riding, eternally flaming bounty hunter. In an interesting twist, young Johnny's morally worthy motivation (he makes the bargain to save his health-impaired father, played by Brett Cullen) earns him brownie points upstairs and enables adult Blaze to turn the tables on his infernal master. Rebellious Ghost Rider vows to use his hellish powers to spite the Devil whenever possible, rather than simply becoming his mindless enforcer or tool.

A decent, committed performance from Nicholas Cage and some startling special effects can't save *Ghost Rider* from ultimately skidding off track by the time a CGI-laden third act rolls around. But the movie's most ambitious set-piece is actually kind of fun, as an alarmed modern metropolis filled with rifle-toting police tries its best to contain a clearly superior supernatural adversary. At one point this awesome entity simply shoos away a hovering helicopter ("You're pissing me off!"). And while Johnny's romance with leading lady Roxanne Simpson (Eva Mendes) is for the most part forgettable, his bond with former Ghost Rider Carter Slade (Sam Elliot) holds our interest throughout, providing the movie's most compelling moments.

Although pretty much panned by critics, *Ghost Rider* made decent money, and it wasn't long (2012) before an even weaker sequel, *Ghost Rider: Spirit of Vengeance*, roared into movie theaters, again with Cage playing Johnny Blaze. The character has since returned to the official Marvel movie fold, awaiting an eventual revival.

95 SWAMP THING 1982

(91) 1.85

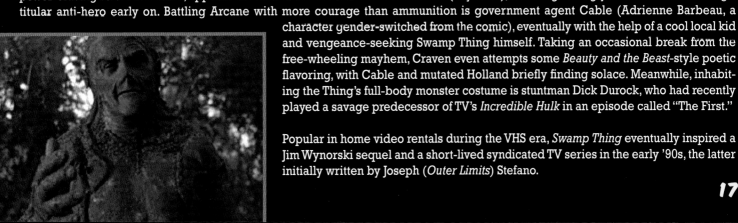

SCIENCE TRANSFORMED HIM INTO A MONSTER.
LOVE CHANGED HIM EVEN MORE!

SWAMP THING
THE COMIC BOOK LEGEND LIVES!

"SWAMP THING" A MELNIKER-USLAN Production of a WES CRAVEN Film **LOUIS JOURDAN** **ADRIENNE BARBEAU** Written and Directed by WES CRAVEN
Based upon characters appearing in magazines published by DC Comics, Inc. Produced by BENJAMIN MELNIKER and MICHAEL E. USLAN

WHO MADE IT:

Embassy Pictures/Swampfilms (U.S.). Director: Wes Craven. Producers: Michael Uslan, Benjamin Melniker. Writer: Wes Craven, based on the comic book by Len Wein and Bernie Wrightson (DC). Cinematography (Technicolor): Robbie Greenberg. Music: Henry Manfredini. Starring Ray Wise (Dr. Alec Holland), Adrienne Barbeau (Alice Cable), Louis Jourdan (Dr. Anton Arcane), Dick Durock (Swamp Thing), David Hess (Ferret), Nicholas Worth (Bruno), Don Knight (Harry Ritter), Al Ruban (Charlie), Ben Bates (Arcane Monster), Nannette Brown (Dr. Linda Holland), Reggie Batts (Jude).

WHAT IT'S ABOUT:

On the verge of a breakthrough in his quest to wipe out world hunger, altruistic botanist Dr. Alec Holland is placed under the protection of special government agent Alice Cable. This doesn't stop crazed outlaw scientist Anton Arcane from attacking Holland's jungle lab in an effort to steal the man's research for his own nefarious ends. An unforeseen accident during the heist transforms Holland into the Swamp Thing, an enormous plant-like creature that fights

back against Arcane's henchmen to save the imperiled Cable. After a series of skirmishes, the monster and the agent are captured, but only temporarily. Arcane's mad plans reach fruition when he uses Holland's serum on himself, providing the Swamp Thing with a worthy, decidedly nonhuman adversary.

WHY IT'S IMPORTANT:

Swamp Thing and Marvel's similarly-themed *Man-Thing* both appeared in 1971, answering the need for a Bigfoot-style swamp monster in comic book form. With a low budget and even lower box office expectations, famed horror director Wes Craven took a whack at DC's shambling monstrosity, ultimately delivering one of the strangest movies ever made.

Blurring the line between gleefully sadistic exploitation thriller and grotesque self-parody, *Swamp Thing* thrusts its fearless cast through a funky scenario of mutated monsters and ruthless criminals. Out of his element, erudite Louis Jourdan relishes every sick line as villainous, power-craving scientist Arcane, opposite number to the virtuous Dr. Alec Holland (Ray Wise), who is agonizingly transformed into *Thing*'s titular anti-hero early on. Battling Arcane with more courage than ammunition is government agent Cable (Adrienne Barbeau, a character gender-switched from the comic), eventually with the help of a cool local kid and vengeance-seeking Swamp Thing himself. Taking an occasional break from the free-wheeling mayhem, Craven even attempts some *Beauty and the Beast*-style poetic flavoring, with Cable and mutated Holland briefly finding solace. Meanwhile, inhabiting the Thing's full-body monster costume is stuntman Dick Durock, who had recently played a savage predecessor of TV's *Incredible Hulk* in an episode called "The First."

Popular in home video rentals during the VHS era, *Swamp Thing* eventually inspired a Jim Wynorski sequel and a short-lived syndicated TV series in the early '90s, the latter initially written by Joseph (*Outer Limits*) Stefano.

17

Campy, childlike approach to the high-flying heroine fails to soar...

SUPERGIRL 1984

105   2.35   🎧

FROM THE PRODUCERS OF THE SUPERMAN MOVIES...

Supergirl

Her first great adventure.

ALEXANDER SALKIND PRESENTS
FAYE DUNAWAY · HELEN SLATER
"SUPERGIRL"™ HART BOCHNER · PETER COOK · MIA FARROW · MARC McCLURE · BRENDA VACCARO
and PETER O'TOOLE as ZALTAR Music by JERRY GOLDSMITH Screenplay by DAVID ODELL Executive Producer ILYA SALKIND
Produced by TIMOTHY BURRILL Directed by JEANNOT SZWARC AN ALEXANDER and ILYA SALKIND PRODUCTION

WHO MADE IT:

TriStar Pictures/Warner Bros/Cantharus Productions (U.S./U.K.). Director: Jeannot Szwarc. Producers: Timothy Burrill, Ilya Salkind. Writer: David Odell, based on the comic book character by Otto Binder and Al Plastino (DC). Cinematography (color): Alan Hume. Music: Jerry Goldsmith. Starring Helen Slater (Kara Zor-El/Linda Lee/Supergirl), Faye Dunaway (Selena), Peter O'Toole (Zaltar), Hart Bochner (Ethan), Mia Farrow (Alura In-Ze), Brenda Vaccaro (Bianca), Peter Cook (Nigel), Simon Ward (Zor-El), Marc McClure (Jimmy Olsen), Maureen Teefy (Lucy Lane), David Healy (Mr. Danvers), Matt Frewer (Eddie).

WHAT IT'S ABOUT:

In the inner space world of Argo City, young Kara loses a precious power source while playing a child's game with her eccentric mentor, Zaltar. The city will waste away unless the Omegahedron is retrieved, so she journeys through a binary chute and enters our universe as Supergirl, a costumed, super-powered female with the same remarkable attributes as her famous cousin, Superman. While blending into our world as teenage schoolgirl Linda Lee, Kara searches the skies by night for the Omegahedron, which has fallen into the eager hands of a poverty-stricken witch named Selena. Seeking world domination and playing with magic far beyond her understanding, Selena conjures cosmic trouble for Supergirl, including an unexpected trip into the Phantom Zone and a dragon-like monster.

WHY IT'S IMPORTANT:

After the success of three *Superman* movies, the Salkinds decided to take a crack at their hero's pretty blonde female cousin, a lesser-known DC character who shared much of the same iconic mythology. Supergirl was not only the distaff Superman, an endearing straight arrow with a passion to help others, she was a teenager for a good deal of her comic book career, offering a fresh demographic to exploit. In a move that seems unfortunate now, the resulting film enthusiastically embraced classic fairy tale flavoring instead of high adventure, with elements of *Snow White* and the *Wizard of Oz* informing both the narrative and the cinematic style.

As dimension-traveling Kara of Argo City, Helen Slater provides enough fresh-faced likeability to keep us interested, but only to a point. Embracing the dated *Batman* TV show's style of self-parody, wicked witch nemesis Selena (Faye Dunaway, fresh from similar chores as Joan Crawford in *Mommie Dearest*) is portrayed as a camp diva suddenly in command of great power. With script adjustments all through production, the storyline seems both fractured and too on-the-nose at the same time. Special effects are at best okay (Supergirl's nocturnal duel with an invisible dragon has its moments), and Jerry Goldsmith's magnificent music score should be counted as a plus, although it often reminds us of how much better it is than the movie itself.

Supergirl bombed with audiences and critics, swiftly ending plans for a *Romeo and Juliet*-like sequel set on another planet, which was part of a hoped-for trilogy. But Kara Zor-El rebounded on the small screen some thirty years later, with savvy TV producers understanding the correct dramatic/fantastical context for this "nice girl" heroine, and young star Melissa Benoist nailing the part... with heart.

Tidbit: Helen Slater went on to play Supergirl's mom in *Smallville*, and her foster mom in Benoist's series.

RIGHT: Kara (Helen Slater) leaves Argo City to retrieve the life-sustaining Omegahedron. BELOW: As Supergirl, she takes on a runaway tractor that threatens Midvale locals.

RIGHT: Kara as schoolgirl Linda Lee Danvers.

ABOVE: Supergirl confronts wicked witch Selena (Faye Dunaway) and her sidekick Bianca (Brenda Vaccaro).

RIGHT: Kara and Zaltar (Peter O'Toole) attempt to escape the Phantom Zone.

Originally, the Supergirl uniform was re-designed to accommodate a Kryptonian headband. Although a more traditional costume was ultimately used, this new look wound up in DC's comics for a while.

So-so futureshock actioner made cartoonish by overstuffed star...

93

BARB WIRE 1996

98 1.85

Poster/photos: © 1996 PolyGram/Gramercy Pictures

WHO MADE IT:

Polygram Filmed Entertainment/Propaganda Films/Dark Horse Entertainment (U.S.). Director: David Hogan. Producers: Todd Moyer, Mike Richardson, Brad Wyman, Peter Heller, Ray Manzella. Writers: Chuck Pfarrer, Ilene Chaiken, based on the Dark Horse comic created by Chris Warner. Cinematography (color): Rick Bota. Music: Michel Colombier. Starring Pamela Anderson Lee (Barb Wire), Temuera Morrison (Axel Hood), Victoria Rowell (Dr. "Cora D" Devonshire), Steve Railsback (Colonel Pryzer), Xander Berkeley (Chief of Police Willis), Jack Noseworthy (Charlie Kopetski), Udo Kier (Curly), Andre Rosey Brown (Big Fatso), Clint Howard (Schmitz), Michael Russo (Santos), Nicholas Worth (Ruben Tentenbaum).

WHAT IT'S ABOUT:

The year is 2017. A sexy nightclub owner named Barb Wire moonlights as a mercenary in Steel Harbor, one of the last free zones in the now fascist United States. When scientist Cora Devonshire wanders into her place, Barb gets roped into a top-secret government plot involving biological weapons, particularly Red Ribbon, a laboratory-manufactured disease derived from the AIDS virus. Soon she is reunited with her old flame Axel Hood, who is now Cora's husband and a guerrilla fighter. But can he be trusted? And how long can even an independent spirit like Barb Wire endure the violence of factions in conflict without taking sides?

WHY IT'S IMPORTANT:

Based on a comic book that seemed designed for a movie sale, Dark Horse's *Barb Wire* offers up blonde bombshell Pamela Anderson as a cynical, super-cool mercenary who runs a nightclub in a near-future totalitarian America. Although the film's visual style is pure *Blade Runner*, the plot is obviously *Casablanca* revisited, with identity-concealing lenses replacing letters of transit and ruthless Washington D.C. fascists standing in for Nazi officers. Unfortunately, this parallel plays less as homage and more like a desperate ploy to kick some interest into predictable material.

Female superheroes derived from comics have had a checkered history on the big screen. Trying to reverse the failure trend, *Barb Wire* was a relatively ambitious project boasting a well-known TV personality, which must have seemed a coup during production. But Pamela Anderson became something of a public self-parody along the way, with the ever-changing size of her bosom getting more press than any worthwhile creative accomplishments. Playing an exaggerated femme fatale to begin with, Anderson's Barb emerges as an uneasy combination of ass-kicking cartoon feminist and iconic bimbo... Jessica Rabbit with a devastating right cross. The critics weren't kind. And audiences generally stayed away, viewing the entire endeavor as something of a bad joke.

On the positive side, David Hogan's movie offers an impressive visual landscape, catching both the decay of a once-great society gone to hell and the cool excitement of potentially dangerous nightlife. Stuntwork is also first-rate, with our heroine's former flame Axel Hood (Temuera Morrison) acquitting himself impressively as a second-tier action hero. But with a cold-as-ice main character played by a limited actress in a hand-me-down scenario gussied up with futuristic trappings, *Barb Wire* cannot help but seem wanting. No sequels to this particular take were announced, although a reboot with 21st Century sensibilities has been bandied about in recent years.

92

THE PUNISHER 2004

(124) [2.35]

Poster/photos © 2004 Lions Gate Entertainment/Marvel characters ™

WHO MADE IT:

Lions Gate Films/Marvel Enterprises (U.S.). Director: Jonathan Hensleigh. Producers: Avi Arad, Gale Anne Hurd. Writers: Jonathan Hensleigh, Michael France, from the Marvel comic book by Gerry Conway, Ross Andru, John Romita Jr. Cinematography (color): Conrad W. Hall. Music: Carlo Siliotto. Starring Thomas Jane (Frank Castle/The Punisher), John Travolta (Howard Saint), Samantha Mathis (Maria Elizabeth Castle), Will Patton (Quentin Glass), Roy Scheider (Frank Castle Sr.), Laura Harring (Livia Saint), Ben Foster (Spacker Dave), Rebecca Romjin (Joan).

WHAT IT'S ABOUT:

FBI agent Frank Castle is a man tragically reborn after criminals murder his family, including his wife and son. Gravely injured in the attack, he is believed to be dead by Howard Saint, the crime lord who ordered the hit. Following his recovery, Castle vows retribution in an exotic, unexpected manner. He transforms himself into a heavily armed vigilante known as the Punisher and will stop at nothing to exact revenge on Saint and dismantle his underworld empire.

WHY IT'S IMPORTANT:

Marvel's badass *The Punisher* has been re-booted cinematically three times in the last few decades. 1989 brought us an Australian-American program starring Dolph Lundgren, and a far more faithful adaptation starring Ray Stevenson hit screens in 2008. Neither was an especially well-made movie.

This 2004 version isn't much better, but it does have a few sharp things going for it: credible performances from John Travolta, Roy Scheider, Ben Foster and Samantha Mathis, evocative photography by Conrad W. Hall, and some genuinely suspenseful sequences Hitchcock might have admired (e.g., hiding from vicious bad guys as they torment a captured ally). Buff lead Thomas Jane, previously seen in *The Crow: City of Angels*, has a certain grim charisma as FBI agent-turned-vigilante Frank Castle. We pretty much believe his happy marriage/cool dad status in those pleasant early scenes, and the brutal massacre of his entire family during an outdoor celebration – an act of mob retaliation – is suitably shocking.

Still, *The Punisher* as envisioned by Marvel works because Castle inhabits a stylized and exaggerated comic book universe. In the bright, revealing sunshine of everyday Florida, the movie's ongoing acts of noir violence often play as ugly and sadistic. It's tough making a genuine hero out of someone so coldly committed, and attempts to humanize Frank by giving him an oddball surrogate family are only partially successful. Actress Rebecca Romijn, who played the blue-skinned mutant Mystique in the original *X-Men* trilogy, is sexily sympathetic as low-rent waitress Joan, while fellow misfits Spacker Dave (Foster) and Bumpo (John Pinette) provide welcome moments of amusement and pathos. The final showdown between Castle and main villain Howard Saint (Travolta) is spectacular, but brutal retribution seems to leave a bad taste in everyone's mouth... including the Punisher, who nearly commits suicide after avenging the death of his loved ones.

Happily, three failed movie launches later, Marvel's brooding dispenser of beyond-the-law justice seems to have found his niche on the small screen, as a key supporting player in the *Daredevil* series (2015 -?).

APRIL 16, 2004
www.punisherthemovie.com

MARVEL

ARTISAN

Ambitious, fanciful take on a cool idea compromised by contrivance...

91 THE LEAGUE OF EXTRAORDINARY GENTLEMEN 2003 (110) 2.35

Poster/photos: © 2003 Twentieth Century Fox

WHO MADE IT:

Twentieth Century Fox Film Corporation/Angry Films (U.S./U.K./Germany/Czech Republic). Director: Stephen Norrington. Producers: Trevor Albert, Mark Gordon, Don Murphy, Sean Connery, Rick Benattar, Michael Nelson. Writer: James Dale Robinson, based on the graphic novel by Alan Moore and Kevin O'Neill. Cinematographer (color): Dan Laustsen. Music: Trevor Jones. Starring Sean Connery (Allan Quatermain), Naseeruddin Shah (Captain Nemo), Peta Wilson (Mina Harker), Tony Curran (Rodney Skinner), Stuart Townsend (Dorian Gray), Shane West (Tom Sawyer), Jason Flemyng (Dr. Jekyll/Mr. Hyde), Richard Roxburgh (Prof. Moriarty alias Fantom/M), Max Ryan (Dante), David Hemmings (Nigel), Tom Goodman-Hill (Sanderson Reed), Terry O'Neill (Ishmael).

WHAT IT'S ABOUT:

In Victorian England, a team of extraordinary figures is enlisted by a mysterious caller to stop a villain intent on turning the nations of the world against one another. These heroes are led by Allan Quatermain and comprise some of the greatest figures from adventure literature: Captain Nemo, Dracula vampiress Mina Harker, invisible man Rodney Skinner, American secret service agent Sawyer, Dorian Gray, and Dr. Jekyll/Mr. Hyde. Working together, this peculiar assortment of titans must combine their special gifts to thwart a mysterious villain and save humanity from certain destruction.

WHY IT'S IMPORTANT:

The comic book that inspired this film was literally conceived as a Victorian version of the *Justice League*, although Marvel's *Avengers* may be a more appropriate parallel, since this League has its own rampaging Hulk. The conceit here was to create a period universe in which all of these significant historical figures could share an equally larger-than-life adventure. The very things that make these heroes "extraordinary" and timeless would provide ongoing interest on many levels, and a super-adversary worthy of their exotic skills would complete the tangy formula.

Fox's movie incarnation added American agent Tom Sawyer (Shane West) to the list of reimagined luminaries, along with Dorian Gray (Stuart Townsend) and his infamous picture. But the story rightfully belongs to an aging, still formidable Allan Quatermain (Sean Connery), fighting the specter of death like a tiger on his last hunt as he leads a curious assortment of allies into one harrowing set-piece after another. Smartly, each League member is given a few good scenes that spotlight their specialty: Mina Harker (Peta Wilson) morphs from beautiful scientist to vampiric she-witch without losing sexual allure – although checking her lips for blood stains by staring into a pocket mirror plays like a misstep. The device of Dr. Jekyll engaging in an ongoing moral debate with brutish alter-ego Mr. Hyde (both Jason Flemyng) has been seen in movies before and since, but is executed fairly well here.

While the novelty of the premise and some impressive sets and production design hold our attention (the Nautilus sailing through a Venice canal is nothing short of breathtaking), *League* eventually sinks from underdeveloped characterizations, an overabundance of fanciful gimmickry, and a noisy, overstuffed third act. Not surprisingly, the success of Marvel's *Avengers* movie series has prompted 20th Century Fox to revisit this similar-enough property, with a reboot currently in development.

Tidbit: Sean Connery, rather unwisely in retrospect, turned down the role of Gandalf in *Lord of the Rings* to appear in this movie.

LEFT: Vampiric Mina Harker (Peta Wilson) flaps into the fray. ABOVE: Three extraordinary gentlemen (Naseeruddin Shah's Nemo, Stuart Townsend's Gray, and Sean Connery's Quatermain) under sudden attack.

ABOVE, LEFT: Captain Nemo's super-sleek Nautilus. ABOVE, RIGHT: The hulking Mr.Hyde (Jason Flemyng). RIGHT: Fatherly Quartermain bonds with young American agent Tom Sawyer (Shane West). LEFT: Nemo takes on a ruthless enemy.

Miniature sets were constructed for the scenes in Venice, a clever combination of physical props and CG magic.

90

PRINCE VALIANT 1954

100 | 2.35

Poster/photos © 1954 Twentieth Century Fox

YOU SEE IT WITHOUT GLASSES IN
CINEMASCOPE

20th CENTURY-FOX presents

Prince Valiant

Technicolor

STARRING

JAMES | JANET | ROBERT | DEBRA | STERLING
MASON · LEIGH · WAGNER · PAGET · HAYDEN

VICTOR McLAGLEN   DONALD CRISP   BRIAN AHERNE   BARRY JONES

MARY PHILIPS   HOWARD WENDELL   TOM CONWAY

PRODUCED BY   DIRECTED BY   SCREEN PLAY BY   Based on King Features Syndicate's
ROBERT L. JACKS   HENRY HATHAWAY   DUDLEY NICHOLS   "Prince Valiant" by Harold Foster

WHO MADE IT:

Twentieth Century Fox Film Corporation (U.S.). Director: Henry Hathaway. Producer: Robert L. Jacks. Writer: Dudley Nichols, based on the comic strip by Hal Foster (King Features). Cinematography (Technicolor): Lucien Ballard. Music: Franz Waxman. Starring James Mason (Sir Brack), Janet Leigh (Princess Aleta), Robert Wagner (Prince Valiant), Sterling Hayden (Sir Gawain), Victor McLaglen (Boltar). Donald Crisp (King Aguar), Brian Aherne (King Arthur), Barry Jones (King Luke), Tom Conway (Sir Kay), Don Megowan (Sir Lancelot), Richard Webb (Sir Galahad), Primo Carnera (Sligon).

WHAT IT'S ABOUT:

After the evil King Sligon exiles his family from Scandia, Prince Valiant vows to become a member of King Arthur's Knights of the Round Table in order to return his father to the throne. As he travels to Camelot, Valiant comes upon the Black Knight, a villain conspiring with Sligon to destroy King Arthur. Under the eye of Sligon's old friend, Sir Gawain, young Valiant trains to be a warrior worthy of the royal court, falls for the beautiful princess Aleta and eventually unmasks the Black Knight.

WHY IT'S IMPORTANT:

Created in 1937 by *Tarzan* comic strip illustrator Hal Foster, *Prince Valiant* was one of the most beautiful examples of the form ever published. Novel in format, the strip dispensed with traditional ballooned dialogue within each panel, employing dense captions below magnificently rendered vistas instead. Valiant himself is a fictional swashbuckler of royal lineage, deftly worked into the fabric of Arthurian legend.

Looking for properties in 1953 that complemented their newly-revealed CinemaScope process, 20th Century-Fox seized on Foster's visually-arresting comic strip. It didn't hurt that MGM had recently scored a triumph with *Ivanhoe*, making noble knights and their maidens fair viable at the boxoffice again.

Bravely sporting Prince Valiant's signature 'page boy' hairstyle, easy, earthy Robert Wagner does his Tony Curtis-like best to appear appropriate as a heroic knight-in-the-making. He's ably supported by villainous James Mason (top-billed here, and seen in *A Star is Born* the same year), gruff ally Sterling Hayden, love interest Janet Leigh, and a cast of game supporting character actors. The plot wraps itself around Valiant's quest to return his Viking father to a rightful throne, not venturing very far from conventional Arthurian adventures presented on the screen. Don't expect any of the outsized sea monsters or Middle Ages-like torture chambers featured prominently in Foster's strip.

Entertaining as Hollywood camp from a bygone era, *Prince Valiant* benefits from excellent location work and some truly dazzling stunts (our hero careening into a curtain and concealing himself within it being a standout). The jousting sequences are also first-rate, making excellent use of early, very wide CinemaScope.

Tidbit: Janet Leigh's English stand-in was none other than teen-aged Shirley Eaton, who would achieve international fame ten years later as Pussy Galore in *Goldfinger*.

Tidbit II: Tall and barrel-chested Don Megowan, cast here as a robust Sir Lancelot, played the title role in *The Creature Walks Among Us* (1956) under a latex monster mask.

ABOVE: Prince Valiant (Robert Wagner) makes his dramatic entrance, diving into the sea with Viking panache. RIGHT: Sir Brack (James Mason) commands the scene even as recovering Valiant listens intently. 20th Century-Fox was smart enough to cast A-list leads along with fine character actors and a pair of dazzling damsels (Debra Paget, Janet Leigh).

BELOW, LEFT: The jousting sequences were highlights of *Prince Valiant*.

Coming on quite strong as Valiant's best friend Sir Gawain is Sterling Hayden (right), a long way from *The Asphalt Jungle*. Richard Webb also appears as Sir Galahad, a role he previously played in *A Connecticut Yankee in King Arthur's Court* (1948).

LEFT: Voluptuous Debra Paget became a staple of Fox period epics; the same year she starred in *Princess of the Nile*, opposite Jeffrey Hunter.

Robert Wagner and Janet Leigh had fun making this film, which was, at the time, the most ambitious adaptation of a comic strip ever made.

THE ONCE AND FUTURE VIKING

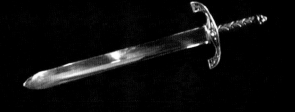

Maiden fair Janet Leigh and virtuous knight Robert Wagner are the attractive young leads of *Prince Valiant*, one of several widescreen period epics produced in the early '50s to lure viewers away from television. A bearded James Mason is also featured as the villainous Black Knight, with real-life Scandinavian Sterling Hayden lending support as Valiant's trusted ally. Wagner endured much friendly mockery over the page boy hairstyle, and seemed ill-at-ease with period dialogue and knightly garb.

2 AMAZING THRILL-THRONGED CHAPTERS

BUCK ROGERS

LARRY CRABBE

Constance MOORE · Wheeler OAKMAN · Jackie MORAN · Philson AHN · Henry BRANDON · Jack MULHALL

WHO MADE IT:

Universal Pictures (U.S.). 12-chapter serial. Directors: Ford Beebe, Saul A. Goodkind. Producer: Barney A. Sarecky. Writers: Norman Hall, Ray Trampe, based on the comic strip created by Philip Francis Nolan. Cinematography (b/w): Jerome Ash. Music: Stock. Starring Buster Crabbe (Buck Rogers), Constance Moore (Wilma Deering), Jackie Moran (George 'Buddy' Wade), Jack Mulhall (Capt. Rankin), Anthony Warde (Killer Kane), C. Montague Shaw (Prof. Huer), Guy Usher (Aldar), Henry Brandon (Capt. Laska).

WHAT IT'S ABOUT:

Captain Buck Rogers, sidekick Buddy Wade, and Buck's sweetheart, Wilma Deering, are piloting an experimental airship when bad weather sends them crashing into the Arctic wastes. A newly developed drug called Nirvano keeps this crew in suspended animation until help arrives; however, it is a full five centuries before Dr. Huer's scientists find them. Operating out of a hidden mountain base, the good doctor is an idealist at odds with fearsome Killer Kane, a criminal chieftain. Buck and his pals join forces with Huer and attempt to find allies on Saturn, unaware that the ringed planet has already fallen to Kane's eager minions.

WHY IT'S IMPORTANT:

After two successful *Flash Gordon* serials, Universal turned to the original comic strip ace of space for a follow-up vehicle, even casting *Flash* star Buster Crabbe in the title role. *Buck Rogers* was a time travel story as much as a galactic adventure, with the hero pulling a Rip Van Winkle in Chapter One, emerging from suspended animation into a future world where only a dedicated band of resourceful rebels challenges the iron-fisted authority of a despot. It's pretty obvious that writer-director George Lucas borrowed key aspects of *Buck*'s storyline for *Star Wars* (a debt he has acknowledged), along with the triangular crawl that sets up the story at the beginning of every chapter.

Unfortunately, *Buck Rogers* lacks the flamboyant flair of the two *Flash* serials. Crabbe is fine as always, but Anthony Warde as swarthy villain Killer Kane is a poor substitute for Charles Middleton's unforgettable Ming the Merciless. Other supporting characters are serviceable but unexceptional: Jackie Moran plays kid sidekick Buddy with gee-whiz enthusiasm, Constance Moore makes an attractive Wilma Deering, and C. Montague Shaw is credible enough as fatherly genius Dr. Huer. Meanwhile, the casting of Asian actors to play residents of Saturn may cause a few raised eyebrows from contemporary viewers. Probably coming off best is Henry Brandon as no-nonsense Captain Laska, a formidable adversary for Buck (Brandon would eventually play John Wayne's nemesis Scar in the 1956 western classic *The Searchers*). Special effects are of the same primitive vintage featured in the *Gordon* serials, although a rather nifty full-size shuttle car is put to good creative use. Thin, angular spaceships replace the Raymond-inspired cylinders previously offered, although the distinctive "electric fan" motor sounds are retained.

Buck Rogers in the 25th Century didn't fare well with critics and audiences, despite the fact that Crabbe and space adventure in general were still popular components. So, instead of producing a second *Rogers* serial as planned, Universal opted for more *Flash*, bringing back Middleton as Ming and Frank Shannon as Dr. Zarkov to join Crabbe's titular hero for *Flash Gordon Conquers the Universe* in 1940. Buck himself would have to wait over ten years for an anemic live-TV series incarnation, and would finally reach the big screen again in 1979, with Glen Larson's theatrically-released TV pilot starring Gil Gerard.

88 SUPERMAN 1948

Poster/photos © 1948 Columbia Pictures/DC characters™

WHO MADE IT:

Columbia Pictures Corporation (U.S.). A 15-chapter serial. Directors: Spencer Gordon Bennet, Thomas Carr. Producer: Sam Katzman. Writers: Lewis Clay, Royal K. Cole, Arthur Hoerl, George H. Plympton, Joseph F. Poland, based on the comic book by Jerry Siegel and Joe Shuster (DC). Cinematography (b/w): Ira H. Morgan. Music: Mischa Bakaleinikoff. Starring Kirk Alyn (Superman/Clark Kent), Noel Neill (Lois Lane), Pierre Watkin (Perry White), Tommy Bond (Jimmy Olsen), Carol Forman (Spider Lady), Herbert Rawlinson (Dr. Graham), Forrest Taylor (Professor Leeds), Nelson Leigh (Jor-El), Luana Walters (Lara), Edward Cassidy (Eben Kent).

WHAT IT'S ABOUT:

The infant Superman is sent to Earth by his parents just as his native planet Krypton blows up. He is raised to maturity by the Kents, a loving farm couple. After their deaths, Clark heads to Metropolis under a bespectacled guise and joins the staff of the Daily Planet in order to be close to the news. On assignment, he investigates a new rock that's been discovered called Kryptonite, and the Man of Steel soon realizes that this remnant of his home world can rob him of super-power and even be deadly. Now in a relationship with fellow reporter Lois Lane, Clark and his caped alter-ego match wits with the

villainous Spider Lady, who is hell bent on ruling the Earth. If she cannot have complete control, she plans on shrinking it with her powerful reducer ray.

WHY IT'S IMPORTANT:

Columbia waited a while before producing their first *Superman* serial, putting the creative brilliance of Max Fleisher's early '40s Technicolor cartoons behind them before tackling the screen's first live-action adaptation. More ambitious than the studio's previous *Batman* serial, *Superman* placed its hopes on handsome, likable lead Kirk Alyn, who threw himself into the showy role and even performed many of his own stunts.

What emerges is a respectful but workmanlike take on the legendary superhero, nicely cast (Noel Neill makes her first appearance as Lois Lane) and relatively daring in pitting a female baddie (Carol Forman) against the Man of Steel. Chapter One even spends an admirable amount of time setting up our hero's origin story on Krypton, with Nelson Leigh adding some class as visionary scientist Jor-El.

But while audiences appreciated these plusses, nothing could compensate for the desperate cartoon animation called into play whenever Superman takes to the skies, or whenever more ambitious visuals are required. It's simply too jarring a gimmick, undermining suspension of disbelief at every turn. Despite this disastrous production choice, the serial made money. Alyn and Neill (along with Lyle Talbot as Lex Luthor) returned a year later in Columbia's sequel serial, *Atom Man vs. Superman*, another live-action experience hampered by animated special effects.

87

FLASH GORDON 1980

(111) [1.37] 🎧

PATHETIC EARTHLINGS...
WHO CAN SAVE YOU NOW?

Music by QUEEN

DINO DE LAURENTIIS Presents FLASH GORDON ★ TOPOL ★ TIMOTHY DALTON
SAM J. JONES ★ MELODY ANDERSON ★ ORNELLA MUTI ★ MAX VON SYDOW ★ Screenplay by LORENZO SEMPLE, JR.
MARIANGELA MELATO as Kala ★ BRIAN BLESSED ★ PETER WYNGARDE ★   A UNIVERSAL RELEASE
Produced by DINO DE LAURENTIIS ★ Directed by MIKE HODGES   [PG] PARENTAL GUIDANCE SUGGESTED
DOLBY STEREO   Read the Novel from Jove Books   Filmed in TODD-AO®

WHO MADE IT:

Universal Pictures/Dino De Laurentiis Company (U.S./U.K.). Director: Mike Hodges. Producer: Dino De Laurentiis. Writers: Lorenzo Semple Jr., Michael Allin, based on the comic strip by Alex Raymond (King Features). Cinematography (Technicolor): Gilbert Taylor. Music: Queen, Howard Blake. Starring Sam J. Jones (Flash Gordon), Melody Anderson (Dale Arden), Max von Sydow (Ming the Merciless), Chaim Topol (Dr. Hans Zarkov), Ornella Muti (Princess Aura), Timothy Dalton (Prince Barin), Brian Blessed (Prince Vultan), Peter Wyngarde (General Klytus), Mariangela Melato (General Kala).

WHAT IT'S ABOUT:

Evil despot Ming the Merciless from the planet Mongo is tormenting the Earth with stratospheric convulsions. To save the world, eccentric scientist Hans Zarkov enlists the unexpected aid of football star Flash Gordon and New York City girl Dale Arden to fly to Ming's planet via spaceship and thwart the attacks. Once there, Flash and his friends must contend with various outlandish perils, even as Ming's seductive daughter Aura falls for the handsome, broad shouldered but rather naïve displaced quarterback. Ming controls various exotic kingdoms on Mongo, each with a leader who has no love for the ruthless emperor. Gordon eventually joins forces with Prince Barin and the winged King Vultan for a final showdown, even as Ming prepares to make a less than receptive Dale Arden his bride.

WHY IT'S IMPORTANT:

Deemed a disaster upon its release, this colorful but inane adaptation of Alex Raymond's legendary comic strip has garnered a perverse following among hipsters in later years. They praise the film for aggressively reveling in its own absurdity, a questionable recommendation at best, but a position they defend with vigorous wit. Reevaluations aside, what's up there on the screen is the definition of a creative mess, a fact fully acknowledged by its own creators in published interviews. With no vision for the film after original director Nicholas Roeg's hasty departure (he wanted class while Dino insisted on camp), *Flash Gordon* ultimately emerged as an unfocused satire of sorts that gleefully transitions from one ridiculous scene to another, sacrificing the evocative adventure fantasy that Raymond conjured in his comics for the sake of "so bad it's good" reverse pleasures. The film's certainly colorful enough in a totally unrealistic way (garish reds and golds a specialty), and the over-the-top sets and funky costumes have an oddball curiosity factor built in. But still, this is all in the service of... ?

Unlike Buster Crabbe, who gave the role of Flash both humor and classical dignity, hunky, long-haired, child-faced Sam J. Jones is game but miscast, making Gil Gerard's 1979 turn as Buck Rogers seem nuanced and sophisticated by comparison. It's hard to dislike Max von Sydow's picture-perfect Ming, but he's undermined by foolish story requirements and dated one-liners every step of the way. Faring a tad better is Topol's silly but humanistic Hans Zarkov, who re-lives his life in reverse during a memory-erasing procedure that provides one of the film's few legitimately inventive sequences. Cute Melody Anderson plays heroine Dale for laughs, while future James Bond Timothy Dalton manages not to embarrass himself as enemy-turned-ally Prince Barin, although his relatively straight performance seems to belong in a different movie. Not very far from the comedic '36 take, Brian Blessed portrays hale and heavy King Vultan of the hawkmen with robust, full-bodied bravado. Once experienced, his "diiiivvvveee!!!" command to winged troops is never forgotten.

With no vision for the film other than excess for its own sake, special effects designers scratched their heads and provided shiny/pretty spaceships and weaponry, which are somehow unblemished by the warfare exploding all around them. Adding its own nutsy "anything goes" quality to the proceedings is an energetic rock score by Queen, with cornball lyrics ("Aha! He'll save every one of us!") enthusiastically quoted by fans at the drop of a space helmet.

ABOVE: Flash Gordon (Sam J. Jones) and Dale Arden (Melody Anderson) are kidnapped by an unhinged Dr. Zarkov (Topol). RIGHT: Flash fights an arena battle with future ally Prince Barin (Timothy Dalton).

ABOVE: Ming's magical ring seduces an increasingly turned-on Dale.

"Who wants to live forever? DIVE!!" famously shouts Prince Vultan of the high-flying Hawkmen, played with robust glee by Brian Blessed.

Here's an original pair of storyboards depicting the revolving platform and whip fight, as visualized for the movie (above image).

58 — SUDDENLY THE DISC STARTS TO TIP — FLASH BEGINS TO SLIDE — HE HEADS BACK TOWARD CENTER

BATTLING BEYOND THE STARS

Space heroes and alien villains were standard fare in comics, and later in the serials and movies derived from them. LEFT: A magnificent poster rendering for the Italian release of *Flash Gordon* (1980), Dino De Laurentiis' bizarre attempt to recapture '60s-style camp decades after popular tastes had changed. ABOVE: Sinestro (Mark Strong) was villainy personified in Warner's equally unsuccessful *Green Lantern* (2011). Despite hopes for movie franchises, there were no sequels to these well-publicized mistakes.

Poster/photos: © 2011 Warner Bros./DC characters™

WHO MADE IT:

Warner Bros./DC Entertainment (U.S.). Director: Martin Campbell. Producers: Donald De Line, Greg Berlanti. Writers: Greg Berlanti, Michael Green, Marc Guggenheim, Michael Goldenberg, based on the comic book by John Broome and Gil Kane (DC). Cinematography (color): Dion Beebe. Music: James Newton Howard. Starring Ryan Reynolds (Hal Jordan/Green Lantern), Blake Lively (Carol Ferris), Peter Sarsgaard (Hector Hammond), Mark Strong (Sinestro), Angela Bassett (Dr. Amanda Walker), Tim Robbins (Robert Hammond), Geoffrey Rush (Tomar-Re, voice), Michael Clarke Duncan (Kilowog, voice).

WHAT IT'S ABOUT:

In a universe as vast as it is mysterious, a small but powerful force has existed for centuries. Protectors of peace and justice, they are called the Green Lantern Corps. A brotherhood of warriors sworn to keep intergalactic order, each Green Lantern wears a ring that grants him superpowers. But when a new enemy called Parallax threatens to destroy the balance of power in the Universe, their fate and the fate of Earth lie in the hands of their newest recruit, the first human ever selected: Hal Jordan. Hal is a gifted and cocky test pilot, but the Green Lanterns have little respect for humans, who have never harnessed the infinite powers of the ring before. But Jordan is clearly the missing piece to the puzzle, and along with his determination and willpower, he has one thing no member of the Corps has ever had: humanity. With the encouragement of fellow pilot and childhood sweetheart Carol, he sets out to quickly master his new powers and find the courage needed to defeat Parallax... becoming the greatest Green Lantern of all.

WHY IT'S IMPORTANT:

Much was expected from *Green Lantern*, the first film adaptation of DC's power-ringed superhero and an ambitious undertaking from all involved. After the unexpected success of Marvel's *Iron Man*, Warner Bros. began to realize that even some of the lesser known comic book demi-gods might click on screen if the right movie was derived from them. That winning formula meant, among other things, showcasing a star worth watching.

Just as *Deadpool* plays to Ryan Reynolds' personal strengths, *Green Lantern* makes him seem worse than he actually is. There is some measure of charm in his reckless pilot-turned-responsible superhero, but it's ultimately not enough to compensate for an avalanche of cosmic mythology that is visually arresting, but only marginally interesting. The Lantern Core member Sinestro, benevolent here but destined to become a villain, is sharply portrayed by Mark Strong with just the right amount of foreboding, while Blake Lively is merely okay as Hal's girlfriend Carol. She and Reynolds do share an amusing moment, however, as a traditional comic book cliché is happily skewered when Carol promptly sees through her boyfriend's flimsy "disguise." Variations on bandit's masks (or eyeglasses) only go so far in concealing a person's identity when 90% of their head is exposed.

Producer/writer Greg Berlanti would survive this high-profile debacle, his embrace of traditional, kinder and gentler comics working exceptionally well on television with series like *The Flash* and *Supergirl*. As for Reynolds, a certain oddball hero from the Marvel side of the fence would soon secure his reputation as a major movie personality, undoubtedly making rival DC green with envy.

Tidbit: James Newton Howard's energetic if unexceptional music score pays homage to John Williams' original *Superman* theme during the helicopter sequence.

ABOVE: Glib Hal Jordan (Ryan Reynolds) tries to activate the mysterious alien lantern with all kinds of goofy word combinations. RIGHT: Green Lantern in his emerald glory, complete with an fx-glowing costume. BELOW: The plight of mutated scientist Hector Hammond (Peter Sarsgaard) reaches violent fruition in act three.

Superhero Green Lantern demonstrates the power ring.

ABOVE, AND RIGHT TOP: Novice Jordan meets his fellow Lanterns in outer space. RIGHT BOTTOM: Carol Ferris (Blake Lively) does her best to keep hotshot test pilot boyfriend Hal psychologically grounded.

Suited-up for his luminous fx costume, actor Ryan Reynolds rehearses some romantic banter with co-star Blake Lively. Reynolds would later mock this gimmicky Lantern uniform in *Deadpool*.

85 BATMAN 1943

260 1.37

WHO MADE IT:

Columbia Pictures (U.S.). 15 serial chapters. Director: Lambert Hillyer. Producer: Rudolph C. Flothow. Writers: Victor McLeod, Leslie Swabacker, Harry Fraser, based on the comic book created by Bob Kane (DC Comics). Cinematography (b/w): James S. Brown Jr. Music: Lee Zahler. Starring Lewis Wilson (Batman/Bruce Wayne), Douglas Croft (Robin/Dick Grayson), J. Carrol Naish (Dr. Daka), Shirely Patterson (Linda Page), William Austin (Alfred Pennyworth).

WHAT IT'S ABOUT:

The U.S. government is terrorized by nefarious Dr. Daka, an emissary from Emperor Hirohito of Japan. He threatens America and democracy itself with atom-smasher ray guns and a device that turns its hapless wearers into zombies. Costumed hero Batman, in truth government operative Bruce Wayne, and Robin the Boy Wonder are aided by lovely Linda Page, whose uncle becomes one of Daka's first victims. Operating out of the Bat Cave, these three crusaders

and Wayne's loyal butler, Alfred, strike out in a convertible to battle their villainous adversary, finally tracking him to an amusement park for a final confrontation.

WHY IT'S IMPORTANT:

The first screen incarnation of DC's cowled and caped detective, Columbia's *Batman* serial was very much a product of its era. Nefarious Dr. Daka is your standard issue Japanese stereotype, while heroic Bruce Wayne/Batman has been reimagined as an operative of the U.S. government… all in the service of a patriotic fifteen-chapter slugfest, filmed at the height of WWII.

Despite these and other superficial adjustments, *Batman* remains fundamentally true to its comic book inspiration. The caped crusader and teenage sidekick Robin catch criminals in Gotham City and turn them over to local authorities. Lead Lewis Wilson borrows a little of Douglas Fairbanks Sr.'s sense of heroic bemusement, clearly enjoying his bizarre double-life as he watches hoods squirm from beneath his devil-eared mask. Alter-ego Wayne is primarily an American Don Diego: rich, easily fatigued and foppish, while sixteen-year-old Douglas Croft is age appropriate as feisty, always ready for action Boy Wonder Robin. Supporting our heroes in their offbeat agenda is William Austin as prissy, often overwhelmed Wayne butler Alfred Pennyworth. His specific characterization established Alfred's persona for all future generations, in both comics and film.

Surprisingly watchable today, *Batman* may be makeshift and cheap (it would be years before a genuine Batmobile would appear on film), but it captures something of the Dark Knight atmosphere evident in early DC comics, compromised but not completely smothered by propaganda requirements of early '40s Hollywood.

WHO MADE IT:

Columbia Pictures/Rastar (U.S). Director: John Huston. Producers: Ray Stark, Carol Sobieski, Joe Layton. Writers: Carol Sobieski, from the stage play by Thomas Meehan and the comic strip by Harold Gray. Cinematography (color): Richard Moore. Music: Charles Strouse. Starring Albert Finney (Daddy Warbucks), Carol Burnett (Miss Hannigan), Ann Reinking (Grace Farrell), Tim Curry (Rooster Hannigan), Bernadette Peters (Lily St. Regis), Aileen Quinn (Annie), Geoffrey Holder (Punjab), Roger Minami (Asp), Toni Ann Gisondi (Molly).

WHAT IT'S ABOUT:

Annie is a plucky, red-haired young girl who dreams of life outside her dreary orphanage. Unexpectedly, she is chosen to stay for one week with the famous billionaire Daddy Warbucks, and share all the benefits of his prosperous lifestyle. That one week turns into many, as the always optimistic toddler gradually wins the heart of her business-minded benefactor, along with other members of the household, including Indian manservant Punjab and Grace, who is employed by Warbucks and secretly cares for her boss. The only person standing in the way of a great new life for Annie is Miss Hannigan, the gin-soaked ruler of the orphanage. When push comes to shove, even she can't be as rotten as she thinks she is, and the goodness of the optimistic orphan wins over a new convert.

WHY IT'S IMPORTANT:

Harold Gray's popular comic strip about the improbable adventures of a plucky orphan found success as a radio show in the early 1930s, and was promptly adapted into two minor movies (1932 and 1938, respectively). It was many years later that Broadway discovered this urban urchin's earthy charms, resulting in the strip's most significant incarnation: a full-blown Tony Award-winning musical. This would eventually inspire a 1982 mega-movie with major stars and a world-class director.

Annie is pretty much a distaff *Oliver Twist* set in America's Depression. Little Aileen Quinn makes for a feisty, two-fisted heroine, nicely supported by Carol Burnett as Miss Hannigan (the villainous orphanage queen turned unexpected ally by film's end) and Albert Finney as gruff but lovable Daddy Warbucks. Other cast members are colorful enough, and the songs manage to retain something of their original verve, reaching a climax with the happy principals warbling "Tomorrow" at FDR's White House... certainly the show's most infectious number.

Unfortunately, Huston's dry and methodical style of directing seems at odds with *Annie*'s required cheery tone. The overall effect is ambitious but perfunctory. Making matters worse, Steven Spielberg's *E.T.* won the hearts of moviegoers that particular summer, leaving Gray's carrot-topped tyke and her bald benefactor in the pop cultural dust. Eventually, a surprisingly good TV adaptation followed, along with a new 2014 movie incarnation that featured an African-American spin on the proceedings.

83 30 DAYS OF NIGHT 2007

WHO MADE IT:

Columbia Pictures/Ghost House Pictures /Dark Horse Entertainment (U.S./New Zealand). Director: David Slade. Producers: Sam Raimi, Ted Adams, Rob Tapert. Writers: Steve Niles, Stuart Beattie, Brian Nelson, based on the comic book by Steve Niles and Ben Templesmith (IDW). Cinematography (color): Jo Willems. Music: Brian Reitzell. Starring Josh Harnett (Sheriff Eben Oleson), Melissa George (Stella Oleson), Danny Huston (Marlow), Ben Foster (The Stranger), Mark Rendall (Jake Oleson), Manu Bennett (Deputy Billy Kitka), Mark Boone Junior (Beau Brower), Nathaniel Lees (Carter Davies), Craig Hall (Wilson Bulosan).

WHAT IT'S ABOUT:

In the sleepy, secluded town of Barrow, Alaska – the northernmost settlement in North America – its citizens are preparing for the annual coming of the Dark, when the sun will set for more than thirty consecutive days and nights. But this year, the event will be terrifyingly different. From across the frozen wasteland, a horde of bloodthirsty vampires descends upon unsuspecting Barrow, mercilessly besieging its residents

with unrelenting horror and swift death. And as the darkness continues, Barrow's only remaining hope lies with Sheriff Eben Oleson and Deputy Stella Oleson, a estranged husband and wife who are torn between saving the town they love and their own survival...

WHY IT'S IMPORTANT:

A great title for an equally brilliant concept, *30 Days of Night* was pitched to both the movies and the comics biz by author Steve Niles. The resulting IDW comic book was promptly sold as a commercial property to Hollywood, and this serviceable movie followed, a generally faithful adaptation directed with cold-blooded gusto by David Slade. Only some off-balance time-line structuring and a pair of dull leads lessen the overall impact.

Once the brilliant premise is set up – towns with month-long polar nights are tailor-made for vampire attacks – the somewhat more familiar concept of a small band of survivors struggling for their lives in an isolated location kicks in. As with *Alien* and various versions of *The Thing*, it's a battle against incredible odds, with increasingly desperate cast members getting whittled down one by one. The black-clad predators that descend upon Barrow are quite convincingly nonhuman. Speaking their own European language (German with a tweak), they appear to be Nosferatu's grandchildren, shark-toothed, ruthless and insatiable. Leader of the pack Marlow (a homage to Mr. Barlow of *Salem's Lot*?), played with ravenous contempt by Danny Huston, somewhat resembles the mouth-breathing maniac zombie from *Night of the Living Dead*'s opening scenes. *30 Days* also re-visits the 'monstrous little girl who bites' concept from *Living Dead*, along with some stylish end titles that utilize still photos for a grim, artful effect.

Suspenseful but strangely uneven, *30 Days of Night* does retain the tragic finale of its comic book source, as noble sheriff Oleson (Josh Harnett), who has turned himself into a vampire to successfully defeat Marlow, perishes in the loving arms of his heartbroken ex-wife (Melissa George) as the sun finally rises on long-awaited Day 30. If we had cared about these people just a little bit more, the dramatic impact of his sacrifice would have been a fine capper to a good thriller.

82 LI'L ABNER 1959

(114) [1.85]

WHO MADE IT:

Paramount Pictures/Triad Productions (U.S.). Director: Melvin Frank. Producer: Norman Panama. Writers: Melvin Frank, Norman Panama, based on the comic strip created by Al Capp. Cinematography (Technicolor): Daniel L. Fapp. Music: Nelson Riddle, Joseph J. Lilley. Starring Peter Palmer (Li'l Abner Yokum), Leslie Parrish (Daisy Mae), Stubby Kaye (Marryin' Sam), Howard St. John (General Bullmoose), Julie Newmar (Stupefyin' Jones), Stella Stevens (Appassionata Von Climax), Billie Hayes (Mammy Yokum), Joe E. Marks (Pappy Yokum), Bern Hoffman (Earthquake McGoon), Al Nesor (Evil Eye Fleagle), Robert Strauss (Romeo Scragg).

WHAT IT'S ABOUT:

In the colorful community of Dogpatch, USA, comely Daisy Mae plans on catching boyish giant Li'l Abner on Sadie Hawkins Day, so he'll be forced to marry her. But just before this much-anticipated event, the small town gets some very bad news: apparently Dogpatch has been declared the most useless place in the country and is slated to become an atomic test bomb site, unless the locals can prove their community has worth. Abner's mother, Mammy Yokum, could have the answer – but even her miraculous Yokumberry tonic might not be enough to save Dogpatch.

WHY IT'S IMPORTANT:

Al Capp's *Li'l Abner* was one of the most popular comic strips ever published, running from 1934 until 1977. It was also one of the most respected, credited with upgrading the form with satiric humor and thoughtful content... "the Mark Twain of cartoonists," both *Journalism Quarterly* and *Time* said of Capp. Even Charlie Chaplin was enamored with the award-winning artist and his famous creation.

The hillbilly residents of Dogpatch, U.S.A., were certainly colorful caricatures, and their adventures often came tinged with political jabs. Most of this social commentary was missing from early radio adaptations, not to mention a generally anemic 1940 movie produced by RKO Radio Pictures. But satire of sorts is evident in the popular Broadway play from 1956, and the resulting movie adaptation from 1959. Although it's a joyful musical with amazing character costumes and make-ups (the sets are deliberately designed to look artificial, reminding viewers of the stage production) it maintains a reasonable edge, with musical statements like "What's Good for General Bullmoose, is Good for the USA" pretty much spelling out Capp's post-war attitude about unrestrained capitalism (the lyric was a parody of a specific statement made by General Motors' head Charles E. Wilson at a Senate subcommittee in 1952). It's unfortunate that the even more subversive "Progress Is The Root Of All Evil" number didn't make it into the picture, but what was included happily captures the sly Al Capp subtext without detracting from *Abner*'s spirited sense of cornball fun.

With a bright cast (although lead Peter Palmer didn't have much of a film career) that was mostly inherited from the stage version, Paramount's *Li'l Abner* is a three-strip Technicolor time capsule that still entertains viewers today. Although presenting lower-income Southerners as backward hillbillies or hicks is politically incorrect by modern standards, the eternally endearing aspects of Dogpatch's cartoonish population seem to override any complaints. Natcherly!

81 SUPERMAN RETURNS 2006

(154) 2.35

WHO MADE IT:

Warners Bros./Legendary Pictures/Peters Entertainment (U.S.). Director: Bryan Singer. Producers: Jon Peters, Bryan Singer, Gilbert Adler. Writers: Michael Doughty, Dan Harris, based on the comic book by Jerry Siegel and Joe Shuster (DC). Cinematography (color): Newton Thomas Sigel. Music: John Ottman. Starring Brandon Routh (Clark Kent/Superman), Kate Bosworth (Lois Lane), Kevin Spacey (Lex Luthor), James Marsden (Richard White), Parker Posey (Kitty Kowalski), Frank Langella (Perry White), Sam Huntington (Jimmy Olsen), Eva Marie Saint (Martha Kent).

WHAT IT'S ABOUT:

Following a mysterious absence of five years, the Man of Steel comes back to Earth from his home planet Krypton, which was supposedly destroyed. While old enemy Lex Luthor plots to render him powerless once and for all with crystals stolen from the Fortress of Solitude, Superman faces the heartbreaking realization that the woman he loves, Lois Lane, has moved on with her life. She is now engaged, has a son whose parentage is a bit uncertain, and has won a Pulitzer for an article about why the world doesn't need the caped wonder from Krypton. In an attempt to protect Earth from cataclysmic destruction, Superman embarks on an epic journey of redemption that takes him from the depths of the ocean to the far reaches of outer space.

WHY IT'S IMPORTANT:

Sometimes a fan's enthusiasm can get in the way of forward-moving creativity. Instead of envisioning a new, modern *Superman* movie mythology, Bryan Singer abandoned his profitable *X-Men* franchise (if briefly) to film a sequel of sorts to the old Richard Donner movie(s) from the late '70s that meant so much to him as a youngster. Given the unique psychiatric/sociological problems many people have accepting a 21st Century Superman to begin with, this may have seemed a safe and logical approach at the outset. But as Singer's movie ultimately proves, turning back the clock is never the answer.

Despite a first class production with all the trimmings, everything in *Superman Returns* plays like a warmed-over version of Donner's 20th Century ideas. Top-billed Brandon Routh cannot help but be compared to Christopher Reeve, and this clearly isn't fair, either to Routh or to viewers. But Singer's sequel-like take forces the comparison, and the same problem diminishes Lois Lane (Kate Bosworth in the shadow of Margot Kidder) and Lex Luthor, although Kevin Spacey's brand of cold-hearted villainy, while completely out of sync with the rest of the movie, manages to establish its own unsavory identity.

Adding its own problems is the original plot, which makes the Man of Steel the odd man out in his former flame's personal life. The fact that Kal-El has apparently sired a super-child out of wedlock is a radical idea not satisfactorily developed.

Superman Returns earned decent reviews – it's the brightly-colored, old-fashioned Man of Steel many viewers think they want – but the reality of this unfortunate folly hit home before very long. Soon DC would reboot the character with a legitimate 21st Century take (infuriating many), and Bryan Singer would return to his *X-Men*, providing that franchise with some of its best installments.

ABOVE: Young Clark Kent (Stephen Bender) gradually discovers his Kryptonian super-powers. LEFT: As Superman (Brandon Routh), Clark protects the city of Metropolis from a plethora of dangers. BELOW: Lois Lane (Kate Bosworth) and her super-son are menaced by power-seeking Lex Luthor (Kevin Spacey).

ABOVE: Potentially devastating secrets of an advanced alien culture are hijacked by Luthor within the Fortress of Solitude.

Filming the opening scenes. A ten-million-dollar sequence with Kal-El exploring present-day, annihilated Krypton was shot, but cut from the final release version.

AVP: ALIEN VS. PREDATOR 2004 (101) [2.35] 🎧

WHOEVER
WINS...
WE
LOSE.

AVP

ALIEN VS. PREDATOR

08.06.04

WHO MADE IT:

Twentieth Century Fox Film Corporation/Davis Entertainment/ Brandywine Productions (U.S.). Director: Paul W. S. Anderson. Producers: Gordon Carroll, John Davis, David Giler, Walter Hill, Mike Richardson, Thomas M. Hammel. Writers: Paul W. S. Anderson, Dan O'Bannon, Ronald Shusett, inspired by the Dark Horse comic books. Cinematography (color): David Johnson. Music: Harald Kloser. Starring Sanaa Lathan (Alexa Woods), Raoul Bova (Sebastian de Rosa), Lance Henriksen (Charles Bishop Weyland), Ewen Bremner (Graeme Miller), Colin Salmon (Maxwell Stafford), Tommy Flanagan (Mark Verheiden), Tom Woodruff Jr. (Grid), Ian Whyte (Scar).

WHAT IT'S ABOUT:

A group of elite archeologists is assembled by billionaire Charles Bishop Weyland for an expedition near the Antarctic to investigate a mysterious heat signal. Weyland hopes to claim this find for himself, and his team soon discovers a pyramid below the surface of a whaling station. Hieroglyphs and sculptures reveal that the structure is a hunting ground for extraterrestrials (Predators), who kill another galactic species (Aliens), as a rite of passage. The humans suddenly find themselves caught in the middle of a full-fledged battle between these two monstrous species. Eventually, resilient scientist Alexa Woods finds common cause with one combatant for an unlikely alliance that ironically benefits mankind.

WHY IT'S IMPORTANT:

The idea of combining two unrelated properties in one movie goes way back. *Frankenstein Meets the Wolf Man* was pretty much the template for *Alien vs. Predator* (a clip of the older movie is included in *AvP*, to remind us of the connection.) This particular combo concept started out as a series of successful comic books for Dark Horse; since both *Alien* and *Predator* were 20th Century Fox-owned, it was one-stop shopping in terms of licensing. Pulling together the initially resistant producers of both properties to make a movie version proved a little more difficult, but eventually a deal was made and the film began taking shape.

Although the hunt-driven Predators have always been Earth visitors, the Aliens paying a call was something legitimately new. Rather than have these primo monsters duke it out in everyday, densely-populated surroundings (something *AvP's* grisly sequel would do), director Paul W. S. Anderson chose a remote location in Antarctica... which is almost like being on an inhospitable alien planet. Following the formula of both franchises, a crack team is assembled to investigate curious phenomena, only to find itself in the crossfire between two warring species.

While not on the same sophisticated level as a Ridley Scott or James Cameron sci-fi epic, *Alien vs. Predator* provides a number of creative elements that resonate. The ancient pyramid our heroes soon find themselves in is a compelling arena, ripe with interesting back stories (a flashback of young Predator hunters preparing for battle is a CG standout), and the cast of mostly competent performers seems game for the inevitable mayhem. Recruited from the movie universe of *Alien* is older but still formidable Lance Henriksen, and Sanaa Lathan is a standout as a fearless young woman who bonds with an extraterrestrial for a final confrontation with its rampaging opposite number.

Alien vs. Predator made money, enough to put that previously mentioned sequel into production. Fox and Dark Horse should have quit while they were ahead. Although no prize winner, Anderson's modest thriller offers reasonable excitement and a measure of style, taking humanity's relationship with an ET race that views us as hunt-worthy to a curious and unexpected new level.

ABOVE: Inside an Antarctic pyramid, Weyland's team discovers the remains of a Facehugger. RIGHT: The titular monsters square off. BELOW: An interesting CGI flashback explores why Predators do what they do, and how long they've been at it. Although *Alien* and *Predator* were both movies before they became comic books, combining the duo was an original Dark Horse concept.

Actor Lance Henriksen, who famously played a heroic android in *Aliens*, returns to the franchise (or half of it) as human billionaire Charles "Bishop" Weyland, caught in the crossfire of two alien species.

Having less in common with humans, the Aliens are portrayed as vicious killing machines, while sentient Predators have a sense of warrior's honor.

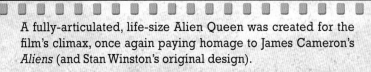

A fully-articulated, life-size Alien Queen was created for the film's climax, once again paying homage to James Cameron's *Aliens* (and Stan Winston's original design).

Impressive wartime espionage adventure enhanced by a game Lloyd Bridges...

SECRET AGENT X-9 1945

(246) [1.37] 🎬

WHO MADE IT:

Universal Pictures (U.S.). A 12-chapter serial. Directors: Lewis D. Collins, Ray Taylor. Producer: Morgan Cox. Writers: Joseph O'Donnell, Harold Channing Wire, Patricia Harper, based on the comic strip by Dashiell Hammett and Alex Raymond (King Features). Cinematography (b/w): Maury Gertsman, Ernest Miller. Music: Milton Rosen, Paul Sawtell. Starring Lloyd Bridges (Phil Corrigan aka Agent X-9), Keye Luke (Ah Fong), Jan Wiley (Lynn Moore), Victoria Horne (Nabura), Samuel S. Hinds (Solo), Cy Kendall (Lucky Kamber), Jack Overman (Marker).

WHAT IT'S ABOUT:

A neutral stretch of land in the Pacific called Shadow Island, which is just above the island of Formosa, is run with an iron fist by American gangster Lucky Kamber. Both sides during World War II find themselves in this location as they seek to control the secret of element 722, which can be used to create synthetic aviation fuel. Intrepid Secret Agent X-9 of the United States joins forces with two-fisted colleagues from China and Australia as they take on the Nazi thugs and try to prevent 722 from falling into enemy hands.

WHY IT'S IMPORTANT:

Produced toward the end of World War II, *Secret Agent X-9* is the second of two espionage-themed serials Universal made based on the moderately successful Dashiell Hammett/Alex Raymond comic strip, which had been created as an answer to Chester Gould's *Dick Tracy*. It is a surprisingly good chapterplay experience, benefitting from an exotic location (Shadow Island, well art directed and photographed), and some genuinely suspenseful plotting.

Most impressive of all is a young Lloyd Bridges in the title role. Bridges was a fine actor, and had already appeared in small but memorable A-movie parts (his turn in Bogart's popular *Sahara* two years earlier was noticed by many). As Phil Corrigan, the Agent X-9 of the title, he takes a standard issue two-fisted hero and imbues him with legitimate personality, rare indeed for a venue with generally little use for nuance or characterization. Bridges is ably assisted by a cast that includes reliable talents like Keye Luke, Samuel S. Hinds, and as the implacably evil Nabura, Victoria Horne (who would play a spinster in both *The Ghost and Mrs. Muir* and Universal's *Harvey* within the next few years).

Although, like all serials, creative elements were borrowed from pre-existing sources (an uncredited music theme is lifted from Hitchcock's *Saboteur*, and stock footage is liberally borrowed from *Gung Ho!*), *Secret Agent X-9* stands as a class act among chapterplays, ably transferring the latter, more exotic incarnation of King Feature's strip (after both Hammett and Raymond had left) to the Saturday afternoon big screen.

For the record, Universal's original take on *Secret Agent X-9* featured a different hero, Agent Dexter, who appeared in the early days of the 1934 comic strip. The plot involved a master thief, Blackstone, and a plot to steal the crown jewels of Belgravia. It starred Scott Kolk, Henry Brandon, and Jean Rogers of *Flash Gordon* fame.

TIMECOP 1994

WHO MADE IT:

Universal Pictures/Largo Entertainment/JVC (US./Canada/Japan). Director: Peter Hyams. Producers: Moshe Diamant, Sam Raimi, Robert Tapert. Writers: Mark Verheiden, Mike Richardson, based on the comic book by Verheiden and Richardson (Dark Horse). Cinematography (color): Peter Hyams. Music: Mark Isham, Robert Lamm. Starring Jean-Claude Van Damme (Max Walker), Mia Sara (Melissa Walker), Ron Silver (Sen. Aaron McComb), Bruce McGill (Com. Eugene Matuzak).

WHAT IT'S ABOUT:

In 2094, Max Walker is a cop working for the Time Enforcement Agency, assigned to prevent time travel and the disastrous consequences that could result from use of this dangerous new technology. But when he discovers that a corrupt senator overseeing the agency, Aaron McComb, has been manipulating the past for financial gain, he travels back in time to thwart the politician's convoluted

scheme... and maybe, if he is lucky, alter the thread of history that resulted in his wife Melissa's untimely murder ten years earlier.

WHY IT'S IMPORTANT:

Based on a minor comic book property from Dark Horse, *Timecop* was clearly inspired by three highly regarded science fiction films of the '80s: *The Terminator*, *Robocop*, and *Back to the Future*. Fashioned as a classy vehicle for its star, martial arts personality Jean-Claude Van Damme, the film benefits from Peter Hyam's directorial flourishes and a twistier script than usual for an action outing. It wound up becoming Mr. Van Damme's most successful achievement at the box office.

As every writer from H.G. Wells to Rod Serling has learned, the device of time travel enables a plethora of intriguing "what if?" scenarios to play out dramatically. *Timecop* specifically deals with the policing of this procedure, as the possibilities for misuse are all too obvious. History can be changed and individuals wiped out of existence by crafty manipulators from the future. Protagonist Max Walker (Van Damme) is a cop-turned-TEC agent who suddenly finds himself in the middle of an elaborate temporal conspiracy instigated by an ambitious, amoral senator (Ron Silver). The inevitable time-twists come thick and fast, often leaving even the most willing viewer more than a little bewildered. What James Cameron set up simply and with relative clarity in *The Terminator* is taken to far more confusing heights here.

But as with the films that inspired it, *Timecop*'s saving grace is its human element, which ties all those headache-inducing plot twists together. Is Walker's pregnant wife Melissa (Mia Sara) destined to be murdered, or can the line of destiny be altered? Using the miracle of time travel to fix what is broken on a personal level was driven home beautifully in 1985's *Back to the Future*, and director Hymas tries to tap into that same cathartic sensibility here. By no means a classic, *Timecop* deserves some credit for managing to have it both ways: it provides Jean-Claude Van Damme fans with all the energetic slugfests they crave, while filling in the gaps with a twisty sci-fi conceit that allows for some provocative questions to be asked.

45

Poster/photos: © 2012 Columbia Pictures/Marvel characters™

WHO MADE IT:

Columbia Pictures Corporation/Marvel Enterprises (U.S.). Director: Marc Webb. Producers: Avi Arad, Matt Tolmach, Laura Ziskin, Kevin Feige. Writers: James Vanderbilt, Alvin Sargent, Steve Kloves, based on the comic book created by Stan Lee and Steve Ditko (Marvel). Cinematography (color): John Schwartzman. Music: James Horner. Starring Andrew Garfield (Peter Parker/Spider-Man), Emma Stone (Gwen Stacy), Rhys Ifans (Dr. Curt Connors/The Lizard), Denis Leary (Captain George Stacy), Martin Sheen (Ben Parker), Sally Field (May Parker), Irrfan Khan (Dr. Ratha), Chris Zylka (Flash Thompson).

WHAT IT'S ABOUT:

Peter Parker is an outcast high schooler who was abandoned by his parents as a boy, leaving him to be raised by his Uncle Ben and Aunt May. Like most teenagers, Peter is trying to figure out who he is and how he got to be the person he is today. Peter is also finding his way with his first high school crush, Gwen Stacy, and together, they struggle with love, commitment, and secrets. As Peter discovers a mysterious briefcase that belonged to his father, he begins a quest to understand his parents' disappearance – leading him directly to Oscorp and the lab of Dr. Curt Connors, his father's former partner. Before long, Spider-Man is set on a collision course with Connors' alter-ego, the monstrous Lizard, even as Peter prepares to to use his powers and shape his destiny as a hero.

WHY IT'S IMPORTANT:

Learning all the wrong lessons from Christopher Nolan's *Batman Begins*, the producers of this ambitious reboot wrongly concluded that seriousness and darkness for its own sake was the key to an improved *Spider-Man*, not taking into account that every superhero character is subtly different and the tone of his universe is a reflection of his or her specific persona. Gone is Sam Raimi's jovial tone, which perfectly matched Stan Lee's original '60s stories. Instead we have a dry, *Dark Knight*-like narrative that ill fits everyone's friendly neighborhood webhead.

To direct this fresh launch, Columbia hired newcomer Marc Webb, most recently the praised auteur of the very Woody Allen-like romantic comedy *300 Days of Summer*. As a result, Andrew Garfield and Emma Stone make a charming Peter Parker and Gwen Stacey, their scenes together refreshingly natural, almost as if they are improvising. Although a touch too handsome, Garfield actually resembles the Parker seen in comics, and he exhibits a less nerd-chirpy, more guttural East Coast accent than previous attempts at the character. This youthful hero really sounds like someone you'd bump into on the streets of Manhattan.

Far less successful is Webb's take on the Lizard (Rhys Ifans), one of the most terrifying villains in the Spider-Man canon, and promised to movie fans as early as *Spider-Man* I. This is a truly missed opportunity, as the gradual disintegration of Peter's latest surrogate scientist dad would have been exciting and disturbing if played á la Jekyll and Hyde, utilizing make-up appliances. Instead, this potential is thrown away by an inevitable, unconvincing CGI interpretation. Reflecting notions from the comic, Stacy's police captain dad (Denis Leary) is a no-nonsense law and order type, an ideological foe to everything Spider-Man's vigilante hero stands for. But in terms of movie foils, even this ultimately plays like a somewhat familiar antagonistic relationship… Stacy amounts to a drier version of J. Jonah Jameson, sans the flat-top hair style.

Webb would make one more *Spider-Man* movie before Columbia called it quits and wisely decided to share the titular web-slinger with Marvel Studios for future movie development.

ABOVE: Uncle Ben (Martin Sheen), Aunt May (Sally Field), Peter Parker (Andrew Garfield). BELOW: Gwen Stacy (Emma Stone) and Peter. FURTHUR BELOW: Dr. Curt Connors (Rhys Ifans) and his alter-ego, the Lizard.

Awed science student Peter Parker begins to understand the depth of his newly-acquired spider-like powers.

Stunt coordinators prepare the upside-down, ceiling crawling hero (fearlessly played by Andrew Garfield) in a N.Y. subway car set.

47

GUARDIANS OF THE EAST COAST

Although many of Marvel's superheroes are native New Yorkers, two of them seem to embody their respective urban neighborhoods: Peter Parker/Spider-Man (Andrew Garfield) is the classic Queens kid working a daily grind in the Big Apple, while Hell's Kitchen of downtown Manhattan plays a significant part in the past and present of "Man Without Fear" Matt Murdock/Daredevil (Ben Affleck). Garfield played the wall-crawler in two films directed by Marc Webb, battling the grotesque Lizard in his first adventure (LEFT: notice the claw marks), high voltage super-villain Electro in the second. Affleck never made a *Daredevil* sequel, although co-star Jennifer Garner repeated her role of assassin-for-hire Elektra in a 2005 spinoff movie.

The blind angle is well-realized in this otherwise workmanlike adventure...

76 DAREDEVIL 2003

Poster/photos: © 2003 Twentieth Century Fox /Regency/Marvel characters™

WHO MADE IT:

Twentieth Century Fox Film Corporation/New Regency Pictures (U.S.). Director: Mark Steven Johnson. Producers: Avi Arad, Gary Foster, Arnon Milchan. Writer: Mark Steven Johnson, based on the comic book created by Stan Lee and Bill Everett (Marvel). Cinematography (color): Ericson Core. Music: Grame Revell. Starring Ben Affleck (Matt Murdock/Daredevil), Jennifer Garner (Elektra Natchios), Colin Farrell (Lester Poindexter/Bullseye), Michael Clarke Duncan (Wilson Fisk/Kingpin), Jon Favreau (Franklin "Foggy" Nelson), Joe Pantoliano (Ben Urich), David Keith (Jack Murdock), Scott Terra (Young Matt).

WHAT IT'S ABOUT:

Attorney Matt Murdock was blinded by toxic waste when he was a young boy, but his other four senses function with superhuman sharpness. As a result, Murdock represents the downtrodden in the courtrooms of New York City by day. But when darkness falls, he becomes the masked, crimson-garbed vigilante Daredevil, a relentless avenger of justice. When criminal mastermind Wilson Fisk aka the Kingpin hires an assassin named Bullseye to kill Daredevil, Murdock must rely on his hyper senses while trusting the motives of the exceptional woman he loves, Elektra, whose traumatic past mirrors his own.

WHY IT'S IMPORTANT:

In some ways, Daredevil was Marvel Comics' answer to Batman: a devil-horned creature of the night on a rampage against urban crime. Upping the conceptual ante is the fact that this masked vigilante is blind; he must call upon his extraordinarily heightened senses to prevail over underworld enemies. What could have been a condescending gimmick in lesser creative hands flourished on the comic book page, with *Daredevil* adding a new, streetwise dimension to Marvel's universe.

This major studio movie incarnation, put into production after the runaway success of Sam Raimi's *Spider-Man*, gets it half right. A game Ben Affleck does what he can with this generic version of lawyer Matt Murdock, aided and abetted by future *Iron Man* director Jon Favreau as droll best friend, "Foggy" Nelson. Serving as both love interest and occasional martial arts opponent, Jennifer Garner tears into the role of emotionally scarred Elektra Natchios, a bad girl/good girl, who also dons exotic wear for nocturnal skirmishes on rooftops. Murdock's romantic relationship with Elektra is doomed from kiss one (the heroine's vicious slaying is a famous piece of comic book history) but Affleck and Garner have an easy chemistry that makes their limited courtship watchable. On the villainious side of the fence, immense Michael Clarke Duncan makes an intimidating Kingpin, while Colin Farrell's unique, death-flicking assassin Bullseye often looks weakly pathetic, a character flavor perhaps not intended.

Although fight scenes are handled with expected big screen aplomb, the film's most impressive creative achievement is enabling the audience to share Matt Murdock's inner ability to "see" via his accelerated senses. Achieved with relatively simple special effects and just the right degree of wonderment, these interludes have a soothingly surreal quality that distinguishes them from the rest of the movie.

Although Fox passed on a sequel for the Man Without Fear, they approved one for Garner's *Elektra*, which softened the heroine and ultimately failed to find an audience. Daredevil himself would return in 2015 as a television series for Marvel, capturing the original comic's flavor far better than this occasionally stylish but generally workmanlike movie adaptation.

BEN AFFLECK JENNIFER GARNER

DAREDEVIL

WWW.DAREDEVILMOVIE.COM 2.14.03

Daredevil may have met his match in Elektra Natchios (Jennifer Garner), who endures a tainted past similar to his own. BELOW, LEFT: Young Matt (Scott Terra).

ABOVE: Card-tossing hitman Bullseye (Colin Farrell). LEFT: Murdock clashes with Wilson Fisk (Michael Clarke Duncan).

Actors Affleck and Garner practiced their martial arts moves extensively before filming began. Garner would reprise her Elektra role two years later.

75 FROM HELL 2001

(122) [2.35]

e than the legend will survive.

JOHNNY
DEPP

HEATHER
GRAHAM

FROM
HELL

OCTOBER R

WHO MADE IT:

Twentieth Century Fox Film Corporation/Underworld Pictures (U.S.). Directors: Albert Hughes, Allen Hughes. Producers: Don Murphy, Jane Hamsher. Writers: Terry Hayes, Rafael Yglesias, based on the graphic novel created by Alan Moore and Eddie Campbell. Cinematography (color): Peter Deming. Music: Trevor Jones. Starring Johnny Depp (Inspector Abberline), Heather Graham (Mary Kelly), Ian Holm (Sir William Gull), Robbie Coltrane (Sergeant Peter Godley), Ian Richardson (Sir Charles Warren), Jason Flemyng (Netley, the Coachman), Katrin Cartlidge (Dark Annie Chapman), Terence Harvey (Benjamin Kidney), Susan Lynch (Liz Stride), Paul Rhys (Dr. Ferral).

WHAT IT'S ABOUT:

In 1888 London, Scotland Yard inspector Frederick Abberline has the uncanny ability to see crimes before they happen and sense who commits the deeds through dreams and visions. When the elusive serial killer known as Jack the Ripper emerges, Abberline is called in to solve the case and stop the unprecedented, murderous rampage

that has all London horror-stricken. As he and his partner Godley investigate, they become acquainted with various prostitutes who were friends and colleagues of the victims. Soon Abberline begins to fall in love with one of them, Mary Kelly, who just happens to be the Ripper's current target.

WHY IT'S IMPORTANT:

Yet another Alan Moore graphic novel brought to the screen with uneven results, *From Hell* crams much of Moore's heavily-researched work about Jack the Ripper into an acceptable pseudo-supernatural thriller, paying occasional lip service to the source material's graphic component with some striking digital vistas of the period. Key to this take on Jack's reign of terror is a subplot embracing a widely discredited government conspiracy theory, suggesting that the Ripper's victims were witnesses who needed to be silenced to protect those in the highest of places.

Johnny Depp gives a solid performance as the story's investigating hero, Inspector Abberline, still grieving over the death of his wife years after the fact. He manages to find temporary solace with red-headed prostitute Mary Kelly (Heather Graham) and Watson-like support from gruff but sympathetic Sergeant Godley (Robbie Coltrane). An added gimmick: mystery-solver Abberline happens to be a genuine psychic who receives periodic flashes of the brutal murders, particularly while under the influence of opium.

Ian Holm, fresh from playing the occasionally possessed Bilbo Baggins in Peter Jackson's *Lord of the Rings* films, deftly shifts from venerable royal doctor to ritual-obsessed madman, a nice addition to cinema's catalogue of Ripper portraits. There's even a canny nod to Nicholas Meyer's seminal JTR tale, *Time After Time*, with the hero mistaking Jack's latest victim for the woman he loves.

Watchable but unremarkable, *From Hell* was met with indifference upon release, neither Jack the Ripper nor the graphic novel angle sparking much interest. Alan Moore had little use for the changes made to his tough lead character (necessitated by star Depp's more civilized persona), and the movie stands today as a curious oddity... part historical melodrama, part exaggerated fantasy-thriller.

Inoffensive but unremarkable adventure borrows from better films...

74

THE PHANTOM 1996

100 2.35

Poster/photos: © 1996 Paramount Pictures/Ladd Company

WHO MADE IT:

Paramount Pictures/Ladd Company (U.S./Australia). Director: Simon Wincer. Producers: Robert Evans, Alan Ladd Jr., Graham Burke, Joe Dante, Bruce Sherlock, Greg Coote, Dick Vane. Writer: Jeffrey Boam, from the comic strip by Lee Falk. Cinematographer (color): David Burr. Music: David Newman. Starring Billy Zane (The Phantom/Kit Walker), Kristy Swanson (Diana Palmer), Treat Williams (Xander Drax), Catherine Zeta-Jones (Sala), James Remar (Quill), Cary-Hiroyuki Tagawa (The Great Kabai Segh), Bill Smitrovich (Uncle Dave Palmer), Casey Siemaszko (Morgan), Samantha Eggar (Lily Palmer), Jon Tenny (Jimmy Wells), Patrick McGoohan (Phantom's Dad).

WHAT IT'S ABOUT:

The legendary Skulls of Touganda are ancient relics from the jungled island of Bengalla that harbor an astonishing energy source unlike anything known to man. Ruthless, power-craving Xander Drax will stop at nothing to obtain and control these artifacts, putting him on a collision course with another Bengallan legend – a masked figure of mystery, garbed in purple, who for over 400 years has served as protector of the jungle: The Phantom!

WHY IT'S IMPORTANT:

Some interesting people were involved with this film, including producers Bob Evans (*Popeye*) and Joe Dante (who always wanted to make a *Plastic Man* movie, but never managed). What emerges is a typical adventure-fantasy from this period; inspired by biggies *Batman* and *Dick Tracy*, *The Phantom* is decidedly tongue-in-cheek, as Bryan Singer's straighter approach to comics adaptation was still a few years away. So while the tale's hero (Billy Zane) is unspoiled, he's also cool and charming, a superhero born in the jungle with the education and panache of a seasoned world traveler. Following the formula first established in Richard Donner's *Superman* (1978), Phantom's opposite number Xander Drax is a broad caricature, played fearlessly by Treat Williams. The ladies, meanwhile, are nicely represented by Kristy Swanson as famous reporter Diana Palmer (good girl) and Catherine Zeta-Jones as seductive Sala (bad girl who turns good girl). Finally, an aging but game Patrick McGoohan chews up some expensive scenery as a special "ghost" star, our titular hero's murdered father... the first Phantom.

Borrowing liberally from *Raiders of the Lost Ark* during early jungle scenes, *The Phantom* also provides echoes of other popular comics-inspired films. When our hero visits New York City to catch his quarry, for example, a meeting of top crooks results in one member refusing Drax's big scheme. Is there any doubt this rebel will be toast before the scene is finished? Still, the always-likable Zane manages to keep things buoyant. His relationship with feisty Diana (they knew each other in college when Phantom assumed the identity of Kit Walker) is familiar but reasonably engaging, while Sala's conversion from vile villainess to helpful ally is possibly the most weakly motivated in movie history ("Don't you care about anything?" asks a captured Diana indignantly, and it is this insightful query that somehow spurs the wicked dragon lady's change of heart).

Nicely produced, photographed, and scored, *The Phantom* is not a terrible movie. But when all is said and done, Lee Falk's legendary Ghost Who Walks simply couldn't stand out from the already-overcrowded pack of retro-heroes that proliferated in the '90s (Alec Baldwin as *The Shadow* from Universal and Disney's *Rocketeer* come to mind). Far better than the Columbia serial made some 50 years earlier, Bob Evans' foray into superhero cinema is colorful but undistinguished.

53

73

CONSTANTINE 2005

(105) 2.35

Poster/photos: © 2005 Lonely Film Productions

THE WAGER
BETWEEN
HEAVEN AND HELL
IS ON EARTH

KEANU REEVES

CONSTANTINE.

COMING SOON

WHO MADE IT:

Warner Bros./Village Roadshow Pictures (U.S.). Director: Francis Lawrence. Producers: Lauren Shuler Donner, Akiva Goldsman, Erwin Stoff, Lorenzo di Bonaventura, Michael Uslan, Benjamin Melniker. Writers: Kevin Brodbin, Frank A. Capello, based on the comic book *Hellblazer* created by Jamie Delano and Garth Ennis (DC). Cinematography (color): Philippe Rousselot. Music: Klaus Badelt, Brian Tyler. Starring Keanu Reeves (John Constantine), Rachel Weisz (Angela Dodson/Isabel Dodson), Shia LaBeouf (Chas Kramer), Djimon Hounsou (Midnite), Max Baker (Beeman), Pruitt Taylor Vince (Father Hennessy), Gavin Rossdale (Balthazar), Tilda Swinton (Gabriel), Peter Stormare (Satan),

WHAT IT'S ABOUT:

Renegade occultist John Constantine has literally been to hell and back. Saved from death after an attempt at suicide, he must now atone for his actions by acting as a guardian in the middle ground between Paradise and Hell. When Constantine teams up with a skeptical policewoman named Angela Dodson to solve the mysterious suicide of her twin sister, their investigation takes them through the world of demons and angels that exists just beneath the landscape of contemporary Los Angeles. Caught in a catastrophic series of otherworldly events, the two become inextricably involved and seek to find their own peace at whatever cost.

WHY IT'S IMPORTANT:

Constantine is an occult mystery-adventure rich in imaginative ideas. The main character, played by Keanu Reeves, is a cynical exorcist dying of lung cancer who is destined for Hell because of a previous suicide; now he's keeping evil entities at bay to buy his way into Heaven, and time is running out. Nice set-up. Happening at the same time is a major effort by the Son of Satan, Mammon, to invade Earth with marauding demons by using the retrieved Spear ofDestiny. Constantine finds himself at the heart of this rule-breaking coup attempt.

As with most occult adventures, arcane events come a little too thick and fast, dissipating interest about mid-way through. Director Francis Lawrence does his best to keep us focused on Constantine's personal plight, which is certainly convoluted enough. Although not a Liverpool lad as in the comics, Reeves is a reasonable casting choice, appropriately bitter and ill-mannered (he never asked for the power to see half-breed monsters, another idea created for the movie) as he undergoes one fantastic experience after another. Rachel Weisz's character and her twin sister are part of Mammon's larger scheme, which ties in with Constantine's second suicide and the foiling of what would literally be Hell on earth. Speaking of Hell, some of the film's best sequences take place there. Not since *Dante's Inferno* (1935) has the torment of countless doomed souls been depicted so unnervingly. Also something of a standout is Tilda Swinton as winged, untrustworthy Gabriel, who believes God has been partial to ungrateful humanity andwelcomes pseudo-Armageddon as a way of improving the stock.

Although it flopped big-time in the U.S., *Constantine* made a pile of money internationally and is viewed as something of a success. There were never any plans for a sequel, but a short-lived NBC TV series was produced in 2014.

72

BUCK ROGERS IN THE 25TH CENTURY 1979

(89) [1.85]

WHO MADE IT:

Universal Pictures (U.S.). Director: Daniel Haller. Producers: Glen A. Larson, Richard Caffey, Andrew Mirisch, Leslie Stevens. Writers: Glen A. Larson, Leslie Stevens, based on the comic strip created by Philip Francis Nowlan. Cinematography (Technicolor): Frank Beascoechea. Music: Stu Phillips. Starring Gil Gerard (Capt. William "Buck" Rogers), Pamela Hensley (Princess Ardala), Erin Gray (Col. Wilma Deering), Henry Silva (Kane), Tim O'Connor (Dr. Elias Huer), Joseph Wiseman (Draco), Duke Butler (Tigerman), Felix Silla (Twiki), Mel Blanc (Twiki's voice), Caroline Smith (Delta Section).

WHAT IT'S ABOUT:

On a mission to launch a space probe in 1987, Captain William "Buck" Rogers is frozen in suspended animation by a meteor storm. He is revived in the year 2491 by the Draconian Princess Ardala, and returned to Earth in his space shuttle with a homing beacon planted aboard in order to track a path to Earth's defense barrier. Torn between the past and a very dangerous present, as well as between rival factions, Buck befriends Colonel Wilma Deering and Dr. Elias Huer, who help him adjust to the somewhat more sterile 25th Century. But the threat of invasion from Ardala's alien forces remains constant, causing the displaced astronaut to become both a fighter pilot and a spy in a battle for the Earth itself.

WHY IT'S IMPORTANT:

The success of *Star Wars* in 1977 inspired producer Glen Larson to develop two space-based TV series, *Battlestar Galactica* and a brand new version of *Buck Rogers in the 25th Century*. The famed comic strip spaceman had been filmed by Universal once before in an unsuccessful 1939 serial with Buster (Flash Gordon) Crabbe, and there had even been a brief 1950s black-and-white TV show, filmed live with mistakes aplenty. 1979's theatrical release of the feature-length pilot was a kind of super-trailer for the NBC series that followed.

The "take" of this shiny new Buck was "Burt Reynolds in space," referring to the macho, devil-may-care superstar who brought a sense of sexy fun to his movie adventures back in the '70s. Star Gil Gerard has vaguely similar charm, and gives the producers pretty much what they asked for. Very pleasant to look at is former model Erin Gray as Rogers' uptight new ally, Col. Wilma Deering, who would become progressively less severe in the resulting TV series. She and voice-of-reason Dr. Huer (Tim O'Connor) promptly become the displaced astronaut's surrogate family, along with a "cute" robot sidekick named Twiki (Felix Silla) that follows him everywhere. Meanwhile, the main villain of this tale is a petulant villainess, portrayed with scene-stealing relish by former *Marcus Welby* regular Pamela Hensley. Her Queen Ardala vampishly romances the back-on-duty captain, while traditional *Buck Rogers* bad guy Kane (the always watchable Henry Silva) operates slyly in her shadow.

With decent special effects (some impressive matte paintings) and reasonably persuasive starship battles, *Buck Rogers in the 25th Century* just about passed as a theatrical feature. It was better produced than the series it spawned, and occasionally a naughty bit-of-business gets a laugh ("Your father's seat is the last thing on my mind," our glib hero tells an amorous Princess Ardala). There is also some cleverness in the catchy theme song provided by Stu Phillips, which sounds a bit like a lullaby as it plays over opening title images of sleeping, time-suspended Buck, sci-fi's answer to Rip Van Winkle.

WHO MADE IT:

New Line Cinema/Golden Harvest/Limelight (U.S.). Director: Steve Barron. Producers: Simon Fields, David Chan, Kim Dawson. Writers: Todd W. Langen, Bobby Herbeck, based on the comic book by Kevin Eastman and Peter Laird. Cinematography (color): John Fenner. Music: John Du Prez. Starring Judith Hoag (April O'Neil), Elias Koteas (Casey Jones), Josh Pals (Raphael, in suit/voice), Michelan Sisti (Michelangelo, in suit), Robbie Rist (Michelangelo, voice), Leif Tilden (Donatello, in suit), Corey Feldman (Donatello, voice), David Forman (Leonardo, in suit), Brian Tochi (Leonardo, voice), Kevin Clash (Splinter, voice), Michael Turney (Danny Pennington), Jay Patterson (Charles Pennington), James Saito (The Shredder).

WHAT IT'S ABOUT:

In New York City, mysterious radioactive ooze has mutated four sewer turtles into talking, upright-walking, crime-fighting ninjas. These intrepid heroes have been named after famous Renaissance artists: Michelangelo, Donatello, Raphael, and Leonardo. With personal behavior that approximates adolescent boys (including a love for pizza), they are trained in the Ninjutsu arts by their equally unique rat sensei, Splinter. When a villainous rogue ninja, who is a former pupil of Splinter, arrives in town and begins spreading lawlessness, it's up to the feisty turtles, along with a bewildered but sympathetic reporter named April O'Neal and a local named Casey Jones, to thwart these evil plans.

WHY IT'S IMPORTANT:

Swiftly made to cash in on the Turtles' popularity as a late '80s cartoon series, this 1990 comedy-adventure was sandwiched between two high-profile blockbusters, Tim Burton's *Batman* and Warren Beatty's *Dick Tracy*. It holds up surprisingly well for a modest production, in spite of or perhaps because of the practical, on-set special effects employed (no CGI). Even more important, a sharp script and savvy direction by Steve Barron managed to hit precisely the right tone, avoiding the obvious pitfalls that demolished *Howard the Duck* a few years earlier.

Each of the Turtle characters has a specific adolescent personality (just as their masks have different colors for easy identification), and the most memorable of the group, brooding loner Raphael (Josh Pals), is given a classic lower east side New York accent… smart move, considering that most of the Ts' trademark lines are clearly California-derived (Cowabunga!). Their humanoid rat surrogate father Splinter is a standard issue Master Po, imparting wisdom at every turn, but he seems almost disturbing alive at times. Speaking of alive, it's a credit to the casting director that the movie's human leads – top-billed Judith Hoag as feisty TV reporter April O'Neal and Elias Koteas as ass-kicking vigilante Casey Jones – are just as agreeable and breezy as their scene-stealing amphibian co-stars.

Teenage Mutant Ninja Turtles does a fine job in bridging the gap between kid movies and comic book action-adventure. The premise of runaway children being tricked and used by criminals who offer the illusion of family solace may be familiar to anyone who's read *Oliver Twist*, but it serves the needs of this property well. It also functions as a fine parallel to the genuine warmth Splinter has for his emotionally needy half-shell "boys."

Successful enough to inspire two less enjoyable sequels back in the '90s, the pizza-craving critters would re-emerge as animated TV stars before making a major movie comeback in 2014. Motion-capture photography from ILM and Megan Fox as April O'Neal were the principal attractions of this critically-panned Michael Bay reboot, which nevertheless managed to spawn a slightly better-liked sequel two years later.

ABOVE: The noble Splinter is held hostage. LEFT: Pizza is Turtle soul food, although delivery in the sewer can be problematic.

April O'Neil (Judith Hoag) is a trusted ally of the amphibious four.

Sworn enemy of the Ninja Turtles is ultra-ruthless, vengeance-seeking Shredder (James Saito) one of Splinter's former pupils, now a renegade ninja with nefarious goals. Only an offbeat alliance between the Turtles and some courageous, resourceful humans saves an unsuspecting NYC from certain doom.

Muppet impresario Jim Henson (left) created the weirdly convincing *Ninja Turtles* costumes.

70 POPEYE 1980

214   2.35

BLOW ME DOWN! IT'S COMINK FOR CHRISTMAS!

I YAM WHAT I YAM!

ROBIN WILLIAMS is POPEYE AND SHELLEY DUVALL is OLIVE OYL

PARAMOUNT PICTURES CORPORATION AND WALT DISNEY PRODUCTIONS PRESENT A ROBERT EVANS PRODUCTION A ROBERT ALTMAN FILM ROBIN WILLIAMS SHELLEY DUVALL POPEYE MUSIC & LYRICS BY HARRY NILSSON EXECUTIVE PRODUCER C.O. ERICKSON SCREENPLAY BY JULES FEIFFER PRODUCED BY ROBERT EVANS DIRECTED BY ROBERT ALTMAN READ THE AVON MOVIE NOVEL™ SOUNDTRACK ALBUM FROM THE BOARDWALK ENTERTAINMENT CO.

© MCMLXXX by Paramount Pictures Corporation and Walt Disney Productions. All Rights Reserved

WHO MADE IT:

Paramount Pictures/Walt Disney Productions (U.S.). Director: Robert Altman. Producer: Robert Evans. Writer: Jules Feiffer, based on the comic strip created by E.C. Segar (King Features). Cinematography (color): Giuseppe Rotunno. Music: Harry Nilsson. Starring Robin Williams (Popeye), Shelley Duvall (Olive Oyl), Paul L. Smith (Bluto), Paul Dooley (Wimpy), Richard Libertini (George W. Geezil), Ray Walston (Poopdeck Pappy), Donald Moffat (The Taxman), Robert Maxwell (Nana Oyl), Donovan Scott (Castor Oyl), Wesley Ivan Hurt (Swee'Pea), Robert Fortier (Bill Barnacle), Linda Hunt (Mrs. Oxheart), Dennis Franz (Spike).

WHAT IT'S ABOUT:

Popeye the Sailor rows to the community of Sweethaven in search of his father, or "pap." There he encounters an assortment of bizarre, often hostile inhabitants, including Olive Oyl, her family, Wimpy, and the local bully, Bluto. Eventually, after much confusion and mayhem, Popeye's father is revealed, and he's cantankerous, bull-headed, and seemingly selfish. In the end, Poopdeck Pappy joins his son as they attempt the daring rescue of Olive and little Swee'Pea, taking on both a sea monster and Bluto's eager fists. Reverse psychology enables Popeye to consume spinach courtesy of his arch-enemy, allowing the Sailor Man to make a startling comeback.

WHY IT'S IMPORTANT:

Making a live-action movie out of *Popeye* might be described as a fool's gamble, which explains why only one notably eccentric filmmaker has ever attempted it. Nevertheless, encouraged by the success of Warner Bros. *Superman* films in the late '70s, Paramount and Walt Disney joined considerable forces to make an original movie musical out of Segar's aggressively strange comic strip.

Casting the lead threatened to hold up production, but the ascendency of zany-hip TV comedian Robin Williams seemed to solve that particular problem. Shelley Duvall, meanwhile, was born to play Olive Oyl. Original tunes were to be provided by popular composer Harry Nilsson, and no one seemed especially concerned that the principal players were all non-singers. For the kind of gentle tunes Nilsson was crafting, it really didn't matter.

And to direct? Producer Robert Evans rolled the dice and bravely hired *M.A.S.H.*'s irreverent guru Robert Altman. For better or worse, *Popeye* was shaping up as a Disney family film with subversive art house deconstruction around the edges. Not exactly a fool's gamble, but pretty close. Screenwriter Jules Feiffer insisted on doing "Segar's Popeye" rather than a variation of the classic Fleischer cartoons produced by Paramount in the '30s and '40s. That meant setting sail for Sweethaven (in truth Malta), a picturesque, semi-fairy tale hamlet as weird as the urchins who inhabit it.

Robin Williams, hoping to conquer the big screen as he had TV, gives his comedic all, which is considerable. That said, and despite Feiffer's insistence on authenticity, this portrait of Popeye is far sweeter than anything Segar ever conceived, more in keeping with the character's kid-friendly associations in later years. He is also given something of an arc: this turns out to be the "origin story" of how Popeye came to appreciate the value of spinach after years of apparently rejecting the potent but bitter-tasting vegetable.

While it's fun to imagine what could have been if producer Evans had said 'wait a minute, let's embrace the Fleischer cartoons, not avoid them,' the movie we actually got does manage some legitimate offbeat charm, and deserves credit for having been tried at all.

Actor/comic Robin Williams brought his unique blend of manic behavior and sweet sensitivity to the unusual role of Popeye. RIGHT: Honored actress Shelley Duvall was equally well-cast as gangly Sweethaven resident Olive Oil. BELOW: Popeye with a captive Poopdeck Pappy (Ray Walston) discuss the virtues of spinach.

BELOW: Bluto bribes Wimpy (Paul Dooley) as Swee'Pea (Wesley Ivan Hurt) looks on.

Two-fisted Popeye faces fights in the ring, and with arch-nemesis Bluto (Paul L. Smith, directly above) during the movie's frenetic climax.

The delightfully cartoon-like community of Sweethaven was created from scratch on the island of Malta.

69 BARBARELLA 1968

98 2.35

PARAMOUNT PICTURES presents
A DINO DE LAURENTIIS PRODUCTION

JANE FONDA

The space age adventuress whose sex-ploits are among the most bizarre ever seen.

SEE
BARBARELLA
DO HER THING!

STARRING
JOHN PHILLIP LAW · MARCEL MARCEAU
DAVID HEMMINGS UGO TOGNAZZI

WHO MADE IT:

Dino De Laurentiis Cinemaografica, Marianne Productions/Paramount Pictures (Italian/U.S.). Director: Roger Vadim. Producers: Dino De Laurentiis. Writers: Terry Southern, Roger Vadim, based on the comic strip and book by Jean-Claude Forest. Cinematography (Technicolor): Claude Renoir. Music: Charles Fox. Starring Jane Fonda (Barbarella), John Phillip Law (Pygar), Anita Pallenberg (The Great Tyrant), Milo O'Shea (Concierge/Durand-Durand), Marcel Marceau (Professor Ping), Claude Dauphin (President of Earth), David Hemmings (Dildano), Ugo Tognazzi (Mark Hand), Veronique Vendell (Captain Moon).

WHAT IT'S ABOUT:

In the distant future, double-rated, five star astro-navigatress Barbarella must interrupt her idyllic existence when the President of Earth assigns her to locate and pacify the renegade scientist Duran Duran. Wide-eyed but committed to her mission, beautiful Barbarella risks the dangers of a hostile, uncivilized part of the galaxy. Soon she's menaced by killer dolls, deadly attacking birds, and a unique machine designed to doom its victim with maximum, unrelenting sexual pleasure. With the aid of winged angel Pygar, sympathetic Professor Ping and freedom-loving revolutionary Dildano, Barbarella succeeds in challenging Sogo's nefarious Black Queen and unmasking Duran Duran... who is now bent on ruling the universe with his positronic ray weapon. Only the evil, unstable liquid energy being known as the Matmos can thwart this mad scheme.

WHY IT'S IMPORTANT:

Jean-Claude Forest's *Barbarella* was better known than most European comic creations in the '60s, partially because it was a take-off on the popular *Flash Gordon*, but also because the title character was visually inspired by international sex kitten Brigette Bardot. Upping the pop culture ante, director Roger Vadim (Bardot's former husband) cast current wife Jane Fonda as the comely space adventurer. Wrapping herself in sexy abbreviated outfits and enduring all manner of fetishistic "perils," she made the role uniquely her own... a 1960s flower child who must occasionally put pacifism on hold and take raygun in hand to rescue the universe from a mad scientist's tyranny.

It was critic Pauline Kael who correctly categorized Fonda's Barbarella as a relatively innocent, wide-eyed American actress lost in a dirty old Frenchmen's cavalcade of funky sci-fi perversions. For the most part, this conceit works: Fonda is a better actress than Bardot ever was, and her flair for light comedy is on full display here (as is the actress herself, performing a zero-gravity striptease under the winking opening titles). Like Dorothy in *The Wizard of Oz*, but a good deal friskier, Barbarella has lots of odd BFFs to help her on her all-important mission, most notable among them the blinded alien angel Pygar (John Phillip Law), although Ugo Tognozzi, Marcel Marceau (in a speaking part) and *Blow Up*'s David Hemmings are also on hand for various forms of assistance. On the side of badness are Black Queen Anita Pallenberg and fugitive genius/would-be universe conqueror Milo O'Shea.

Occasionally groanable (this was just a few years after *Batman*'s campy influence), but more often than not entertaining and imaginative, *Barbarella* made a lot of money when first released. Enlivened by production design, costumes, and special effects that do a fine job in replicating Forest's stylish universe, it gets the job done with European verve and a cheerfully perverse smile.

ABOVE: Barbarella's zero-gravity striptease was a credit sequence delight for adolescent male viewers, who weren't used to nudity on the screen in 1968. LEFT: Barbarella (Jane Fonda) is taken prisoner by the Black Queen (Anita Pallenberg) as renegade scientist Duran Duran (Milo O'Shea), posing as the Queen's Concierge, looks on with bemusement. Winged captive Pygar (John Phillip Law, far left) is unable to help his besieged Earthling friend.

Barbarella endures a succession of bizarre and sometimes stimulating perils before disorganized rebel Dildano (David Hemmings) joins forces with her.

Director Roger Vadim directs his then-wife Jane Fonda as two tiny twin tots take her captive early in the storyline.

ON THE WINGS OF AN ANGEL

The majestic, sightless, high-flying character of Pygar, last of the Ornithanthropes, became iconic for Jean Claude-Forest's *Barbarella* comic strip, almost as memorable as the super-sexy heroine herself. He was perfectly realized by lean, muscular John Phillip Law, who also appeared in Mario Bava's *Danger: Diabolik* the very same year (1968). Right: Blinded and thrown into the Labyrinth, Pygar is nursed back to health by Professor Ping (Marcel Marceau). It's doubtful that any scene like this was actually filmed, although clearly someone went to a little trouble preparing this captivating moment for an on-set photo.

68

FANTASTIC FOUR: RISE OF THE SILVER SURFER 2007

WHO MADE IT:

Twentieth Century Fox Film Corporation/Constantin Film Produktion/1492 Pictures, Marvel Enterprises (U.S./Germany). Director: Tim Story. Producers: Avi Arad, Bernd Eichinger, Ralph Winter. Writers: Don Payne, Mark Frost, John Turman, based on the comic book created by Stan Lee and Jack Kirby (Marvel). Cinematography (color): Larry Blanford. Music: John Ottman. Starring Ian Gruffudd (Reed Richards/Mr. Fantastic), Jessica Alba (Sue Storm/Invisible Woman), Chris Evans (Johnny Storm/Human Torch), Michael Chiklis (Ben Grimm/The Thing), Julian McMahon (Dr. Victor von Doom/Doctor Doom), Kerry Washington (Alicia Masters), Doug Jones (Norrin Radd/Silver Surfer; voiced by Laurence Fishburne).

WHAT IT'S ABOUT:

The superhero team known as the Fantastic Four – Mr. Fantastic, the Invisible Woman, Thing and the Human Torch – renew their ongoing feud with power-craving Dr. Doom, the evil genius they thought they'd destroyed. But Doom takes a back seat to a new, far more devastating threat: a mysterious being of immeasurable power known as the Silver Surfer has been dispatched to herald the coming of something so huge and destructive, the entire planet Earth may be in jeopardy. With the potential end of the world coming on the heels of Reed Richards' and Sue Storm's marriage, the combined might of the world's greatest superheroes is yet again put to the test. Relying upon each of their unique cosmic skills, the Fantastic Four power into action... with Doom, the Silver Surfer and ultimately the mighty Galactus proving to be super-formidable adversaries.

WHY IT'S IMPORTANT:

Tim Story's first *Fantastic Four* movie wasn't exactly a critical darling, but it did well at the box office. So a sequel was logically launched, with the producers wisely aware that the titular Four themselves – including a pre-Captain America Chris Evans as the Human Torch – weren't setting viewers' hearts aflame. So they gave equal billing and a good amount of screen time to the Silver Surfer, one of Marvel's most elegant and striking characters.

Also front-and-center is the wedding of Sue Storm (Jessica Alba) and Reed Richards (Ian Gruffudd). Back in the early '60s, this union was a major Marvel event, with all the heroes from their made-up universe (such as it was then) making fun cameos. The concept is used reasonably well here, the "reaching a new personal plateau" theme reflected in the gradual but steady evolution of Johnny Storm (Evans) from carefree clown to responsible member of the team.

But the Surfer's where the action is, leaving behind some picturesque vistas of mass destruction. Probably the film's best scene is the super-powered chase between the Torch and SS, both beings morphing through buildings and across dense landscapes before finally winding up in outer space... a problem for Mr. Flame On. The ultimate confrontation with Galactus is oddly-conceived (an indistinct entity), disappointing fans who were expecting something more closely resembling what they'd experienced in the comics.

Profitable but not super-profitable, the *Fantastic Four* movie series á la Story came to a close with this decent-enough adventure, best appreciated by younger viewers. While most of the film may be unexceptional, its respectful depiction of the Silver Surfer really can't be faulted. As for the First Family of Comics, they'd face a disastrous big screen reboot from 20th Century Fox a few years later, making these workmanlike efforts from the mastermind behind *Barber Shop* seem quaintly charming by comparison.

Reprising their roles from the original movie: Johnny Storm/Human Torch (Chris Evans), Ian Gruffudd (Reed Richards/Mr. Fantastic), Sue Storm/Invisible Woman (Jessica Alba), and Ben Grimm/The Thing (Michael Chiklis). RIGHT: The Silver Surfer (Doug Jones).

The sleek, super-fast Silver Surfer appears to be a threat to planet Earth, prompting the Fantastic Four into emergency action. Visible, sympathetic Sue tries to reason with this elegant alien, who regards her quizzically.

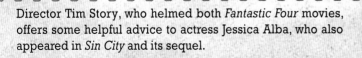

Director Tim Story, who helmed both *Fantastic Four* movies, offers some helpful advice to actress Jessica Alba, who also appeared in *Sin City* and its sequel.

67 BATMAN 1966

(105) 1.85 ♪

WHO MADE IT:

Twentieth Century Fox Film Corporation/Greenlawn Productions (U.S.). Director: Les Martinson. Producers: William Dozier, Charles B. Fitzsimons. Writers: Lorenzo Semple Jr., based on the comic book created by Bob Kane (DC Comics). Cinematography (color): Howard Schwartz. Music: Nelson Riddle. Starring Adam West (Batman/Bruce Wayne), Burt Ward (Robin/Dick Grayson), Lee Meriwether (Catwoman/Kitka), Cesar Romero (The Joker), Burgess Meredith (The Penguin), Frank Gorshin (The Riddler), Alan Napier (Alfred), Neil Hamilton (Commissioner Gordon), Stafford Repp (Chief O'Hara), Madge Blake (Aunt Harriet Cooper), Reginald Denny (Commodore Schmidlapp).

WHAT IT'S ABOUT:

Dynamic Duo Batman and Robin have their work cut out for them when the greatest villains of all time team up to conquer Gotham City... and the world. With their usual flamboyant glee, Joker, Penguin, Riddler and Catwoman succeed in turning the U.N. Security Council into dehydrated dust, even as the feline fury, disguised as Miss Kitka, attempts to seduce unsuspecting Bruce Wayne. An overzealous shark and a waterfront bomb that Batman has a tough time getting rid off add to the challenging adventure, and in the end, a slight mishap with the finally restored leaders suggests that a more understanding, better-governed world might be in the offing.

WHY IT'S IMPORTANT:

Originally intended as an introduction to the 1966 *Batman* television series, this feature film incarnation actually didn't go into production until after the TV show had been successfully launched. With most American families still watching black-and-white TV, it gave viewers their first sustained look at the now-famous Dynamic Duo and their oddly attired arch-villains in full color.

Although not as good as many first-season episodes, this passable self-parody ups the weekly ante by providing several scene-chewing baddies on screen at the same time. All perform as expected, with future *Time Tunnel* actress Lee Meriwether stepping into Catwoman's skin-tight outfit for the first and only time (original Catwoman Julie Newmar was busy on location filming the Gregory Peck western *McKenna's Gold*).

Writer Lorenzo Semple Jr. has fun finding satire in the least likely of places, with gags ranging from the prudent use of shark repellent (extremely effective against goofy-looking predators) and, in one standout sequence, the problems faced by a resourceful crimefighter when trying to dispose of a cartoonish explosive ("Some days you just can't get rid of a bomb!").

Riding the wave of Batmania in 1966, this modest theatrical movie did reasonable business, and enabled many fans to see their favorite heroes in the flesh, as Adam West and Burt Ward took part in an extensive personal appearance campaign linked to Fox's release. Just as significantly, the picture's higher budget allowed for some newfangled Bat-weapons and vehicles, which would promptly reappear as both props and stock footage in second-season episodes of the TV series.

Unexceptional but moderately entertaining, *Batman '66* successfully replicates whatever it was that made the campy TV take so amazingly popular in its day.

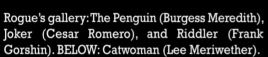

Rogue's gallery: The Penguin (Burgess Meredith), Joker (Cesar Romero), and Riddler (Frank Gorshin). BELOW: Catwoman (Lee Meriwether).

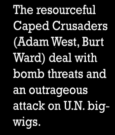

The resourceful Caped Crusaders (Adam West, Burt Ward) deal with bomb threats and an outrageous attack on U.N. big-wigs.

The movie's relatively high budget allowed for some showy new creations, such as the Batcopter and the speedy Batboat.

WHO MADE IT:

Universal Pictures/Marvel Enterprises (U.S.). Director: Ang Lee. Producers: Avi Arad, Larry J. Franco, Gale Anne Hurd, James Schamus. Writers: James Schamus, Michael France, John Turman, based on the comic book created by Stan Lee and Jack Kirby (Marvel). Cinematography (color): Frederick Elmes. Music: Danny Elfman. Starring Eric Bana (Dr. Bruce Banner/Hulk), Jennifer Connelly (Betty Ross). Sam Elliott (General Thunderbolt Ross), Josh Lucas (Major Glenn Talbot), Nick Nolte (Dr. David "Dave" Banner), Cara Buono (Edith Banner), Celia Weston (Mrs. Krenzier).

WHAT IT'S ABOUT:

A top secret military project hires prestigious university students to assist in the creation of a cell altering machine called the "gammasphere." Leader of this elite group is brilliant scientist Bruce Banner, whose adult emotional life has been compromised by abuse he suffered as a child. Banner is assisted by compassionate colleague Betty Ross, daughter of a seemingly unfeeling father. When the gammasphere goes wrong, Banner is suddenly afflicted with the ability to turn himself into a mammoth, green-skinned creature with incredible strength. Soon dubbed the Hulk, this uncontrollable being is a manifestation of Banner's long suppressed inner demons, and the metamorphosis begins when his emotions flare up. These unstable and now quite dangerous feelings are traced directly to the scientist's haunted childhood, leading to a final father-son confrontation threatens more than just the lives of two human beings.

WHY IT'S IMPORTANT:

Ang Lee's *Hulk* is a curious animal. The idea of making a comic book movie that can transcend the limitations of its genre and emerge as a work of cinema art is certainly exciting, and there are times when Lee's movie hits that high note. Other times, it seems overdone and, in the special effects department, not

very convincing. There are moments when this dour-looking Hulk resembles a Claymation take on Li'l Abner.

The idea of scientist Bruce Banner (Eric Bana) being an abused child comes from the comics, Peter David's contributions specifically, and it's a heavy burden for an audience-friendly film of this kind. It's clear before very long that Lee is exploring a "sins of the fathers" scenario, and there is certainly enough malice to go around. Nick Nolte is positively frightening as the unhinged dad of Banner, a true human monster, and Sam Elliot is a by-the-book cold fish as General Thunderbolt Ross, father of Bruce's love interest, Betty Ross (Jennifer Connelly). Soon all are faced with a gamma-radiated giant in their midst, along with other assorted mutants. After various chases and captures, the final confrontation is between the two Banners, an art house battle of wills and genetic abnormalities gone amok.

Nowhere near as effective as Ken Johnson's 1977 TV pilot, *Hulk* made money and garnered some decent reviews, but was ultimately deemed an ambitious misfire. Significantly, Marvel's stand-alone take on the character starring Ed Norton a few years later must be counted as another creative failure. It took actor Mark Ruffalo and the use of Hulk as a supporting "hero" in the Marvel universe for the character to be palatable on screen, as he has been ever since the first *Avengers* movie.

65 MYSTERY MEN 1999

121 | 1.85

Poster/photos: © 1999 Universal Studios

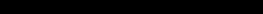

WHO MADE IT:

Universal Pictures/Golar Productions (U.S.). Director: Kinka Usher. Producers: Lawrence Gordon, Lloyd Levin, Mike Richardson. Writers: Neil Cuthbert, Bob Burden, based on Flaming Carrot Comics created by Bob Burden (Dark Horse). Cinematography (color): Stephen H. Burum. Music: Stephen Warbeck. Starring Hank Azaria (Jeff/The Blue Raja), Ben Stiller (Roy/Mr. Furious), Claire Forlani (Monica), Janeane Garofalo (Carol/The Bowler), Eddie Izzard (Tony P.), Greg Kinnear (Lance Hunt/Captain Amazing), William H. Macy (Eddy/The Shoveler), Kel Mitchell (Invisible Boy), Lena Olin (Dr. Anabel Leek), Paul Reubens (The Spleen), Geoffrey Rush (Casanova Frankenstein), Wes Studi (The Sphinx).

WHAT IT'S ABOUT:

When Captain Amazing, Champion City's legendary superhero, falls into the hands of the evil madman Casanova Frankenstein and his disco-dancing henchmen, there's suddenly a chance for the aspiring super-heroes to show what they can do. They're the Mystery Men... a ragtag team of su-perhero wannabes featuring: Mr. Furious, whose power comes from his boundless rage; The Shoveler, a father who shovels "better than anyone"; The Blue Raja, a fork-flinging mama's boy; The Bowler, who fights

crime with the help of her father's skull; The Spleen, whose power is pure flatulence; Invisible Boy, who's only invisible when no one's watching and The Sphinx, a cliche-spewing philosopher.

WHY IT'S IMPORTANT:

Live-action parodies of comic book subjects run the risk of being silly, inconsequential affairs, best suited to brief *Saturday Night Live* sketches than feature-length presentations. *Mystery Men*, which boasts an A-level cast and some genuine imagination in a num-ber of areas, occasionally rises above this pitfall, but more often than not plummets into it. The movie's funny and engaging, just not funny or engaging enough. The whole thing's based on a snarky comic book cre-ated by Dark Horse at the high of the company's fashionability in the late '80s/early '90s. Ironically, *MM*'s most famous member, Flaming Carrot, doesn't appear in the film. What we do have is a team of unmasked, blue collar "superhero" losers out to rescue a genuine superman (played with pre-fab charm by Greg Kinnear) who is the captive of doom-planning villain Casanova Frankenstein (Geoffrey Rush). Typical of their ineptitude, our stalwart heroes wind up killing the hapless captain instead of saving him. And that's just the beginning of their problems. In all fairness, it's quite a team: Ben Stiller was born to play high-strung Mr. Furious, Hank Azaria's a scream with his fruity British accent, Janeane Garofalo looks like she really knows how to bowl, and William H. Macy brings his usual brand of cracked goodwill to hardhat hero the Shoveler... who twirls a mean one. Let's not even talk about the Spleen (Paul Reubens) and his regrettable super-power. It all adds up to a pokey parody with occasional wit and inevitable heart, not a bad combination.

Mystery Men provides some mild amusement, nice turns by a bunch of comedy pros (mustn't forget Louise Lasser as Blue Raja's sympathetic mom), and some pretty colorful production design. There was no sequel, and none is currently planned.

64 THE ROCKETEER 1991

(138) 2.35 🎧

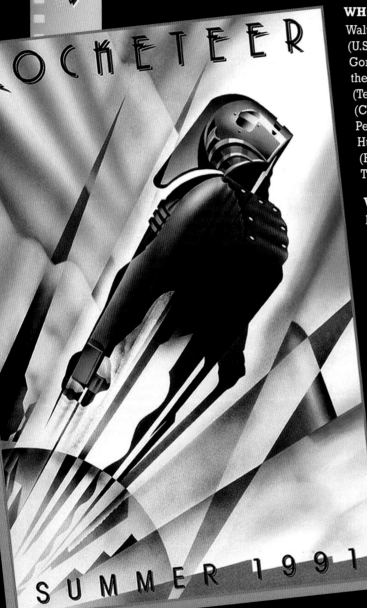

WHO MADE IT:

Walt Disney Pictures/Touchstone Pictures/Silver Screen Partners IV (U.S.). Director: Joe Johnston. Producers: Charles Gordon, Lawrence Gordon, Lloyd Levin. Writers: Danny Bilson, Paul De Meo, based on the comic book by Dave Stevens (Pacific Comics). Cinematography (Technicolor): Hiro Narita. Music: James Horner. Starring Billy Campbell (Cliff Secord), Jennifer Connelly (Jenny Blake), Alan Arkin (A. "Peevy" Peabody), Timothy Dalton (Neville Sinclair), Terry O'Quinn (Howard Hughes), Ed Lauter (Fitch), James Handy (Wooly), Paul Sorvino (Eddie Valentine), Jon Polito (Bigelow), Clint Howard (Mark), Tiny Ron Taylor (Lothar).

WHAT IT'S ABOUT:

In 1938 Los Angeles, an eager young pilot named Cliff Secord finds himself in possession of a stolen, top secret jet-pack that gives him the ability to fly. As he and his mechanic pal Peevy experiment with the astonishing device, Cliff soon learns that popular screen-star Neville Sinclair is in fact a traitor and will stop at nothing to get his hands on the rocket pack so he can give it to the Nazis. Caught between enemy agents and the FBI, with actress girlfriend Jenny Blake endangered by Sinclair, young Secord uses the pack to become the costumed hero Rocketeer and set things straight. A final, explosive confrontation between the forces of good and evil atop an airborne blimp finally settles the score.

WHY IT'S IMPORTANT:

The Rocketeer seemed to rocket out of nowhere in the 1980s, Dave Stevens' exquisitely drawn comics feature an immediate fan favorite. It was quite a coup for independent publisher Pacific Comics to sell this cult creation to both Touchstone Pictures and Walt Disney, even as the far more famous *Dick Tracy* was being prepped by Disney as an answer to Tim Burton's *Batman* (1989).

Inspired by the *Commando Cody* "rocket man" serials from the post atomic era, Stevens' *Rocketeer* was really a tribute to wartime-era Hollywood, with real-life personalities like model Betty Page and "monster without make-up" Rondo Hatton as supporting characters. Unfortunately, what played as fanciful and fun on the four-color page emerges as a smorgasbord of partially-interesting ideas when given film reality, especially in the workmanlike hands of director Joe Johnston.

The titular hero, to begin with, is about as cool as a bewildered cootie in a costume that accentuates his awkwardness (it doesn't help that Rocketeer's "learning curve" has him screwing up more than once). You couldn't find more attractive leads than Bill Campbell and Jennifer Connelly, but both suffer from a severe case of the blands. Alan Arkin is mostly wasted as the hero's earthy father figure and mentor, although Terry O'Quinn has a fun moment as Howard Hughes, a big believer in outrageous dreams ("So what if the damn thing never worked," he says of his famous but eternally grounded Spruce Goose, even as he helps our heroes with their newfangled rocket suit). Most controversial of all was the satiric jab at Errol Flynn embodied in the character of swashbuckling star Neville Sinclair (Timothy Dalton). The old Hollywood wives' tale of Flynn being a Nazi spy is given free reign here. It may be blatantly unfair, but it fits into this wacky revisionist take on a Tinseltown that never was, as does the explosive explanation for the removal of "LAND" from the famous "Hollywoodland" hillside letter arrangement.

Despite some agreeably mad notions, *The Rocketeer* is about a third as enjoyable as it needs to be, ultimately emerging as a lowercase Indiana Jones adventure set in the States. Not surprisingly, boxoffice was tepid, and no sequels were produced.

Cliff Secord (Billy Campbell) has the experimental rocket-pack adjusted by trusty mechanic/best pal Peevy (Alan Arkin).

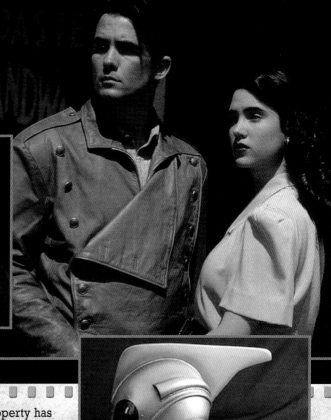

LEFT: Lothar (Tiny Ron Taylor) and Neville Sinclair (Timothy Dalton).

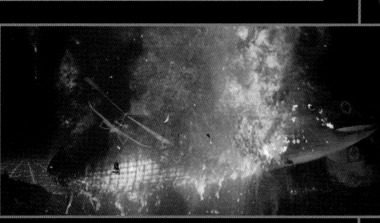

ABOVE: the explosive fx finale. RIGHT: Secord and his actress sweetheart, Jenny Blake (Jennifer Connelly).

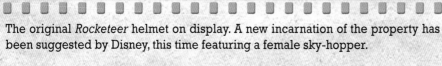

The original *Rocketeer* helmet on display. A new incarnation of the property has been suggested by Disney, this time featuring a female sky-hopper.

63 BLADE II 2002

(117) [1.85] 🎧

WHO MADE IT:

New Line Cinema/Amen Ra Films/Imaginary Forces/Marvel Enterprises (U.S.). Director: Guillermo del Toro. Producers: Avi Arad, Michael De Luca, Peter Frankfurt, Andrew J. Horne, Jon Divens, Lynn Harris, David S. Goyer, Wesley Snipes. Writer: David S. Goyer, based on the comic book character created by Marv Wolfman and Gene Colan for *Tomb of Dracula* (Marvel). Cinematography (color): Gabriel Beristain. Music: Marco Beltrami. Starring Wesley Snipes (Blade), Kris Kristofferson (Whistler), Ron Perlman (Reinhardt),

WHAT IT'S ABOUT:

Half-vampire and half-human, Blade is a fierce vampire hunter who lives on a serum that allows him to resist the urge for blood. He is aided in his missions by mentor and father figure Whistler, thought dead but now infected by a vampire virus, and pot-smoking slacker Scud. Blade soon learns that his greatest enemy, vampire leader Damaskinos wants to joins forces in a monumental struggle against the Reapers, mutated super-bloodsuckers on a rampage of murder. Wary, Blade agrees to a truce and reluctantly joins the Bloodpack, an elite squad of commandos originally

WHY IT'S IMPORTANT:

Impressed with the success of Warren's *Vampirella* comic series in the '70s and determined to mine every sub-genre of fantasy imaginable, Marvel delved into the world of undead bloodrinkers with *Tomb of Dracula* and the black variation *Blade*, both written by Mark Wolfman. As with Vampirella, heroic Blade depends on a blood serum substitute to keep from feeding on humans, a serviceable gimmick later appropriated by TV's *True Blood* series.

Pitting martial artists against supernatural forces is something Asian cinema does effortlessly. It's a lot harder to pull off with American comic book properties, as the comparatively vulgar slugfests that are required at periodic intervals have a less sophisticated, all-too raw physical tangibility about them. This works against the inherent elegance and poetry that generally allows for a willing suspension of disbelief. *Blade* and its sequel tried to compensate with imaginative variations of classic vampire lore and no-nonsense, street-smart flavoring. An unsmiling Wesley Snipes as Blade certainly fits the bill visually, although audiences rarely get below the surface of his relentlessly super-cool anti-hero.

Acclaimed fantasy director Guillermo del Toro tackled *Blade II*, providing more stylish set-pieces and even weirder creatures for Snipes to battle with. But what works so brilliantly in dark fairy tales for children (*Pan's Labyrinth* is still del Toro's finest work) often hits a heavy wall in his comic book adaptations, which are pitched on an entirely different emotional wavelength. Only in the film's final moments, with Blade holding a dying vampire ally (Leonor Varela) in his arms so that she can see the sun before being disintegrated by it, does the film achieve a degree of poetic validation.

62

THE WOLVERINE 2013

WHO MADE IT:

Twentieth Century Fox Film Corporation/Marvel Entertainment/Donner's Company (U.S./U.K.). Director: James Mangold. Producers: Lauren Shuler Donner, Hutch Parker. Writers: Mark Bomback, Scott Frank, based on the comic book character by Chris Claremont and Frank Miller (Marvel). Cinematography (color): Ross Emery. Music: Marco Beltrami. Starring Hugh Jackman (Logan/Wolverine), Tao Okamoto (Mariko Yashida), Rila Fukushima (Yukio), Hiroyuki Sanada (Shingen Yashida), Svetlana Khodchenkova (Dr. Green/Viper), Brian Tee (Noboru Mori), Haruhiko Yamanouchi (Yashida), Will Yun Lee (Kenuichio Harada), Famke Janssen (Jean Grey).

WHAT IT'S ABOUT:

Logan aka Wolverine, living in isolation like an animal since the death of his beloved Jean Grey, finds himself in modern day Japan to bid an old friend from World War II farewell. Just hours before passing away, this friend, Yashida, the country's most powerful tech mogul, implores Logan to protect his granddaughter Mariko whom he has personally chosen to take over the family business – much to the chagrin of her plotting father, Shingen. When the yakuza attempt a high-profile kidnapping of Mariko during Yashida's funeral, Wolverine comes to her rescue. Out of his depth in an unknown world he faces his ultimate nemesis in a life-or-death battle that will leave him forever changed.

WHY IT'S IMPORTANT:

After the relative disappointment of *X-Men Origins: Wolverine*, Fox decided not to move forward with the planned *X-Men Origins: Magneto* (eventually reborn as *X-Men: First Class*). Instead, a new solo Wolverine adventure was put into production, this one inspired by a popular *Wolverine* comic book story set in Japan.

As with a good James Bond movie, the snappy change of locales adds color and zest to the proceedings; Logan travels from the wintery Yukon to the exotic Far East (with only a few exteriors actually shot on location; most of the movie was filmed in Australia). The central conflict between rival heirs that Wolverine entangles himself with is nothing special in itself. It just provides a serviceable adventure for our taloned protagonist as he continues to search

for inner peace, or at least a rationalization of his immortality. Surprisingly, Logan's affection for Mariko (Tao Okamoto) plays as more than just required romance; his tortured remorse over Jean Grey's death provides the emotional rationale for it. Ultimately, all roads lead to an inevitable CG slugfest, with Wolverine squaring off against the scene-stealing Silver Samurai, an electromechanical suit of Japanese armor that clearly knows how to defend itself.

In an end credits moment, Logan's X-Men partners show up for a brief "next movie" tease that had some audience members groaning. Do we really need any more of these films, many pondered aloud? The answer was a surprising yes, as *The Wolverine*'s immediate follow-up, *X-Men: Days of Future Past*, itself a sequel to 2011's *X-Men: First Class*, unexpectedly raised the bar for the good professor and his cronies.

FLASH GORDON CONQUERS THE UNIVERSE 1940 220 1.37

WHO MADE IT:

Universal Pictures (U.S.). A 12-chapter serial. Directors: Ford Beebe, Ray Taylor. Producer: Henry MacRae. Writers: George H. Plympton, Basil Dickey, Barry Shipman, based on the comic strip by Alex Raymond (King Features). Cinematography (b/w): Jerome Ash, William A. Sickner. Music: Stock. Starring Buster Crabbe (Flash Gordon), Carol Hughes (Dale Arden), Charles Middleton (Emperor Ming), Anne Gywnne (Sonja), Frank Shannon (Dr. Zarkov), John Hamilton (Prof. Gordon), Shirley Deane (Princess Aura), Roland Drew (Prince Barin), Lee Powell (Capt. Roka), Don Rowan (Capt. Torch), Victor Zimmerman (Lieutenant Thong), Edgar Edwards (Captain Turan), Ben Taggart (General Lupi).

WHAT IT'S ABOUT:

Earth is being ravaged by a mysterious plague of interstellar origin known as the Purple Death. Investigating in his spaceship, Dr. Zarkov discovers that a craft from the planet Mongo is seeding our atmosphere with this deadly poison. It's clear that vengeful despot Ming the Merciless is once again threatening our world, prompting arch-adversaries Flash Gordon, Dale Arden, and Zarkov himself to venture into outer space for a final showdown on Mongo. There, the Earth team is joined by allies Prince Barin of Arboria and Queen Fria. Warding off ongoing attacks from Ming, Flash and his friends journey to the frozen northern land of Frigia in search of polarite, an antidote to the Purple Death.

WHY IT'S IMPORTANT:

After their production of *Buck Rogers* proved more miss than hit, Universal cancelled plans for a second Buck serial and returned to *Flash Gordon* for inspiration. With Buster Crabbe once again facing off against Charles Middleton's Ming, *Conquers the Universe* served as the final entry of what became a trilogy of spacefaring chapterplays.

Although burdened by a reduced budget, *FGCTU* plays as slightly more sophisticated than its predecessors, reflecting the sensibilities of a new, soon to be war-besieged decade. Even Dale Arden evolves from Jean Rogers' helpless hunny-bunny to a full-fledged space adventurer enacted by Carol Hughes, a decent match for irresistible bad girl Sonja (Anne Gwynne). Prince Barin is no longer overweight and awkward, but, as played by Roland Drew, svelte and self-assured. Indeed, for a good portion of *Conquers the Universe*, the lead heroes behave more like Robin Hood and his feather-capped followers than futuristic star warriors.

As always, each chapter ends with an outrageous cliffhanger, and stock music is liberally applied at every turn... although this is the first of Universal's *Flash* serials to extensively utilize Franz Lizst's *Les Preludes* as the main heroic theme. It works amazingly well, providing a fine substitute for the previous, *Invisible Man*-derived *Flash* theme.

In a curious try at poetry, Chapter 12's final lines of dialogue explain the serial's title, which appears to characterize heroic Flash as some kind of interplanetary despot. By conquering Ming, who had declared himself "the universe," Gordon achieves a towering status even the Gods might envy, at least according to Dr. Zarkov. It's a fitting conclusion to a legendary serial trilogy that, to this day, remains the definitive adaptation of Alex Raymond's great comic strip.

Buster Crabbe, Frank Shannon, and Charles Middleton return for a third outing as Flash Gordon, Dr. Zarkov, and Ming the Merciless, respectively, with Carol Hughes replacing Jean Rogers as Dale Arden.

Back for more spit-firing fun are the serial's distinctive spaceships.

Flash and Dale battle mechanical men during the course of their third adventure.

"THE PURPLE DEATH"

Chapter 1

This original 1940 lobby card for Chapter 1 offers the stalwart space heroes in more conventional garb.

60 DICK TRACY 1990

(105) 1.85

WHO MADE IT:

Touchstone Pictures/Buena Vista Pictures/Silver Screen Partners IV/Mulholland Productions (U.S.). Director: Warren Beatty. Producers: Beatty, Jon Landau, Art Linson. Writers: Jim Cash & Jack Epps Jr., based on the comic strip created by Chester Gould. Cinematography (color): Vittorio Storaro. Music: Danny Elfman, Stephen Sondheim (songs). Starring Warren Beatty (Dick Tracy), Al Pacino ("Big Boy" Caprice), Madonna (Breathless Mahoney), Glenne Headly (Tess Trueheart), Charlie Korsmo (The Kid), Jeames Keane (Pat Patton), Seymour Cassel (Sam Catchem), Michael J. Pollard (Big Bailey), Charles Durning (Chief Brandon), Dick Van Dyke (DA Fletcher), Dustin Hoffman (Mumbles), Mandy Patinkin (88 Keys), William Forsythe (Flattop), Ed O'Ross (Itchy), R.G. Armstrong (Pruneface), Paul Sorvino (Lips Manlis), James Caan (Spud Spaldoni), Catherine O'Hara (Texie Garcia).

WHAT IT'S ABOUT:

Hard-boiled detective Dick Tracy is searching for evidence that proves Alphonse "Big Boy" Caprice is the city's most dangerous crime boss. He may have found the key to unraveling this powerful cretin's illegal empire in Breathless Mahoney, a sultry barroom singer who has witnessed some of Caprice's crimes firsthand. But Mahoney seems more set on stealing Dick away from his long-suffering girlfriend, Tess Trueheart, than helping him solve the case of his career. Meanwhile, a homeless youngster is saved from a savage beating by Tracy, who, along with Tess, befriends the boy. Ultimately, Breathless tries to manipulate events while disguised as the enigmatic No-Face, but dies in a final skirmish with framed and furious Big Boy, who finally plummets to his own well-deserved demise.

WHY IT'S IMPORTANT:

This big studio, family-friendly *Dick Tracy* was created very much in the shadow of Tim Burton's recent *Batman* (1989), with an always-game Warren Beatty amping up the stylization so that it deliberately calls attention to itself. From the outlandish make-ups of freakish criminal characters to an unreal landscape of primary colors, this loopy, ultimately entertaining take on Chester Gould's hard-boiled detective strip dishes up some classic camp comedy. Put another way: It has Al Pacino practically chewing our noses as explosive, oft-quoting Big Boy Caprice, in striking counterpoint to his dour Michael Corleone of *Godfather III* that same year.

Just as worthwhile in a far more subdued way is Beatty as the titular hero. He's beyond merely an attractive caricature of do-gooding, registering as an honest, often sad anachronism who finds his unswerving sense of moral righteousness unexpectedly challenged by seductive bad girl Breathless Mahoney (Madonna). The movie ultimately rewards him with a swell girlfriend and a very handy surrogate offspring named Kid – this scene-stealing brat saves Tracy's life twice. *Dick Tracy*'s mini-mystery really isn't much of a mystery, and, given the film's self-aware tone, it may be that we're intended to know that it's Breathless under that No Face mask, playing both ends against the middle in classic style. It's relationships and star power chemistry that are important here, and the fun of watching an already over-the-top villain go completely berserk for a kitschy and visually arresting climax. Even fireworks are conveniently provided.

Far more interesting than Ralph Byrd's off-the-rack G-man, as seen in serials and cheap features, filmmaker Beatty's naïve-yet-savvy Dick remains a rocksteady symbol of law and order. He may be sympathetic to offbeat expressions of love, but certainly not bribery and the sacrifice of basic principles as he understands them. In the final analysis, Tess Trueheart has nothing to worry about.

Warren Beatty's vision for *Dick Tracy* required an artfully unreal "comic book" world for the master sleuth to inhabit. RIGHT: Madonna added her own brand of seductive unreality to her role as showgirl Breathless Mahoney.

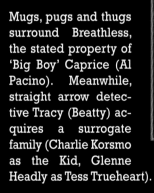

Mugs, pugs and thugs surround Breathless, the stated property of 'Big Boy' Caprice (Al Pacino). Meanwhile, straight arrow detective Tracy (Beatty) acquires a surrogate family (Charlie Korsmo as the Kid, Glenne Headly as Tess Trueheart).

Visual effects supervisors Michael Lloyd and Harrison Ellenshaw presided over the unique metropolitan vistas created for the film, which won three Oscars.

59 BATMAN RETURNS 1992 (126) 1.85

WHO MADE IT:

Warner Bros./The Guber-Peters Company (U.S.). Director: Tim Burton. Producers: Peter Guber, Jon Peters, Tim Burton, Denise Di Novi, Larry Franco, Benjamin Melniker, Michael Uslan. Writers: Daniel Waters, Sam Hamm, based on the comic book created by Bob Kane (DC). Cinematography (color): Stefan Czapsky. Music: Danny Elfman. Starring Michael Keaton (Batman/Bruce Wayne), Danny DeVito (Penguin/ Oswald Cobblepot), Michelle Pfeiffer (Catwoman/Selina Kyle), Christopher Walken (Max Shreck), Michael Gough (Alfred Pennyworth), Michael Murphy (The Mayor), Cristi Conaway (Ice Princess), Pat Hingle (Commissioner Gordon).

WHAT IT'S ABOUT:

Batman's skirmish with a troupe of criminal circus performers is only the beginning of a daunting new adventure. Hideously deformed scion of a wealthy Gotham City family, the foul Penguin plots with evil businessman Max Schreck to become mayor of a city he hopes to transform into a cathedral of crime. Upon overhearing these plans, Schreck's mousy secretary Selena Kyle is tossed from a high-rise window by her boss. Emerging alive but half-mad, Selena transforms herself into the leather-clad avenger Catwoman. Although she teams with the Penguin and Schreck to foster crime and help discredit Batman, she also has her own score to settle.

WHY IT'S IMPORTANT:

Following the spectacular box office success of *Batman* (1989), director Tim Burton was given a freer creative hand with its eagerly-awaited sequel. This was good in some ways – Burton fashioned a bizarre but irresistible Catwoman (Michelle Pfeiffer) that, in her makeshift sexy costume and with a deep, dark voice to die for, nearly steals this colorful show. On the other hand, Burton's Penguin take (played with disgusting relish by Danny De Vito), a deformed creature who dresses like something out of a silent-era horror movie, is a little too gross for his own good.

The Caped Crusader himself (or Dark Knight) takes something of a backseat to these two, or three, with Christopher Walken skulking about as a corrupt bigwig and the remorseless murderer of innocent secretaries who hear more than they should. The plot is a convoluted affair involving a Mayoral run by Oswald (Penguin) Cobblepot and the aggressive antics of a criminal circus, but it's really just an excuse to bring together Batman and Catwoman (and even more importantly, Bruce Wayne and Selina Kyle) for a brief, funny, ultimately tragic relationship. It's the heart of the movie and, despite or because of all the candy-coated eccentricity involved, it resonates.

Although uneven and alienating to many, *Batman Returns* is nevertheless a most competent rollercoaster ride, with Burton improving his skill with superheroic action sequences and epic-filmmaking in general. Batman's final attack on Cobblepot is thrilling tour-de-force, as his enemy's apocalyptic plans for Gotham City (armies of bomb-toting penguins advancing on the city, one of the film's more childish ideas) are dramatically thwarted. Meanwhile, Catwoman's heartbreaking final moments with an unmasked Bruce Wayne provide just the right emotional capper, bringing *Batman Returns* to an exciting but melancholy end.

For Tim Burton as director/creative prime-mover, this was the end of the line. The *Batman* movie series would now be helmed (for two additional entrees, anyway) by Joel Schumacher. With *Batman Forever*, this changeover was met with enthusiastic applause. By the time movie number two, *Batman and Robin*, came along, viewers were drifting away in droves. Yet another rebirth was required, this time without bat-nipples on our hero's chestplate and a far more sophisticated treatment worthy of the subject matter.

ABOVE: Batman (Michael Keaton) finds an ideal companion in Catwoman (Michele Pfeiffer), a hyper-insecure secretary abruptly transformed into Gotham's leading femme fatale through an act of shocking violence.

Catwoman joins forces with the wretched Penguin (Danny DeVito) to launch a crime wave in Gotham City… with Batman their mutual nemesis.

The romantic relationship between villain/victim Selena (Pfeiffer) and Bruce Wayne (Keaton) is charmingly tragic.

LEFT: sculpt of Catwoman's distinctive cowl.
RIGHT: Costumed Pfeiffer and Keaton are directed by Tim Burton.

58 CAPTAIN AMERICA: THE FIRST AVENGER 2011

(124) [2.35]

WHO MADE IT:

Marvel Entertainment/Paramount Pictures (U.S.). Director: Joe Johnston. Producers: Kevin Feige, Alan Fine, Louis D'Esposito, Stephen Broussard, Mitch Bell, Nigel Gostelow. Writers: Christopher Markus, Stephen McFeely, based on the comic book created by Joe Simon and Jack Kirby (Timely Comics/Marvel Comics). Cinematography (color): Shelly Johnson. Music: Alan Silvestri. Starring Chris Evans (Captain America/Steve Rogers), Hayley Atwell (Peggy Carter), Sebastian Stan (James Buchanan "Bucky" Barnes), Tommy Lee Jones (Colonel Phillips), Hugo Weaving (Johann Schmidt/Red Skull), Dominic Cooper (Howard Stark), Stanley Tucci (Dr. Abraham Erskine), Samuel L. Jackson (Nick Fury), Toby Jones (Dr. Zola).

WHAT IT'S ABOUT:

Born during the Depression, Steve Rogers grows up a frail youth in a poor family. He is inspired to enlist in the army, but is rejected because of his poor health and physical state. Overhearing the boy's earnest plea, General Phillips offers Rogers the opportunity to take part in a unique experiment. He is injected with a "super soldier" serum that bombards him with powerful vita-rays. After months of intensive physical and tactical training, he is given his first assignment as the costumed, patriotic icon Captain America. Armed with an indestructible shield, this sentinel of justice proceeds to wages a one-man war against evil and sets his sights on a his Nazi opposite number, the Red Skull.

WHY IT'S IMPORTANT:

Marvel needed to create a few "stand-alone" superhero movies before the studio could combine them for *The Avengers*. Patriotic shield-thrower Captain America was problematic due to the changing social view of the U.S. in foreign markets, and no one wanted a chest-beating flag waver pushing traditional values in the 21st Century. Marvel solved the problem by producing a nostalgic "origin story" set in World War II, where heroes and villains were more clearly-defined.

Unfortunately, the resulting movie winds up being as bland as its frustrated hero, Steve Rogers (Chris Evans), which is hardly the fault of the actors or producers. Evans' take on this key character would spring to life in the vastly superior follow-up movies helmed by Joss Whedon and the Russo brothers. But here, under Joe Johnston's predictably lackluster direction, Steve Rogers fades into the woodwork, his relationship with equally nondescript love interest Hayley Atwell (Peggy Carter) generating zero chemistry. Cap's final confrontation with Nazi super-villain Red Skull (Hugo Weaving) is also far less exciting than it should be. Coming off best in this pedestrian entry are ill-fated sidekick Bucky (Sebastian Stan) and, briefly, Stanley Tucci as the sympathetic Dr. Erskine.

Captain America, as portrayed by Evans, would soon evolve as a modern patriot with serious misgivings about the direction his own government has taken. For those seeking a dramatization of this super-soldier's origin, *First Avenger* provides fans with the basics... and little else.

57 WANTED 2008

(110) [2.35] 🎧

SUMMER 2008
www.wantedmovie.com

WHO MADE IT:

Universal Pictures/Spyglass Entertainment/Relativity Media (U.S./Germany). Director: Timur Bekmambetov. Producers: Marc Platt, Jason Netter, Iain Smith, Jim Lemley. Writers: Chris Morgan, Michael Brandt, Derek Hass, based on the graphic novel by Mark Millar and J.G. Jones. Cinematography (color): Mitchell Amundsen. Music: Danny Elfman. Starring James McAvoy (Wesley Gibson), Morgan Freeman (Sloan), Angelina Jolie (Fox), Thomas Kretschmann (Cross), Common (Earl Spellman aka "The Gunsmith") Konstantin Khabensky ("The Exterminator"), Marc Warren ("The Repairman"), Dato Bakhtadze ("The Butcher"), Terence Stamp (Pekwarsky), David O'Hara (Mr. X), Chris Pratt (Barry), Lorna Scott (Janice).

WHAT IT'S ABOUT:

After the murder of a father he never knew, mundane, 25-year-old account manager Wes Gibson discovers powers beyond his dreams. He becomes the latest recruit in the Fraternity – a secret society of assassins – and develops lightning-quick reflexes with superhuman agility. Guided by wickedly brilliant tutors, Wes morphs into a killing machine and dutifully carries out the death orders of the mythological Fates, weavers of every man's lifeline. But before long he discovers that his compatriots are not exactly the enforcers of justice they claim to be, and that dispensing death can be a lot easier than controlling one's own life.

WHY IT'S IMPORTANT:

Some decent performances add luster to *Wanted*, an over-the-top action thriller about a secret society of professional assassins known as the Fraternity. Frustrated civilian Wesley Gibson (James McAvoy) is their reluctant new recruit; his recently-murdered father was part of the organization, and now Wesley's being targeted by the same killer, appropriately named Cross (Thomas Kretschmann). Our young hero goes from harassed office worker to super hit man, ushered into a world of violence by head honcho Sloan (dignified as always Morgan Freeman) and seasoned field pro Fox (Angelina Jolie, adding another sexy action babe to her resume). Recognizing its obligation to work comic book-style fantasy into the proceedings, the movie conveniently plagues Wesley with ultra-weird panic attacks. These are actually adrenaline rushes that inexplicably grant him superhuman strength, speed, and a heightened sense of perception... certainly handy skills for his new profession.

Aiming at its core audience, *Wanted* offers an endless series of high-octave action sequences, making little pretense to be about much else. Although director Timur Bekmanbetov strays somewhat from his comic book inspiration (no super villains), there is a suggestion of Mark Platt's "we're all losers" theme, whether we are wasting our time watching staccato shoot-em-ups like *Wanted* or actually participating in the storyline as Wesley is (Platt's comic suggested that a love of escapism turns people into monsters). But this grim self-awareness is fairly limited by design; *Wanted* is mostly well-crafted, nicely polished adrenaline-rush entertainment for mainstream audiences, everything its original creator had misgivings about.

Surprisingly, the movie earned mostly positive reviews ("...the cinematic equivalent of an energy drink," said critic David Fear), and was even nominated for two Academy Awards, both in the sound category. A sequel was discussed, but nothing came of it.

Serio-comic crime world fantasy a showcase for hot-as-a-pistol Carrey...

56 THE MASK 2008

(110) 2.35

WHO MADE IT:

New Line Cinema/Dark Horse Productions (U.S.). Director: Charles Russell. Producer: Bob Engelman. Writers: Mike Werb, Michael Fallon, Mark Verheidan, based on the comic created by John Arcudi and Doug Mahnke (Dark Horse). Cinematography (color): John R. Leonetti. Music: Randy Edelman. Starring Jim Carrey (Stanley Ipkiss/The Mask), Cameron Diaz (Tina Carlyle), Peter Greene (Dorian Tyrell), Richard Jeni (Charles Schumaker), Peter Riegert (Lt. Mitch Kellaway), Jim Doughan (Det. Doyle), Amy Yasbeck (Pegg Brandt), Orestes Matacena (Niko), Nancy Fish (Mrs. Peenman).

WHAT IT'S ABOUT:

Girlfriend-deprived Stanley Ipkiss is a shy bank clerk who is too nice for his own good, a personality trait that often makes him a pushover when it comes to confrontations. After one of the most trying days of his life, he finds a mask by the sea that depicts Loki, the Norse night god of mischief. Now, whenever he puts it on, Stanley unleashes his inner self upon the world: a cartoony romantic wild man. Dubbed "The Mask" by the media, this live-wire entity soon earns the wrath of small-time crime boss Dorian Tyrel. They wind up on a collision course, as Ipkiss' green-skinned alter ego sets out to eliminate every gangster in the city.

WHY IT'S IMPORTANT:

Long before Deadpool there was Jim Carry's take on *The Mask*, a hyper-snarky and colorful pseudo-superhero based on a minor comic book from Dark Horse. The comic itself was inspired by a 1961 Canadian horror film of the same name ("Put the Mask on now!"), and early drafts by screenwriter Mike Fallon contain ritual scenes set in Africa, home of the accursed object. This origin would be altered significantly to accommodate Carry, with story material re-worked in general.

From a Hollywood perspective, this was one of the key movies that propelled Jim Carrey to super-stardom in the '90s and beyond. The fantasy involved affords the young actor a unique showcase for his considerable comedic talents, with the film itself never losing focus on the simple fable being presented. The writers do manage some unexpected twists along the way, one of them making a comely Cameron Diaz, in one of her early high-profile roles, even more agreeable as a character.

Visually, *The Mask* owes much to the fx technology developed for Robert Zemekis' *Who Framed Roger Rabbit*, computer-generated animation with a shading and fluidity that makes drawn characters appear almost lifelike. Shoehorned into the storyline is the protagonist's fondness for wise-ass cartoons, which enables a wild tableau of Tex Avery-like imagery to stun our eyes and blow our minds. Even the gangland motif is a leftover from *Rabbit*, although *The Mask*, for all its eccentricity and special effects, remains essentially a real-world movie with some very unreal things happening within it.

Sitting on a huge hit, New Line happily offered Jim Carrey the lead in their planned sequel... but the millions he was now being paid for bigger projects scuttled those plans. A sequel was announced anyway, with original villain Dorian returning and a female Mask to be introduced. Nothing came of that desperate take. Finally, and without the participation of Carrey, *Son of the Mask* was released to a less-than-enchanted public in 2004, ending what was once a potent fantasy franchise.

Hapless but likeable Stanley Ipkiss (Jim Carrey) suddenly finds himself seduced by vixen Tina Carlyle (Cameron Diaz). He returns the favor on the dance floor,

The Mask (Carrey) wreaks havoc about town, making life impossible for a small-time crime boss. All manner of bizarre complications follow, resulting in a third act free for all.

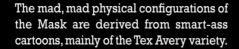

The mad, mad physical configurations of the Mask are derived from smart-ass cartoons, mainly of the Tex Avery variety.

On display is Jim Carrey's facial mask. This unique anti-hero was brought to movie life in a variety of inventive ways.

83

LEND AN EAR, HAVE A HEART

LEFT: An early example of CGI gone wild… The Mask (Jim Carey) does his thing, bringing a variety of cartoon-like body distortions to surreal life. Almost as magical are the scientific creations of Dr. Tony Stark (Robert Downey Jr., ABOVE), not the least of which is an artificial heart that keeps him alive and ready for the next super-battle. Stark is seen here with Gwyneth Paltrow as Pepper Potts in a promotional image for *Iron Man 3*.

55 IRON MAN 3 2013

WHO MADE IT:

Marvel Studios/Walt Disney Studios Motion Pictures (U.S.). Director: Shane Black. Producer: Kevin Feige. Writers: Drew Pearce, Shane Black, based on the comic book created by Stan Lee, Don Heck, Larry Lieber, Jack Kirby (Marvel). Cinematography (color): John Toll. Music: Brian Tyler. Starring Robert Downey Jr. (Tony Stark/Iron Man), Gwyneth Paltrow (Virginia "Pepper" Potts), Don Cheadle (Col. James "Rhodey" Rhodes/Iron Patriot), Guy Pearce (Aldrich Killian), Rebecca Hall (Dr. Maya Hansen), Stephanie Szostak (Brandt), James Bade Dale (Savin), Ben Kingsley (Trevor Slattery), Jon Favreau (Happy Hogan).

WHAT IT'S ABOUT:

Barely recovering from his battle with alien forces, brash-but-brilliant industrialist titan Tony Stark/Iron Man faces off against a super-terrorist whose reach knows no bounds. After Stark finds his personal world abruptly shattered by an audacious enemy attack, he sets out to find those responsible. This harrowing journey tests the scientist's mettle at every turn. Backed against the wall, he is left to survive by his own devices, literal and otherwise, relying on ingenuity and sharpened instincts to protect those closest to him. As he fights his way back to combat readiness, Stark discovers the answer to the question that has secretly haunted him: does the man make the suit or does the suit make the man?

WHY IT'S IMPORTANT:

After the relative disappointment of Jon Favreau's *Iron Man 2*, Robert Downey Jr. brought his old pal Shane Black into the white-hot series, who promptly infused it with a vitality and hipness that caught many viewers by surprise. Clearly, this particular story was designed to bring the Tony Stark saga to some kind of emotionally-satisfying conclusion. But Marvel wasn't about to retire their most flamboyant and bankable actor, an irresistible personality that pretty much launched the MCU back in 2008.

In *Iron Man 3*, semi-depressed Stark shares the screen with everyone from a precocious child to a bogus terrorist (Ben Kingsley), still allowing time for co-star Gwyneth Paltrow (as loving, loyal Pepper Potts) to don an automated soldier suit herself and mix it up with the boys. Although overkill is the order of the day here, Black carries it off with wiseass panache and an infectious sense of self-assurance. That said, the overstuffed climax involving a plethora of Iron Men costumes buzzing about can be confusing and headache-inducing, even for die-hard fans. Indeed, 17 optical effects companies contributed to this movie, among them Scanline VFX, Digital Domain, and Weta Digitial. They were rewarded for their impressive, if sometimes overwhelming conceptions by an Academy Awards Best Visual Effects nomination.

Embraced by critics, *Iron Man 3* did amazingly well at the box office, convincing Robert Downey Jr. to continue with the role that resurrected his acting career, and made him a multi-millionaire in the process. Although an *Iron Man 4* was considered and actually briefly announced, Downey Jr. next played Stark in *The Avengers: Age of Ultron,* followed by *Captain America: Civil War,* and finally 2017's *Spider-Man: Homecoming,* where the emotionally exhausted but still formidable adventurer becomes something of an Obi-Wan Kenobi to fledging hero Peter Parker.

A precocious boy and his pals wreak lovable havoc in this groundbreaking comedy...

54 SKIPPY 1931

(85) [1.33]

IN THE MOVIES NOW
in person
Skippy

JACKIE COOPER, ROBERT COOGAN
MITZI GREEN *and* **JACKIE SEARL**

FROM THE STORY *by* PERCY CROSBY
DIRECTED *by* NORMAN TAUROG

a Paramount Picture

WHO MADE IT:

Paramount Pictures (U.S.). Director: Norman Taurog. Producers: Louis D. Lighton. Writers: Joseph L. Mankiewicz, Normand Z. McLeod, Sam Mintz, based on the comic strip by Percy Crosby. Cinematography (b/w): Karl Struss. Music: John Leipold. Starring Jackie Cooper (Skippy), Robert Coogan (Sooky), Mitzi Green (Eloise), Jackie Searl (Sidney), Willard Robertson (Dr. Skinner), Helen Jerome Eddy (Mrs. Wayne).

WHAT IT'S ABOUT:

Skippy is the precocious, somewhat spoiled son of well-respected Dr. Skinner, in charge of health programs for the local community. A chatterbox who grumbles incessantly but always sees a way out of any problem,

young Skippy is surrounded by various colorful friends, including the obnoxious Sidney and loud, irritating Eloise. His best pal is a new kid from Shantytown, the becapped Sooky. When Sooky's dog Penny is nabbed by the local dog-catcher, the two boys desperately try to raise money to buy a license. One of their schemes is putting on a show for kids in the neighborhood, with star performer Eloise paying for the privilege to entertain. Although Dr. Skinner is late to realize his young son's emotional needs, he becomes a true friend and supporter in the end.

WHY IT'S IMPORTANT:

Percy Crosby's beautifully-illustrated comic strip (1923-45) is something of an American classic. The inspiration for *Peanuts*, *Dennis the Menace*, and countless others, it made kid adventures more life-size, smartly balancing humor with pathos. Skippy himself was one of the strangest boy heroes of this era, an offbeat but ultimately agreeable mix of emotional ups and downs.

Paramount's 1931 movie version is an impressive achievement in itself. It won director Norman Taurog an Oscar for Best Picture, and provided rising young star Jackie Cooper an ideal vehicle for his considerable talents. As with the strip, Skippy is a spoiled grumbler part of the time, a bright-eyed idealist and friend to the end in other situations. He is ably supported by a wonderful cast of youthful performers, with Mitzi Green's Eloise something of a showstopper. The story takes us from the zaniness of a makeshift neighborhood "show" worthy of an *Our Gang* tale, to the palpable grief felt by Sooky (Robert Coogan) after a tragic revelation. Taurog maintains long tracking shots of the boys in ongoing conversation, enabling viewers to live through their escalating troubles. There is also a potent theme about social injustice bubbling just below the surface, with the good Dr. Skinner's priorities and dismissive view of Shantytown suggesting a form of class snobbery.

Although *Skippy* was a big success and earned a sequel the same year (*Sooky*), creator Percy Crosby hated Hollywood's take and legally barred all future movie adaptations. Nevertheless, the spirit of his unique creation lives on, not only in the countless films and TV shows that were inspired by it, but in the moniker of a certain peanut butter company that has been satisfying youngsters for generations.

Nutsy John Hughes farce fueled by adolescent fantasies...

...s all in the name of science. Weird Science.

With a lot of wishful thinking and a little help from the supernatural, Wyatt and Gary accidentally brought Lisa, their ultimate fantasy, to life.

Now she's showing them how to live with fast cars, expensive clothes and a party that's getting wilder and weirder.

A JOHN HUGHES Film A HUGHES/SILVER Production "WEIRD SCIENCE" Written and Directed by JOHN HUGHES
ANTHONY MICHAEL HALL ILAN MITCHELL-SMITH and KELLY LeBROCK Written and Directed by JOHN HUGHES
Music by IRA NEWBORN Director of Photography MATTHEW F. LEONETTI, A.S.C. Produced by JOEL SILVER A UNIVERSAL PICTURE
Soundtrack available on MCA Records & Cassettes. DOLBY STEREO

WHO MADE IT:

Universal Pictures (U.S.). Director: John Hughes. Producer: Joel Silver. Writer: John Hughes, based on EC Comic from the 1950s. Cinematography (Technicolor): Matthew F. Leonetti. Music: Ira Newborn, Jimmy Iovine. Starring Anthony Michael Hall (Gary Wallace), Ilan Mitchell-Smith (Wyatt O'Donnelly), Kelly LeBrock (Lisa), Bill Paxton (Chet O'Donnelly), Robert Downey Jr. (Ian), Robert Rusler (Max), Suzanne Snyder (Deb), Judie Aronson (Hilly), Vernon Wells (Lord General).

WHAT IT'S ABOUT:

A pair of nerdy high school teens, Gary Wallace and Wyatt Donnelly, are dateless as usual on Friday night. How can these apparent losers ever wind up with a beautiful woman? Easy. They somehow manage to create one, making extraordinary use of their computer. Living and breathing "Lisa" is the utterly breathtaking girl of their dreams, the perfect female, answering every adolescent prayer Gary and Wyatt ever had. But fortunately for them, she is pre-programmed to boost their confidence level by placing them in situations where they are forced to behave like responsible men rather than salivating geeks.

WHY IT'S IMPORTANT:

Arguably the least impressive of John Hughes' 1980s teenage confections, *Weird Science* is distantly based on an all-but-forgotten EC Comic of the same name that entertained readers in the pre-code '50s. It takes its central idea (and little else) from a specific Al Feldstein yarn called "Made of the Future!" which appeared in issue #5. *Weird Science* and its companion title *Weird Fantasy* never reached the profitable heights of EC's *Tales from*

the Crypt (horror traditionally outsells sci-fi), but they were impressive comic book titles in their own right, eventually even boasting sanctioned adaptations of Ray Bradbury stories.

Hughes' movie version is centered around a pair of teenage nerds (Anthony Michael Hall, Ilan Mitchell-Smith) who, inspired by a viewing of *Bride of Frankenstein* on TV, scientifically conjure up the babe of their dreams, Lisa (Kelly LeBrock). Regressive male fantasies notwithstanding, it's clear that this stunning computer-driven genie has only the best interests of her pimply young "masters" at heart, teaching them to stand up for themselves in a series of increasingly bizarre set-pieces. Our nerd heroes must somehow find the fortitude to deal with all manner of adversity, starting with standard-issue school bullies (Robert Downey Jr. in an early role). Many have commented that this movie's scenario rightfully belonged in an hour episode of Steven Spielberg's *Amazing Stories*, which seemed to specialize in teen hijinks and over-the-top whimsical fantasy.

Regardless, *Weird Science* was a relative success, inspiring a popular syndicated TV series in the '90s with equally bodacious Vanessa Angel (originally cast as *Xena, Warrior Princess*) taking over for LeBrock. It is rumored a 21st Century reboot is underway.

52

RED 2010

STILL ARMED. STILL DANGEROUS. STILL GOT IT.

OCTOBER 15
Red-TheMovie.com

WHO MADE IT:

Summit Entertainment/Di Bonaventura Pictures (U.S.). Director: Robert Schwentke. Producers: Lorenzo di Bonaventura, Mark Vahradian. Writers: Jon Hoeber, Erich Hoeber, based on the comic book by Warren Ellis and Cully Hamner (DC/Homage). Cinematography (color): Florian Ballhaus. Music: Christopher Beck. Starring Bruce Willis (Francis "Frank" Moses), Morgan Freeman (Joe Matheson), John Malkovitch (Marvin Boggs), Helen Mirren (Victoria Winslow), Karl Urban (William Cooper), Mary-Louise Parker (Sarah Ross), Rebecca Pidgeon (Cynthia Wilkes), Brian Cox (Ivan Simanov), Richard Dreyfuss (Alexander Dunning), Julian McMahon (Vice President Robert Stanton), Ernest Borgnine (Henry), James Remar (Gabriel Singer).

WHAT IT'S ABOUT:

Lonely, bored and retired former CIA agent Frank Moses does his best to adjust to a conventional life that offers little challenge or meaning. His only solace comes from periodic conversations with his equally dissatisfied pension case worker, Sarah. One fateful day, Frank's home is attacked by heavily-armed masked assailants, which suddenly thrusts him back into his old, life-threatening line of work. With help from both Sarah and Russian operatives, he reconnects with former associates Joe, Marvin, and Victoria in a daring scheme to combat security forces. Like Frank, these seasoned agents are all classified 'R.E.D.'... Retired Extremely Dangerous.

WHY IT'S IMPORTANT:

Red is one of the few DC properties (published through imprint Homage/Wildstorm) that was not produced by studio parent Warner Bros., which passed when it was offered. Instead, Lorenzo di Bonaventura and less prestigious Summit Entertainment became involved, promptly assembling a cast to die for.

Somewhere along the line a significant decision was made to go "funny," possibly in reaction to the more over-the-top melodrama of the far drier, excessively violent and brutal comic. Bruce Willis fits comfortably into the reimagined role of retired CIA agent Frank Moses, who, according to colleague Victoria Winslow (a gun-toting Helen Mirren), is all "gooey" inside, a sentimental softie who compensates by being one of the most dangerous operatives imaginable. This results in an improbable romance with the slightly crazy, adventure-craving case worker (Mary-Louise Parker) who sends Moses pension checks and indulges in boy-girl chitchat with him over the phone. It also leads to an audacious scheme where Moses and his retired compatriots strike back at their former bosses and take on both a wealthy manipulator (Richard Dreyfuss) and the Vice President of the United States (Julian McMahon), all involved in shady past operations.

This movie's sense of fun stems from a simple idea: How can people so heavily involved with life-and-death spy operations simply hang it up and become placid senior citizens? They can't. Along the way, themes of friendship, the need for love, and the significance of kindred sensibilities are explored (Moses and his young CIA pursuer Cooper, played by Karl Urban, are variations of each other at different ages).

Red amused most critics and performed better than expected at the box office, inspiring a less than successful sequel in 2013. A *Red 3* is currently in development.

A wild, perverse combination of sex, satire and super-adventure, á la Bava...

51 DANGER: DIABOLIK 1968 105 1.85

Aka Baron Prasil   Poster/photos © 1968 Paramount Pictures, Inc.

WHO MADE IT:

Dino De Laurentiis Cinemagraphica, Marianne Productions/Paramount Pictures (Italian/French/U.S.). Director: Mario Bava. Producers: Dino De Laurentiis. Writers: Dino Maiuri, Brian Degas, Tudor Gates, Mario Bava, based on the Italian comic book *Diabolik* created by sisters Angela and Luciana Giussani in 1962. Cinematography (Technicolor): Antonio Renaldi. Music: Ennio Morricone. Starring John Phillip Law (Diabolik), Marisa Mell (Eva Kant), Michel Piccoli (Inspector Ginko), Adolfo Celi (Ralph Valmont), Claudio Gora (Police Chief), Mario Donen (Sergeant Danek), Terry-Thomas (Minister of Interior/Minister of France), Renzo Palmer (Assistant).

WHAT IT'S ABOUT:

In a nameless European country, Diabolik is a somewhat twisted criminal mastermind and killer who has just pulled off a spectacular heist. He spends most of his time in an extravagant underground lair with his drop-dead gorgeous girlfriend Eva, who helps her super-crook steal millions from the government. At one point, befuddled police minister Ginko is approached by a rival master criminal named Valmont, who proposes to use his underworld connections to catch Diabolik for the authorities. Soon, both Eva and her black-suited paramour are being chased by both dogged mobsters and frustrated cops... a pursuit that ultimately leads to a bizarre, glittering, solid-gold fate.

WHY IT'S IMPORTANT:

After spreading his wings as an extraterrestrial angel in *Barbarella* (also produced by Dino De Laurentiis), John Phillip Law proved equally striking as the black-costumed Diabolik, master thief, adventurer, and lover. His *Phantomas*-inspired character was created for Italian comics by a pair of enterprising sisters in the early '60s. Like *Barbarella*, Mario Bava's film version was a European response to a decade's worth of James Bond adventures and campy comic book adaptations, most notably TV's *Batman*. But the Euro comics were always harsher, more sophisticated, and laced with heavy doses of sado-masochism. The movie adaptations followed suit, becoming real eye-openers for kids who had never been exposed to this kind of material before.

Law is excellent in the title role, as is Marisa Mell as Eva Kent, our thief's ultra-sexy woman of choice and a frequent partner in his various heists. As a matter of fact, Diabolik's only motivation seems to be the need to shower his beloved Eva with riches; they literally make love in a bed of cash at one point. This core relationship gives the tale its necessary through line, as does the pursuit of dogged but doomed-to-fail Inspector Ginko (Michel Piccoli). Reminding viewers of the camp factor, Terry-Thomas has a hilarious cameo as the haplessly besieged Minister of the Interior/Minister of Finance. Laughs aside, there is some potent social satire here, with Diabolik not only thumbing his nose at authority figures, but ultimately wreaking havoc with the unnamed country's financial structure and allowing its bemused citizens the privilege of not paying their taxes!

Apart from the compelling visuals and some startling violence (Diabolik kills on reflex, using knives rather than guns), Bava's movie is enhanced greatly by composer Ennio Morricone's original music score, a riveting combination of Indian influences, Bondian jazz, and some of the "waa-waa" flavoring of his Italian western creations. And while a few of the matte paintings designed for Diabolik's elaborate hideout come across as artificial, they somehow contribute to the film's overall tone of gleeful, unrestrained absurdity. Rarely seen today, *Danger: Diabolik* is a nutty and superbly stylish ride, one worth taking for fans of the comic genre and fantasy cinema in general.

LEFT: the film's striking anti-hero Diabolik (John Phillip Law) and his equally sexy lover Eva Kant (Marisa Mell). ABOVE: a bed of cool cash. BELOW: In his avant garde '60s lair, Diabolik and Eva stand ready for their next groovy adventure.

RIGHT: Diabolik's memorable climax traps the titular hero in a totally unique and fitting way. Not surprisingly, Eva is along for her lover's final wink (zoom it, Mario).

Elements of science fiction and fantasy-horror work their way into this comics/caper film, reflecting director Bava's deft experience with these related genres.

Director Mario (*Mask of Satan*) Bava and his crew film the outlandish 'bed of money' sequence (see above image).

WHO MADE IT:

First National Pictures/John McCormick Productions (U.S.). Director: Alfred E. Green. Producer: John McCormick. Writers: Frank Griffin, Mervyn LeRoy, George Marion Jr. (titles), based on the comic strip created by William M. Conselman and Charles Plumb. Cinematography (b/w): Arthur Martinelli. Starring Colleen Moore (Ella Cinders), Lloyd Hughes (Waite Lifter), Vera Lewis (Ma Cinders), Doris Baker (Lotta Pill), Emily Gerdes (Prissy Pill), Mike Donlin (Film Studio Gateman).

WHAT IT'S ABOUT:

A small-town girl named Ella who is mad about the movies wins a talent contest supposedly sponsored by a film studio. She shows up in Hollywood for a promised screen test, only to discover that the contest was a sham. Disheartened but not discouraged, Ella vows to make it in Tinseltown one way or another. Fate takes a hand when she reacts in genuine terror to a fire that breaks out on a movie test, providing her with a most impressive screen test. Ella achieves her dream of becoming a star, but is given pause by the arrival of hometown boyfriend Waite, who offers her a very different lifetime contract.

WHY IT'S IMPORTANT:

A farcical take on the *Cinderella* story, Conselman and Plumb's original comic strip squeezed the most out of this familiar rags-to-riches parable. So does the enjoyable silent movie based on it, produced in large part to showcase the charms of star Colleen Moore. Offering naïve determination that never escalates into outright defiance, Moore seems to embody kind-hearted but constantly beleaguered Ella. Her eyeball acrobatics alone are worth applause, and she's never less than pleasing to watch.

The satiric depiction of Ella's vile family is, as one might expect, on-the-nose and serviceable, with love interest Waite Lifter (Lloyd Hughes) less offensive than he could have been. Our heroine's Hollywood misadventures follow the "big ball" sequence, making all that transpires in the film's second half a tad anti-climactic. Still, some of *Ella Cinders'* most interesting sequences are featured in the movie-making sequences. A staged fire that gets out of hand and an escaped lion (!) add to the plucky gate-crasher's trials and tribulations.

The comic strip stopped publication in 1961, and stories about poor, abused girls finding eventual bliss with hunky Prince Charmings went out of style during this period. Even so, resilient Ella Cinders becomes a full-fledged movie star based on her own perseverance and skills (and a submitted photo that accidentally showcases her crossed eyes), and her decision to settle down with Waite – who turns out to be more than just the local iceman – comes from a position of career strength and inner acceptance. Sometimes nice girls don't finish last... especially the ones who have both charm and a wacky sense of humor working for them.

49

BRIDE OF THE INCREDIBLE HULK 1978

(95) [1.37] 🔊

WHO MADE IT:

Universal Studios (television; U.S.). Director: Kenneth Johnson. Producers: Nicholas Corea, James G. Hirsh, Chuck Bowman, Kenneth Johnson. Writer: Kenneth Johnson, based on the comic book created by Stan Lee and Jack Kirby (Marvel). Cinematography (Technicolor): John McPherson. Music: Joseph Harnell. Starring Bill Bixby (Dr. David Banner), Mariette Hartley (Dr. Caroline Fields), Lou Ferrigno (Hulk), Jack Colvin (Jack McGee), Brian Cutler (Brad), Diane Markoff (The Girl), Duncan Gamble (Mark), Meeno Peluce (The Boy).

WHAT IT'S ABOUT:

Still seeking a cure from the gamma ray contamination that transforms him into a green-skinned mutation whenever he gets angry, David Banner enlists the aid of Dr. Caroline Fields, an expert in hypno-therapy. But Dr. Fields is dying of a rare blood disease, and soon both empathetic individuals are fighting against time to solve their mutual medical problems. Along the way, they fall deeply in love, and are married. David and Caroline must face the recurring problem of the Hulk and the threat of a raging tropical storm as passion and science join forces in a desperate, heart-wrenching fight for survival.

WHY IT'S IMPORTANT:

Bride of the Incredible Hulk was in actuality the second season premiere episode of the popular CBS television series, a well-crafted two hour drama helmed by series creator Kenneth Johnson. Like his 1977 feature pilot, it was released theatrically in countries outside the U.S., and continued the personal, sensitive dramatic style that came to characterize Johnson's "non-comic book-ey" approach to this material. A story of two lonely but vital people who fall in love and must face death together, it's a Marvel movie for anything but the Marvel target audience.

Johnson has a ball exploring Banner's unpredictable relationship with his own alter-ego through a series of monitored dream sequences, with Hulk seemingly contained by various hi-tech cages in David's unconscious, only to escape from each and every one. A clever final image has both figures traveling the same straight line at exactly the same pace; their fates are entwined, for better or worse.

Front and center is the genuine affection that develops between Banner and his doomed psychiatric ally, Caroline Fields (Mariette Hartley). Both are smart, humanist professionals with everything to live for, a fact that underscores their mutual tragedies. Bixby and Hartley are wonderful together, and this warm chemistry earned the actress an Emmy award for performance – one of the first times in TV history that a sci-fi/ fantasy series was acknowledged for something other than makeup or special effects. It also led to both stars being cast in a rom-com series called *Goodnight, Beantown* in 1983.

Likeable child actor Meeno (*Voyagers!*) Peluce delivers the film's memorable closing line: "Nobody ever dies, if someone remembers them." The same sentiment would be applied to the temporarily deceased Mr. Spock in Nicholas Meyer's *Star Trek II: The Wrath of Khan* a few years later. It's just as effective here, as grieving David tears up and composer Joe Harnell's "lonely man" piano theme ends this heartfelt drama on a final, bittersweet note.

48 SCOTT PILGRIM VS. THE WORLD 2010 (112) [1.85] 🎧

GET THE HOT GIRL. DEFEAT HER EVIL EXES.
HIT LOVE WHERE IT HURTS.

SCOTT PILGRIM US. THE WORLD

FROM THE DIRECTOR OF
SHAUN OF THE DEAD AND HOT FUZZ

WHO MADE IT:

Universal Pictures/Big Talk Films (U.S./U.K./Japan). Director: Edgar Wright. Producers: Marc Platt, Eric Gitter, Nira Park, Edgar Wright. Writers: Michael Bacall, Edgar Wright, based on the graphic novel by Byran Lee O'Malley. Cinematography (color): Bill Pope. Music: Nigel Godrich. Starring Michael Cera (Scott Pilgrim), Mary Elizabeth Winstead (Ramona Flowers), Kieran Culkin (Wallace Wells), Satya Bhabha (Matthew Patel), Chris Evans (Lucas Lee), Brandon Routh (Todd Ingram), Mae Whitman ("Roxy" Righter), Ellen Wong (Knives Chau), Alison Pill (Kim Pine).

WHAT IT'S ABOUT:

Scott Pilgrim has never had a problem getting a girlfriend. It's getting rid of them that proves difficult. From the girl who kicked his heart's ass – and now is back in town – to the teenage distraction he's trying to shake when Ramona Flowers rollerblades into his world, love hasn't been easy. He soon discovers, however, his new crush has the most unusual baggage of all: a nefarious league of seven exes controls her love life and will do whatever it takes to eliminate him as a suitor. As Scott gets closer to Ramona, he must face an increasingly vicious rogues' gallery from her past – from infamous skateboarders to vegan rock stars and fearsome identical twins. And if he hopes to win his true love, he must vanquish them all before it really is game over.

WHY IT'S IMPORTANT:

Teen-hip and endlessly inventive, *Scott Pilgrim vs. the World* is a peculiar movie helmed by the visionary who gave us *Shaun of the Dead*, Edgar Wright. It's based on a just-as-odd series of graphic novels created by Bryan Lee O'Malley between 2004 and 2010, published by Portland-based indie Oni Press. Both concern 22-year-old Canadian slacker Scott Pilgrim, who plays bass guitar in the band Sex Bob-Omb when he isn't mismanaging one unlikely romantic relationship after another. His "hero's journey" is covered in the movie, with Scott (played with frail confusion by Michael Cera) finding true love at last in the form of sophisticated dream girl Ramona Flowers (Mary Elizabeth Winstead). First, he has to deal with the high school cutie (Ellen Wong) he's currently dallying with. But then, out of left field, comes the insanity of the seven "evil exes," jealous former lovers of Ramona who engage in surreal, videogame-style combat with her hapless and besieged current suitor.

Though wisely set in chilly Toronto, Wright rightfully creates a completely absurd, stylized universe for this unique personal journey. Comic book sound effects graphics are everywhere (harking back to the old *Batman* TV series), and special effects are fully embraced. Interestingly, we aren't viewing this madness through Pilgrim's eyes... it's just the nutsy world he inhabits. And while the gimmicks can get a tad overwhelming at times, our hero's friends and foes are all memorable enough to keep viewers grounded. The seven exes are a scream (some familiar faces here), and all three of Scott's girlfriends present and past (the enigmatic Winstead, heart-broken Wong, and pissed-off drummer Kim Pine) are sympathetic and have palpable emotions that engage us. Underneath all the fantastical visuals and video flavoring, Woody Allen's *Manhattan* seems to be peeking through. Scott even wound up with his underage girlfriend (Wong) in an early cut, until audience reaction insisted he hook up with Ramona instead.

Not exactly perfect, but relentlessly imaginative and ultimately heartfelt, *Scott Pilgrim vs. the World* was a boxoffice disappointment when first released; not surprisingly, it became a cult hit on video. The wiseass gimmicks may be a bit much for some, but for those who can go with Wright's absurdist flow, this coming-of-maturity parable is worth a gander. And a listen, given the cool soundtrack...

ABOVE: Knives (Ellen Wong), Scott (Michael Cera), and Ramona (Mary Elizabeth Winstead) prepare to take on the most reprehensible ex of all. RIGHT: Scott strikes a graphically-styled blow against Matthew Patel (Satya Bhabba), first of the seven exes. BELOW: There's just something about sad-faced siren Ramona Flowers that pushes Scott Pilgrim's love button.

LEVEL UP!
GUTS ·3
HEART ·3
SMARTS ·4
WILL ·4

ABOVE: Having defeated most of Ramona's ex-boyfriends and one ex-girlfriend, Scott has earned "the power of love," which comes to him in the form of a flaming red sword – all part of his heroic, video arcade-stylized journey to maturity. RIGHT: Ramona gets into the action as well, squaring off against jealous Knives Chau in a kickass bout over Scott.

Director/co-writer Edgar Wright finds himself inspired by Mary Elizabeth Winstead as Ramona, who changes her hair color throughout the movie (from shocking pink to blue, and finally green).

THE AVENGERS: AGE OF ULTRON 2015 (141) 2.35

WHO MADE IT:

Marvel Studios/Walt Disney Studios Motion Pictures (U.S.). Director: Joss Whedon. Producer: Kevin Feige. Writer: Joss Whedon, based on the comic book by Stan Lee and Jack Kirby. Cinematography (color): Ben Davis. Music: Brian Tyler, Danny Elfman. Starring Robert Downey Jr. (Tony Stark/Iron Man), Chris Evans (Steve Rogers/Captain America), Scarlett Johansson (Nastasha Romanoff/Black Widow). Mark Ruffalo (Bruce Banner/The Hulk), Chris Hemsworth (Thor), James Spader (Ultron), Samuel L. Jackson (Nick Fury), Jeremy Renner (Clint Barton/Hawkeye), Aaron Taylor-Johnson (Pietro Maximoff/Quicksilver),Elizabeth Olsen (Wanda Maximoff/Scarlet Witch).

WHAT IT'S ABOUT:

When Tony Stark tries to jumpstart a dormant peacekeeping program, things go awry and Earth's mightiest heroes, including Iron Man, Captain America, Thor, the Incredible Hulk, Black Widow and Hawkeye, are put to the ultimate test as the fate of planet Earth hangs in the balance. Widow finds she has much in common with Hulk's lonely alter-ego Bruce Banner, and the two embark on a somewhat surprising romantic relationship, even as Clint Barton/Hawkeye tries to preserve the safety of his secret married life. Meanwhile, with the villainous humanoid techno-being Ultron becoming an ever-increasing threat, it is up to the Avengers to stop him from enacting his terrible plans.

WHY IT'S IMPORTANT:

Joss Whedon's eagerly-awaited sequel to his game-changing *The Avengers* is not an especially bad movie, it's just not fresh or exciting enough to serve as a worthy follow-up. Ostensibly, it's about super-scientist Tony Stark putting hubris before caution by grandly unleashing an A.I. technology that threatens to supplant the human race. With thematic aspects that date back to *Frankenstein* and even earlier, Stark is actually a good candidate for "playing God" in this oft-used but always provocative scenario. Still, there are reasons why *Colossus: The Forbin Project* does justice to this concept and *Age of Ultron* does not, the major unavoidable obstacle being the built-in requirements of a Marvel comic book movie. There is simply no time for a gradual, believable sense of awareness – everything has to happen very quickly, there are endless supporting characters that need to be served, and CG-generated slugfests must occur at regular intervals. On top of everything, we've seen a grandstander like Stark screw-up royally in these movies before; there's nothing especially fresh about exploring his regrets, unless that exploration happens to be exceptional. Here, it's perfunctory.

Ultron's best moments are the in-between stuff, a visit to the home and family of Hawkeye (Jeremy Renner) adding some perspective to his close relationship with Black Widow (Scarlett Johansson). Unfortunately, this is slightly undercut by Nastaha's out-of-left-field romantic relationship with Bruce Banner (Mark Ruffalo). Not that a case couldn't be made for these two lonely outsiders finding themselves. But in the previous movie, Widow was developing something special and meaningful with teammate Steve Rogers (who, in *Ultron*, dismisses her previous behavior as "flirting," therefore negating all that was achieved with their earnest bond), and, in the upcoming *Civil War*, it's Stark she seems to be warming up to. All one can say is, it's nice to have a girl on the team!

Fortunately for Marvel, the Russo brothers eagerly picked up the white-hot ball that Joss Whedon half-dropped, with their effective conspiracy thriller, *Captain America: The Winter Soldier*, providing unexpected vitality, and *Captain America: Civil Wars*, pushing the ongoing storyline inexorably forward.

A well-meaning but impulsive Tony Stark (Robert Downey Jr., above) brings deadly-dangerous artificial being Ultron (James Spader, right) to life. It isn't long before the mighty Avengers are called into action to clean up the milk their comrade spilled.

ABOVE, LEFT: Ultron's eventual foil, the austere and purple-skinned Vision (Paul Bettany) is a dignified entity in the tradition of Marvel's Silver Surfer, and a new addition to the Avengers team.

LEFT: Some make-up touches are required for the Vision.
RIGHT: Director Joss Whedon demonstrates the proper archery technique to Hawkeye (Jeremy Renner).

46 DR. STRANGE 2016

97 | 1.85

WHO MADE IT:

Marvel Studios/Walt Disney Studios. Director: Scott Derrickson. Producers: Kevin Feige, Victoria Alonso, Stephen Broussard, Charles Newirth, David J. Grant. Writers: Jon Spaints, Scott Derrickson & C. Robert Cargill, based on the Marvel comic by Stan Lee and Steve Ditko. Cinematography (color): Ben Davis. Music: Michael Giacchino. Starring Benedict Cumberbatch (Dr. Stephen Strange), Tilda Swinton (The Ancient One), Chiwetel Ejiofor (Mordo), Rachel McAdams (Christine Palmer), Benedict Wong (Wong), Mads Mikkelsen (Kaecilius), Michael Stuhlbarg (Dr. Nicodemus West), Benjamin Bratt (Jonathan Pangborn).

WHAT IT'S ABOUT:

The life of world-famous neurosurgeon Dr. Stephen Strange changes forever after a car accident robs him of the use of his hands. When traditional medicine fails him, Strange is forced to look elsewhere for healing, and hope. He eventually finds both in a mysterious Eastern enclave known as Kamar-Taj. He quickly learns that this is not just a center for spiritual healing but also the front line of a battle against unseen supernatural forces bent on destroying our reality. Before long Dr. Strange – armed with newly acquired magical powers – is forced to choose whether to return to his life of fortune or leave it all behind to defend the world as the most powerful sorcerer in existence.

WHY IT'S IMPORTANT:

Although impeccably produced like all Marvel Comics Universe epics, *Dr. Strange* falls strangely short in several key ways, its bewildering metaphysical interludes and endless exposition scenes nearly eclipsing a legitimately compelling premise. Benedict Cumberbatch is fine as an arrogant surgeon who loses the use of his hands in a car accident, propelling him on an anguished journey of spiritual discovery. This far-reaching quest results in the good doctor's relatively abrupt transformation into a master sorcerer, with nothing less than the fate of several universes depending on his ingenuity. Even with equally persuasive Tida Swinton on hand as the wisdom-spouting Ancient One, his soft-spoken, bald-headed mentor, there is simply too much arcane fantasy to digest for one storyline. Instead of an escalating sense of wonder, frustration with the narrative begins to set in mid-way through, and the mind-blowing special effects, startling at first, eventually become redundant and exhausting. The MCU need for traditional villains, tortured turncoats and cosmos-hungry overlords doesn't help. Somewhere in the middle of the muddle is a solid parable of a doctor finding his finer lights, and one wishes the visual and aural noise could be turned down so some grounded drama might soar, rather than just peek around the edges. Ironically, writer Stan Lee and artist Steve Ditko nailed this material far more effectively back in their 1960s comic book series. Even with the limitless potential of imaginative renderings, these storytellers instinctively knew that less was more when it came to the occult; their version of *Dr. Strange* was a supernatural adventure thriller with superhero-style overtones, rather than the other way around. That's what made it unique.

Despite these shortcomings, *Dr. Strange* is to be commended for being a true stand-alone origin tale, increasingly rare in the MCU. Critics reflexively praised the film, and audiences showed up to give Disney and company another mega-hit. But other than serving the overall Marvel "master plan," this ambitious, colorful but ultimately disappointing movie experience required less complicated magic and better-balanced storytelling to achieve its inherently rich potential.

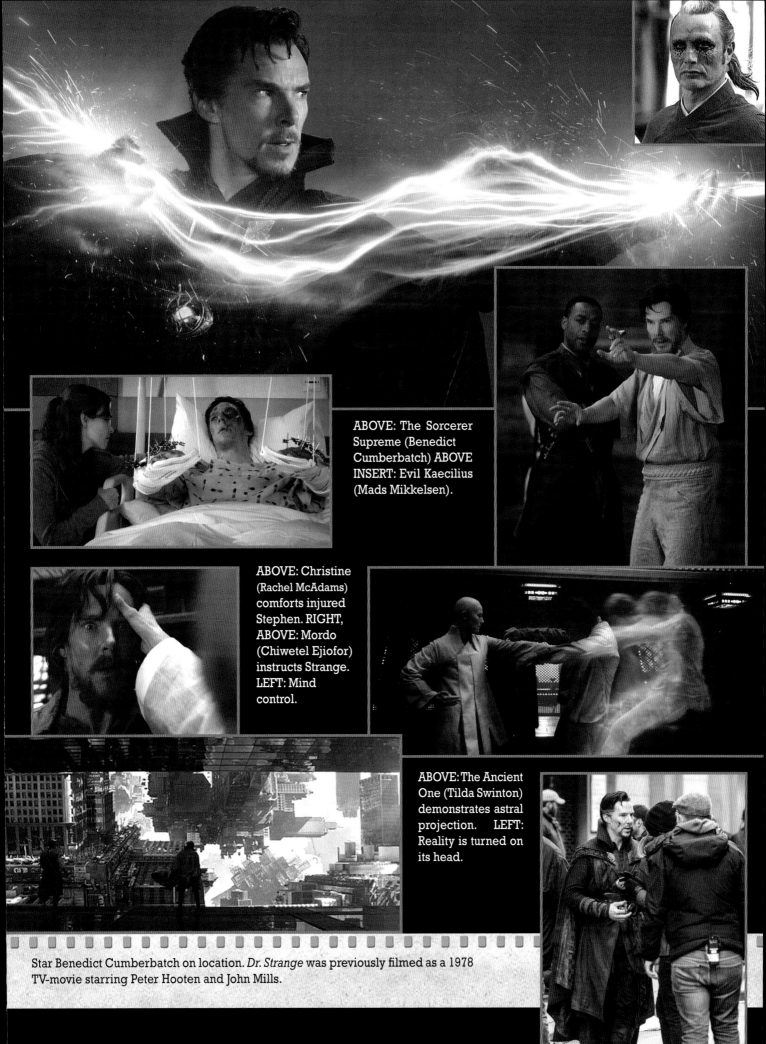

ABOVE: The Sorcerer Supreme (Benedict Cumberbatch) ABOVE INSERT: Evil Kaecilius (Mads Mikkelsen).

ABOVE: Christine (Rachel McAdams) comforts injured Stephen. RIGHT, ABOVE: Mordo (Chiwetel Ejiofor) instructs Strange. LEFT: Mind control.

ABOVE: The Ancient One (Tilda Swinton) demonstrates astral projection. LEFT: Reality is turned on its head.

Star Benedict Cumberbatch on location. *Dr. Strange* was previously filmed as a 1978 TV-movie starring Peter Hooten and John Mills.

45 WATCHMEN 2009

FROM THE VISIONARY DIRECTOR OF '300'

WATCHMEN

03.06.09

WHO MADE IT:

Warner Bros./Paramount Pictures/Legendary Pictures (U.S.). Director: Zack Snyder. Producers: Lawrence Gordon, Lloyd Levin, Deborah Snyder. Writers: David Hayter, Alex Tse, based on the graphic novel by Alan Moore and Dave Gibbons (Vertigo). Cinematography (color): Larry Fong. Music: Tyler Bates. Starring Malin Akerman (Laurie Jupiter/Silk Spectre II), Billy Crudup (Jon Osterman/Dr. Manhattan), Matthew Goode (Adrian Veidt/Ozymandias), Carla Gugino (Sally Jupiter/Silk Spectre), Jackie Earle Haley (Walter Kovas/Rorschach), Jeffrey Dean Morgan (Edward Morgan Blake/The Comedian), Patrick Wilson (Daniel Dreiberg/Nite Owl II), Matt Frewer (Moloch), Stephen McHattie (Hollis Mason/Nite Owl), Robert Wisden (President Nixon).

WHAT IT'S ABOUT:

In an alternate 1985 America, costumed superheroes are part of the fabric of everyday society, and the "Doomsday Clock" – which charts the USA's tension with the Soviet Union – is permanently set at five minutes to midnight. When one of his former colleagues is murdered, the washed-up but no less determined masked vigilante Rorschach sets out to uncover a plot to kill and discredit all past and present superheroes. As he reconnects with his former crime-fighting legion – a ragtag group of retired superheroes, only one of whom has true powers – Rorschach glimpses a wide-ranging and disturbing conspiracy with links to their shared past and catastrophic consequences for the future.

WHY IT'S IMPORTANT:

Arguably the most respected comic book/graphic novel of all time, DC's *Watchmen* came to the screen after various modern-era comics-based melodramas had already familiarized audiences with weird, deconstructed superheroes. Seeing armed and dangerous slimeballs in gimmicky costumes was no longer shocking in 2009, but in 1986, the concept was disturbingly fresh. *Watchmen* in either incarnation presents an unnerving parallel view of history, with America wining the Vietnam war, Nixon presiding over three terms after suppressing Watergate revelations, and the Cold War escalating to the boiling point in the 1980s. Alan Moore's groundbreaking vision is mostly retained by filmmaker Zack Syder, just off *300*, who wisely chose to make this superhero epic a period piece. It adopts the rainswept flavor of neo-noir, emerging as a murder mystery/conspiracy thriller with clever fantasy elements.

Dominating the storyline are an ensemble of complicated characters, one more idiosyncratic than the next. The low-life Comedian, played with cigar-chomping reprehensibility by Jeffrey Dean Morgan, commands our interest right off (he's savagely slain five minutes into the movie), as does reclusive tale-teller Rorschack (Jackie Earle Haley), patterned after Steve Ditko's right-wing comic character Mr. A. All-powerful and always enigmatic is blue-skinned, mild-mannered super-mutant Dr. Manhattan (Billy Crudup), romantically involved with second-generation crusader Silk Spectre II (Malin Akerman), even as earthy, hero-next-door Night Owl II (Patrick Wilson) does his best to keep everyone and everything grounded. Finally, the well-meaning but coldly arrogant Judas figure Ozymandias (Matthew Goode), smartest man on Earth, rounds out this tainted team.

All things considered, *Watchmen* clearly honors its celebrated inspiration. Moore's original ending closely resembled a classic *Outer Limits* episode ("Architects of Fear") but director Synder didn't want his already busy scenario cluttered up with bogus extraterrestrial threats, so the Lovecraftian alien squid planted by Ozymandias in New York City was left out of the screenplay.

Complex, overlong, and often confusing, *Watchmen* probably deserves credit for having been made at all. Graduating to more famous icons, director Synder would continue to explore the role of imperfect heroes in an imperfect world with his Superman and Batman films a few years later.

ABOVE: Group photo from the good old days. FAR LEFT: The Comedian (Jeffrey Dean Morgan) enjoys his work. INSERT: The paranoid, darkly committed Rorschach (Jackie Earle Haley) seeks answers.

Night Owl II (Patrick Wilson) and Silk Spectre II (Malin Akerman) quell a prison uprising while rescuing the framed Rorschach.

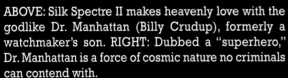

ABOVE: Silk Spectre II makes heavenly love with the godlike Dr. Manhattan (Billy Crudup), formerly a watchmaker's son. RIGHT: Dubbed a "superhero," Dr. Manhattan is a force of cosmic nature no criminals can contend with.

Night Owl II (Wilson, center) and The Comedian (Morgan, right) are directed on set by Zack Snyder, who would go on to helm *Man of Steel* and *Batman v Superman: Dawn of Justice*.

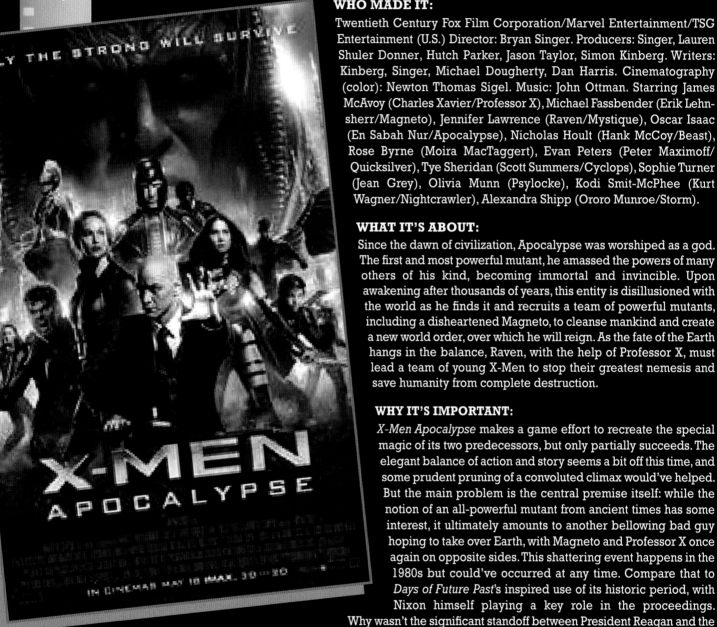

WHO MADE IT:

Twentieth Century Fox Film Corporation/Marvel Entertainment/TSG Entertainment (U.S.) Director: Bryan Singer. Producers: Singer, Lauren Shuler Donner, Hutch Parker, Jason Taylor, Simon Kinberg. Writers: Kinberg, Singer, Michael Dougherty, Dan Harris. Cinematography (color): Newton Thomas Sigel. Music: John Ottman. Starring James McAvoy (Charles Xavier/Professor X), Michael Fassbender (Erik Lehnsherr/Magneto), Jennifer Lawrence (Raven/Mystique), Oscar Isaac (En Sabah Nur/Apocalypse), Nicholas Hoult (Hank McCoy/Beast), Rose Byrne (Moira MacTaggert), Evan Peters (Peter Maximoff/Quicksilver), Tye Sheridan (Scott Summers/Cyclops), Sophie Turner (Jean Grey), Olivia Munn (Psylocke), Kodi Smit-McPhee (Kurt Wagner/Nightcrawler), Alexandra Shipp (Ororo Munroe/Storm).

WHAT IT'S ABOUT:

Since the dawn of civilization, Apocalypse was worshiped as a god. The first and most powerful mutant, he amassed the powers of many others of his kind, becoming immortal and invincible. Upon awakening after thousands of years, this entity is disillusioned with the world as he finds it and recruits a team of powerful mutants, including a disheartened Magneto, to cleanse mankind and create a new world order, over which he will reign. As the fate of the Earth hangs in the balance, Raven, with the help of Professor X, must lead a team of young X-Men to stop their greatest nemesis and save humanity from complete destruction.

WHY IT'S IMPORTANT:

X-Men Apocalypse makes a game effort to recreate the special magic of its two predecessors, but only partially succeeds. The elegant balance of action and story seems a bit off this time, and some prudent pruning of a convoluted climax would've helped. But the main problem is the central premise itself: while the notion of an all-powerful mutant from ancient times has some interest, it ultimately amounts to another bellowing bad guy hoping to take over Earth, with Magneto and Professor X once again on opposite sides. This shattering event happens in the 1980s but could've occurred at any time. Compare that to *Days of Future Past*'s inspired use of its historic period, with Nixon himself playing a key role in the proceedings. Why wasn't the significant standoff between President Reagan and the Soviets directly woven into the central concept? The "apocalypse" of the title would have had far greater significance if it referred to very real potential dangers posed by the long-standing Cold War suddenly getting hot... with both "good" and "bad" mutants at the heart of events.

Missing opportunities and muddled third-act editing aside, *X-Men: Apocalypse* does a great many things right. The characters, both major and minor, are flawlessly cast and performed, with younger performers all given scenes that showcase their considerable talents. Jennifer Lawrence acquits herself well as reluctant hero Mystique, while James McAvoy as Xavier and Michael Fassbender as Lehnsherr are as compelling as ever, the tragic death of Erik's family in Poland providing a standout sequence.

Ironically, the most telling bit of business occurs when Xavier's young heroes kick back and go to the movies (*Return of the Jedi* is playing). There is a fan-familiar argument about whether *Empire Strikes Back* is better than *Star Wars*, but everyone agrees that the third film of such trilogies is generally the least impressive. That happens to be true in *Apocalypse*'s case, as well, and it's downright creepy that the filmmakers seem to know it in advance. But this well-produced movie, which was successful at the box office, is not a creative disaster by any means. It's simply an unfortunate disappointment that is nevertheless worth checking out for intermittent greatness.

ABOVE: Jean Grey (Sophie Turner), Nightcrawler (Kodi Smit-McPhee), Scott Summers (Tye Sheridan). LEFT: As his allies look on in awe, Apocalypse (Oscar Isaac) prepares to destroy civilization in the 1980s and replace it with a new order.

LEFT: Quicksilver (Evan Peters) manages to save everyone from the collapsing X-mansion, including a four-footed inhabitant.

ABOVE: Mystique (Jennifer Lawrence) in Apocalypse's death grip.

ABOVE: Storm (Alexandra Shipp). RIGHT, TOP: Magneto (Michael Fassbender) pours it on. RIGHT, BELOW: The augmented Angel (Ben Hardy).

Several cast members were wired up for various levitation sequences presented in the film. An epilogue suggests the adventures of these super-mutants will continue.

103

43

SUICIDE SQUAD 2016

97   1.85

WHO MADE IT:

Warner Bros./Atlas Entertainment/DC Entertainment (U.S.). Director: David Ayer. Producers: Charles Roven, Richard Suckle, Geoff Johns, Steven Mnuchin, Zack Snyder, Colin Wilson. Writer: David Ayer, based on various DC Comics characters. Cinematography (color): Roman Vasyanov. Music: Steven Price. Starring Will Smith (Deadshot), Jared Leto (Joker), Margot Robbie (Harley Quinn), Joe Kinnaman (Rick Flag), Jai Courtney (George "Digger" Harkness/Captain Boomerang), Viola Davis (Amanda Walker), Jay Hernandez (Chato Santana/El Diablo), Adewale Akinnuoye-Agbaje (Waylon Jones/Killer Croc), Carla Delevinge (June Moone/Enchantress), Karen Fukuhara (Tatsu Yamashiro/Katana), Ike Barinholtz (Griggs).

WHAT IT'S ABOUT:

It feels good to be bad... Assemble a team of the world's most dangerous, incarcerated super-villains, provide them with the most powerful arsenal at the government's disposal, and send them off on a mission to defeat an enigmatic, insuperable entity. U.S. intelligence officer Amanda Waller has determined only a secretly convened group of disparate, despicable individuals with next to nothing to lose will do. However, once they realize they weren't picked to succeed but chosen for their patent culpability when they inevitably fail, will the Suicide Squad resolve to die trying, or decide it's every villain for himself?

WHY IT'S IMPORTANT:

Originally part of DC's *Brave and the Bold* comic series in 1959, *Suicide Squad* was dragged out of mothballs nearly thirty years later for a significant reimagining. No longer a band of respectable Silver Age adventurers, this new, far edgier Squad was a government-sponsored strike team made up of flamboyant and potentially volatile super-villains. Under the watchful eyes of tough-as-nails handlers, they undertake insanely dangerous missions in order to commute their prison terms. This *Dirty Dozen* approach to the company's resident baddies seemed to guarantee an outlandishly amusing "high concept" experience, in comics and eventually on film.

For the most part, this conceit pays off. The assembled cine-villains are all worthy specimens, some of them DC superstars, with powers and temperaments designed to hold interest while moving the plot/high-stakes mission forward. Will Smith has his best role in years as Deadshot, a master sniper with a soft spot for his youthful, criminally unspoiled daughter. Equally engaging is Margot Robbie's little-girl-lost wacko Harley Quinn, a showy role for any actress. Reworked effectively for the big screen, she is given emotional range within limited parameters, and Robbie runs with the opportunity. Although their bizarre mission is promptly compromised by unexpected, internal complications, the protagonists manage to regroup and inevitably save the day by allowing their long-submerged humanity to fully define themselves and their goals. Everyone is doing what they are doing for love, pure and simple, which is something both villains and handlers have in common. Harley's crazed adoration for the mostly irredeemable Joker is handled sympathetically, and even a relatively minor character like Katana (group leader Rick Flag's bodyguard) is given a moment of heartbreaking pathos, speaking to her anguished, sword-imprisoned husband as the others look on, somehow relating in an elemental way.

Outperforming Marvel's *Dr. Strange* at the 2016 box office, *Suicide Squad* leapfrogged over its scathing notices. To most satisfied viewers, it was another *Deadpool*, a wildly irreverent comic book adventure that effortlessly blurred the line between compelling pop-tragedy and wickedly ingratiating camp.

The gang's all here: specifically, the Suicide Squad and the equally badass government operatives who handle them. Left to Right: super-thief Captain Boomerang (Jai Courtney), former psychiatrist Harley Quinn (Margot Robbie), master hitman Deadshot (Will Smith), body-guard Katana (Karen Fukuhara), group leader Rick Flag (Joel Kinnaman), mega-mutant Killer Croc (Adewale Akinnuoye-Agbaje), and firestarter El Diablo (Jay Hernandez).

ABOVE: The Enchantress (Cara Delevinge), formerly archeologist June Moone.

ABOVE, LEFT: Tormented El Diablo. ABOVE: The vile Joker, played by Jay Leto.

LEFT: Filming Batman (Ben Affleck).
RIGHT: Filming the Joker (Leto).

105

42 HELLBOY 2004

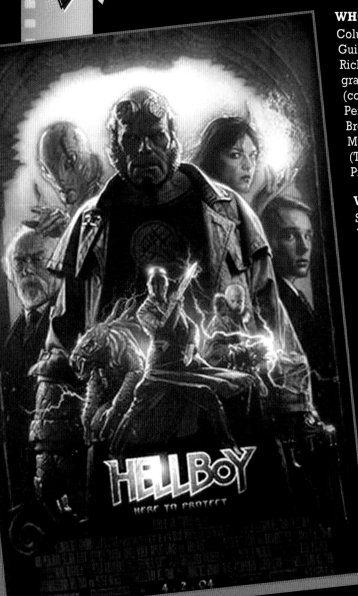

WHO MADE IT:

Columbia Pictures/Revolution Studios/Starlite Films (U.S.). Director: Guillermo del Toro. Producers: Lawrence Gordon, Lloyd Levin, Mike Richardson. Writers: Guillermo del Toro, Peter Briggs, based on the graphic novel created by Mike Mignola (Dark Horse). Cinematography (color): Guillermo Navarro. Music: Marco Beltrami. Starring Ron Perlman (Hellboy), John Hurt (Trevor Bruttenholm aka Professor Broom), Selma Blair (Liz Sherman), Rupert Evans (John Thaddeus Myers), Karel Roden (Grigori Efimovich Rasputin), Jeffrey Tambor (Tom Manning), Doug Jones (Ape Sapien, voiced by David Hyde Pierce), Brian Steele (Sammael), Ladislav Beran (Kroenen).

WHAT IT'S ABOUT:

Sorceror Grigori Rasputin joins forces with Hitler's Germany during World War II to summon a young demon from the pits of Hell, a creature to be used as the ultimate Axis weapon. Instead, this entity is captured by American forces and put in the care of Professor Broom, the founder of a top-secret organization called the Bureau for Paranormal Research and Defense. Sixty years later, the demon, now known as Hellboy, has honed his skills under Broom's tutelage and is part of an elite secret defense team alongside firestarter Liz Sherman and Abe Sapian), an aquatic humanoid with the power of telepathy. Although sworn to doing good, Hellboy must battle his own darkest impulses when Rasputin returns, determined to bring the demon back to his natural ways so that evil may finally rule the world.

WHY IT'S IMPORTANT:

Hellboy, created by artist Mike Mignola and published by Dark Horse, is a decently-written, spectacularly drawn comic book, with Mignola's use of line, shape and composition a breath of fresh air. So impressed with all this visual flair was filmmaker Guillermo del Toro that he jumped at the chance to do a film adaptation.

As a movie, *Hellboy* plays like a lower-case MCU offering without all the gimmick guest heroes to bolster audience interest. As conceived by Mignola and developed by del Toro, the titular character (Ron Perlman) is a standard issue, cigar-chomping, Ben Grimm-esque New Yorker, with Hell his true point of origin. He is discovered in infant form during World War II, and a threat from nefarious occult forces is soon underway. As all of us who have seen *Raiders of the Lost Ark* know, the Nazis were fascinated by supernatural-sourced power and will go to fanatical extremes to master it.

The story proper, set in present day, offers an organization vaguely similar to Professor X's mutant school, in this case the BPRD, where benevolent Professor Broom (John Hurt) watches over various low-profile metahumans, including fishman Abe Sapian (Doug Jones) and firestarter Liz Sherman (Selma Blair), who become Hellboy's best friend and romantic interest, respectively. Under del Doro's assured hand, all play their roles with professional aplomb, Blair's "just got dragged out of bed" deliveries proving especially enjoyable. On the villainous side of the fence is no less than twisted power-seeker Rasputin (Karl Roden), a master sorcerer.

The film is rich in visual imagination, with the various make-ups and body suits for good guys and bad guys alike designed to perfection. But despite a multitude of creative plusses, *Hellboy* never seems to reach its full dramatic potential. It's not as good as the best superhero movies nor as effective as the screen's finest supernatural thrillers. And nothing can replicate what artist Mignola gave us on the page. Still, it's nice to see a non-DC/Marvel character reach the big screen with reasonably impressive results, and this peculiar fire-and-brimstone morality play/slugfest is certainly worth a look.

An opening sequence set in World War II brings the infant Hellboy into our universe. Years later, this crimson demonoid will take on sorcerer Grigori Rasputin and his nefarious allies.

Hellboy finds love in his heart for Liz Sherman (Selma Blair), a firestarter, and kinship with amphibious BPRD colleague Abe Sapien (Doug Jones, right).

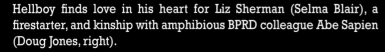

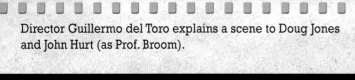

Director Guillermo del Toro explains a scene to Doug Jones and John Hurt (as Prof. Broom).

Tim Burton's urban fairy tale re-defines the Caped Crusader...

41 BATMAN 1989

126 1.85 🎧

Poster/photos: © 1989 Warner Bros./DC characters™

NICHOLSON ◇ KEATON

BATMAN

WHO MADE IT:

Warner Bros./The Guber-Peters Company (U.S.). Director: Tim Burton. Producers: Peter Guber, Jon Peters, Chris Kenny, Barbara Kalish, Benjamin Melniker, Michael Uslan. Writers: Sam Hamm, Warren Skaaren, based on the comic book created by Bob Kane (DC Comics). Cinematography (color): Roger Pratt. Music: Danny Elfman. Starring Michael Keaton (Batman/Bruce Wayne), Jack Nicholson (The Joker/Jack Napier), Kim Basinger (Vicki Vale), Robert Wuhl (Alexander Knox), Pat Hingle (Commisioner James Gordon), Billy Dee Williams (Harvey Dent), Michael Gough (Alfred Pennyworth), Jack Palance (Carl Grissom), Jerry Hall (Alicia Hunt).

WHAT IT'S ABOUT:

Having witnessed his parents' brutal murder as a child, millionaire philanthropist Bruce Wayne fights crime in Gotham City disguised as Batman, a costumed vigilante who strikes fear into the hearts of lawbreakers. He is aided in this unique crusade by his loyal butler, Alfred, and operates out of an excavated, equipment-filled cave directly below his mansion. When a deformed madman called The Joker seizes control of Gotham's underworld and threatens the entire city, Batman must confront his most ruthless criminal nemesis, even as he safeguards both his identity and a woman he has come to care for, reporter Vicki Vale.

WHY IT'S IMPORTANT:

Superman proved to be a money-making franchise in the 1980s for Warner Bros, despite the deteriorating quality of the films themselves. Still, Hollywood was initially reluctant to take a chance on DC's second most important super-hero, the Caped Crusader. At this juncture, he was best remembered as the Campy Crusader from the 1966-69 TV series with Adam West. Unlike *Superman*, *Batman* required more than just a superficial makeover... the character's entire persona and the tonal universe he inhabited called for a major U-turn.

Idiosyncratic filmmaker Tim Burton was never the perfect choice to helm a *Batman* movie – warmer and weirder Spider-Man would have been a better fit. But his 1989 blockbuster is rightly credited with introducing "dark" into the comic book movie vernacular, with heavy gothic trappings and a wet-of-asphalt *Blade Runner*-like urban landscape establishing an unmistakable, if somewhat artificial, ambience. It's candy-colored darkness Burton revels in, akin to a childlike fascination for comforting nightmares. It would take Christopher Nolan and a harsher study to catch the edgy, no-nonsense adult tone required for a modern-era Batman.

Still, Burton and company deliver an agreeably fractured fairy tale that never fails to entertain. Keaton brings an arched-eyebrow strangeness of his own to the dual role of Bruce Wayne/Batman, stepping into a spooky armored suit that can transform even a small-statured man into a formidable warrior. Jack Nicholson's full-out turn as the Joker is so robust it edges toward becoming a little self-satisfied, but ultimately works in an almost elemental way. Most important, the campy do-gooder flavor of the 1966 television series is finally placed in historic perspective, supplanted by a new, very specific persona for Batman – dark and brooding, gothic, operatic. It remains the essential model to this day.

Among the other major plusses: Anton Furst's aggressive production design, and a pseudo classical musical score provided by Danny Elfman. Burton followed up his uber-hit with the somewhat uneven *Batman Returns*, creating both an iconic fantasy take on Catwoman (Michelle Feiffer) and a less satisfying, hard to stomach Penguin (Danny DeVito).

ABOVE: Butler Alfred (Michael Gough) shares a moment with Bruce Wayne (Michael Keaton). RIGHT: Batman (Keaton) rescues Vicki Vale (Kim Basinger). BELOW: The Joker (Jack Nicholson) prepares for more mayhem.

Batman and Vicki race toward the sleek, futuristic Batmobile, which practically becomes a character in the story.

Final showdown at Gotham Cathedral.

Director Tim Burton takes costumed Michael Keaton through his paces. The duo worked previously in the well-received fantasy comedy *Beetlejuice*.

Famed celebrity photographer Herb Ritts shot extensive gallery portraits of the Darknight Detective (Michael Keaton) and Clown Prince of Crime (Jack Nicholson) for Tim Burton's 1989 *Batman*. At the time, Keaton's armored attire was a new and unexpected upgrade from traditional spandex super-tights.

PUTTING ON THE RITTS

40 SPY SMASHER 1942

(215) 1.37

WHO MADE IT:

Republic Pictures (U.S.). A 12-chapter serial. Director: William Witney. Producer: William J. O'Sullivan. Writers: Ronald Davidson, Norman S. Hall, William Lively, Joseph O'Donnell, Joseph Poland, based on the comic book by C.C. Beck and Bill Parker (Fawcett Comics). Cinematography (b/w): Reggie Lanning. Music: Mort Glickman. Starring Kane Richmond (Alan Armstrong/Spy Smasher; Jack Armstrong), Marguerite Chapman (Eve Corby), Sam Flint (Admiral Corby), Hans Schumm ("The Mask"), Tris Coffin (Drake).

WHAT IT'S ABOUT:

After discovering information about Nazi activities in occupied France, Alan Armstrong, aka the costumed vigilante Spy Smasher, is captured by enemy agents and ordered to be executed. He manages to escape back to America and connects with his twin brother Jack, who is incorrectly recognized and killed by a Nazi operative codenamed The Mask. This ruthless villain begins a series of attacks against the United States, ranging from forged money that would imperil the economy to outright destruction of aircraft, oil and munitions intended for Britain. Facing his persistent nemesis Spy Smasher for a final, fateful confrontation, the enraged Mask is killed aboard his own U-Boat in a sea of flaming oil.

WHY IT'S IMPORTANT:

After successfully adapting *Adventures of Captain Marvel* into a 12-chapter serial, Republic Pictures turned to the equally flamboyant *Spy Smasher* one year later, delivering the same kind of quality treatment in all creative departments: cinematography, stuntwork, and special effects (the studio's on-staff Lydecker brothers once again providing perfectly-filmed miniatures). A resourceful detective and vigilante, Alan Armstrong/Spy Smasher was Fawcett Comics's answer to Bruce Wayne/Batman, just as their high-flying Captain Marvel was a variation of DC's Superman.

The plot gimmick of twin brothers impersonating each other was not part of the original comic book premise; rather, this venerable device was created for the serial to add interest, enabling star Kane Richman to tackle a double role. In a fascinating cliffhanger surprise, Jack Armstrong, pretending to be his superhero brother, is ultimately killed by their Nazi nemesis, the Mask (Hans Schumm). It may be the only time in serial history that the life-threatened hero doesn't manage to escape a dastardly end.

After the war was won, Fawcett's *Spy Smasher* became *Crime Smasher*, making him even more like urban-based Batman. Eventually the property was absorbed by DC Comics, as was *Captain Marvel*. Later incarnations of *Smasher* utilized his colorful name for different characters, including, in recent years, a female anti-terrorist operative committed to giving Barbara (Batgirl/Oracle) Gordon ongoing grief.

Responding to the great nostalgia craze initiated by TV's *Batman* in 1966, the original Republic serial was edited down to feature length and released to small screen viewers in the form of a movie, retitled *Spy Smasher Returns*.

39

DREDD 2012

WHO MADE IT:

Lionsgate/DNA Films/Entertainment Film Distributors (U.K./U.S.). Director: Pete Travis. Producers: Alex Garland, Andrew Macdonald, Allon Reich. Writers: Alex Garland, based on the comic strip *Judge Dredd* created by John Wagner and Carlos Ezquerra. Cinematography (color/3D): Anthony Dod Mantle. Music: Paul Leonard-Morgan. Starring Karl Urban (Judge Dredd), Olivia Thirlby (Judge Cassandra Anderson), Lena Headey (Ma-Ma), Wood Harris (Kay), Warrick Grier (Caleb), Domhnall Gleeson (Computer Expert), Deobia Oparei (TJ), Francis Chouler (Judge Guthrie).

WHAT IT'S ABOUT:

In an irradiated future, the only force of order lies with the urban cops called "Judges" who possess the combined powers of judge, jury and instant executioner. Dredd is the ultimate Judge, challenged with ridding Mega City of its latest scourge – a dangerous drug epidemic that has users of "Slo-Mo" experiencing reality at a fraction of its normal speed. Dredd is assigned to train and evaluate Cassandra Anderson, a rookie with powerful psychic abilities thanks to a genetic mutation. A heinous crime calls them to a 200-story vertical slum controlled by prostitute-turned-drug lord Ma-Ma and her ruthless clan, who overtake the compound's control center and wage a dirty, vicious war against the Judges. With the body count climbing and no way out, Dredd and Anderson battle for their survival.

WHY IT'S IMPORTANT:

The second high-profile film adaptation of Britain's perennially popular sci-fi comic, *Dredd* manages to be both repulsive and lyrically beautiful, often at the same time. This unapologetically violent movie, helmed by former social worker Pete Travis, is a decided improvement over the ambitious but misguided Sylvester Stallone vehicle from a decade earlier. Future Dr. McCoy Karl Urban's under the bulky helmet this time, with his jutted chin and a perpetual frown doing most of the acting. Perversely enough, it's a convincing performance, with Urban spouting monotonic RoboCop-like commands to perps occasionally punctuated by subtle, ironic observations. This personal touch makes Dredd a bit more than simply a one-dimensional hero, although most of the heavy dramatic lifting is performed by Olivia Thirlby as Judge's rookie partner Anderson, who happens to be psychic. There is a nice contrast between the unrestrained feelings of those criminals her mind touches, and the numbness-to-violence that must be maintained while performing field duties as a Judge. In the end, an emotionally and physically spent Anderson weighs all the pros and cons, decides she's unfit for the job and resigns, although her senior partner/evaluator Dredd passes her with flying colors. Also making a striking impression is Lena Headey as primary villain Ma-Ma, an incestuous, masochistic harpy with grandiose criminal dreams. And the "block" itself becomes something of a main character, an enormous monolithic skyscraper/slum community that shields itself into a tomb after Ma-Ma takes over.

Filmed flamboyantly in 3D, *Dredd* received mostly positive reviews, but didn't fare especially well at the box office. It may have been too grim, too mean, too exquisitely bloodthirsty for mainstream tastes. But for those superhero action fans looking for a stylish dip in ultra-violent waters, this robust adaptation of John Wagner's future shock scenario will certainly get the job done.

38 TALES FROM THE CRYPT 1972 (92) [1.85]

Poster/photos: © 1972 Amicus Productions, Inc.

WHO MADE IT:

Metromedia Producers Corporation/Amicus Productions (U.K./U.S.). Director: Freddie Francis. Producers: Max Rosenberg, Milton Subotsky, Charles Fries, based on the comic book by William Gaines and Al Feldstein (EC). Cinematography (color): Norman Warwick. Music: Douglas Gamley. Starring Ralph Richardson (Crypt Keeper), Joan Collins (Joanne Clayton), Peter Cushing (Arthur Edward Grimsdyke), Roy Dotrice (Charles Gregory), Richard Greene (Ralph Jason), Ian Hendry (Carl Maitland), Patrick Magee (George Carter), Barbara Murray (Enid Jason), Nigel Patrick (Major Rogers), Robin Phillips (James Elliot).

WHAT IT'S ABOUT:

Visiting a catacomb, five people get lost and find themselves in a crypt. There, they encounter the sinister Crypt Keeper, who tells them five stories involving murder, mayhem, and retribution. The first involves a woman who slays her husband for his insurance on Christmas Eve, and is soon slain herself by a serial killer dressed as Santa Claus. The second concerns a man who abandons his family to run off with his mistress, only something unexpectedly dark happens during their journey. The third is about a kindly janitor who is driven to suicide by a heartless neighbor; he eventually rises from the grave as a figure of retribution. Story Four is built around a legendary statue that can grant three wishes to its owner. The concluding tale punishes the cruel new director of a home for the blind in appropriately cruel fashion. After this last story is told, all five crypt listeners learn, much to their horror, that they are at the gate of hell itself.

WHY IT'S IMPORTANT:

Amicus Productions was Hammer Films' main competitor in the British horror film arena of the '60s and '70s, for the most part specializing in anthology features… movies with five mini-tales and an eerie wraparound story. EC Comics' *Tales from the Crypt* proved an ideal fit, with the nasty/funny yarns spun by New York comics publishers in the '50s easily making the transition to both enterprising producers Rosenberg and Subotsky and English black humor in general.

Providing a striking contrast to the cackling, campy puppet used in the later TV series, Sir Ralph Richardson is austere dread personified as the Crypt Keeper, preparing a group of strangers for their hellish reward by compelling them to relive their respective damning scenarios. All of the yarns are quite good, some better than others. Up first is pre-*Dynasty* Joan Collins as a murderess who bludgeons her husband on Christmas Eve, only to be stalked by a maniacal killer garbed in a Santa Claus costume. Although brief, this single-set thriller is well-staged and dripping in irony: the heroine can't call the police because of the crime she's just committed, and her own little daughter is not only imperiled, but winds up letting Santa inside the house. Our feelings for Collins' character run the gamut from disgust (she's a heartless killer) to primal sympathy (a mother's concern for her endangered child) in a remarkably short time.

Centerpiece of this anthology is Peter Cushing's "zombie" thriller, boasting a distinctive Roy Ashton monster make-up and a nifty rising-from-the-grave sequence that was featured prominently in *Crypt*'s advertising. But the best of a good lot of nasty tales is saved for last: the ingeniously-devised revenge against a sadistic martinet initiated by abused blind man Patrick Magee is EC Comics at its finest, captured on film with maximum efficiency and poetic elegance.

Tales from the Crypt fared well with critics and audiences, inspiring a less-liked sequel, *The Vault of Horror*, just a year later. While the well-produced TV series of the late '80s gave the creepy franchise its most successful take, Freddie Francis' 1972 interpretation has legitimate dark charms of its own, and should not be overlooked.

ABOVE, LEFT: The solemn Crypt Keeper (Sir Ralph Richardson) addresses his clueless, ultimately doomed guests, ABOVE, RIGHT. LEFT: Santa Claus is more naughty than nice in the first tale of terror. RIGHT: Ghastly fates await the five unfortunates who wander into the Crypt Keeper's dank catacomb, including an especially nasty revenge initiated by sinned-upon members of a home for the blind.

Arthur Grims-dyke (Peter Cushing) rises from the grave to even the score with the heartless soul who put him there to begin with.

Actor Peter Cushing rarely wore monster make-up in his horror films. *Tales from the Crypt* was a notable exception, with Roy Ashton transforming him into a zombie.

115

WHO MADE IT:

Universal Pictures (U.S.). A 15-chapter serial. Directors: Ford Beebe, Robert F. Hill. Producer: Barney A. Sarecky. Writers: Ray Trampe, Norman S. Hall, Wyndham Gittens, Herbert Dalmas. Cinematography (b/w): Jerome Ash. Music: Stock. Starring Buster Crabbe (Flash Gordon), Jean Rogers (Dale Arden), Charles Middleton (Emperor Ming), Frank Shannon (Dr. Zarkov), Beatrice Roberts (Queen Azura), Donald Kerr (Happy Hapgood), Richard Alexander (Prince Barin), C. Montague Shaw (Clay King), Wheeler Oakman (Tarnak), Warner Richmond (Zander).

WHAT IT'S ABOUT:

When a mysterious beam of light starts disrupting the Earth's atmosphere, Flash Gordon and his former space companions Dr. Zarkov and Dale Arden, accidentally accompanied by wisecracking reporter Happy Hapgood, journey to Mars. There they encounter their old enemy, Ming the Merciless, who has formed an alliance with the Witch Queen of Mars, Azura. Her nefarious powers include the ability to transmute people into figures of living clay, condemned to live in darkened caves, and she is hated and feared by most of the population. After a series of life-threatening perils, Flash and his intrepid group break up the Ming-Azura alliance and destroy the device that was threatening Earth.

WHY IT'S IMPORTANT:

Universal's first *Flash Gordon* serial was a spectacular success for the studio, so a sequel was immediately prepared. *Flash Gordon's Trip to Mars* proved to be another ambitious undertaking, costing far more than the average 15-chapter extravaganza. Returning were picture-perfect Buster Crabbe as Flash, Charles Middleton as Ming, Jean Rogers as a somewhat dowdy Dale Arden, and Richard Alexander as their ally from Mongo, Prince Barin. New to the proceedings were villainous Witch Queen Azura (Beatrice Roberts) and comedy relief sidekick Hapgood (Donald Kerr).

Trip to Mars picks up exactly where the first serial ends, with safely returned Zarkov and his "stratosphere party" being celebrated for their heroic efforts. This mood is swiftly broken by Ming's latest threat from space, a destructive beam of light projected from Mars. Soon Flash and his friends are once again touching down on alien soil, reunited with old allies and facing a plethora of outlandish perils.

Making a lasting impression are the grotesque but benevolent Clay People, victims of Azura's dark magic. As with the '36 offering, background music was lifted from Universal's theatrical features (mainly *Bride of Frankenstein* and *The Invisible Man*), with the quirky cue composed for a half-drunken Dr. Pretorious in *Bride* serving as the theme for these clay-cursed denizens.

Fun and energetic, *Trip to Mars* lacked the special transcendent qualities of its predecessor, but nevertheless provided Crabbe and company with another opportunity to dash about fanciful sets and clobber exotically-clad stuntmen. It was followed in 1940 with the lower-budgeted but still entertaining *Flash Gordon Conquers the Universe*, last of the three classic serials.

Tidbit: This serial was released in March 1938. In November of the same year, Universal issued a re-edited, feature-length version to theaters, *Mars Attacks the World*.

ABOVE: Flash Gordon (Buster Crabbe), Dale Arden (Jean Rogers), and Dr. Zarkov (Frank Shannon), embark on a second space adventure, this time with reporter Happy Hapgood (Donald Kerr) in tow. LEFT, BELOW: On Mars, they encounter allies old and new, including Prince Barin (Richard Alexander) and the Clay King (Montague Shaw).

Dr. Zarkov and Flash ride the shuttle car, a cramped but efficient high-speed vehicle.

LEFT: A miniature forest of twisted, dead trees was created by Universal's special effects department, intercut and matched with shots of a full-size set.

36

SUPERMAN II 1980

127 | 2.35

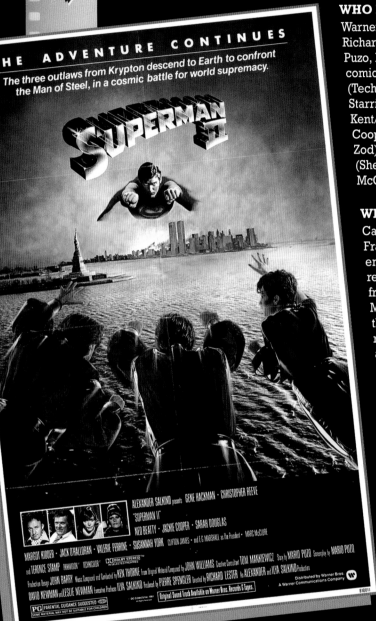

WHO MADE IT:

Warner Bros./Dovemead Limited/Film Export A.G. (U.S./U.K.). Director: Richard Lester. Producers: Pierre Spengler, Ilya Salkind. Writers: Mario Puzo, David Newman, Leslie Newman, Tom Mankiewicz, based on the comic book by Jerry Siegal and Joe Shuster (DC). Cinematography (Technicolor): Robert Paynter, Geoffrey Unsworth. Music: Ken Thorne. Starring Gene Hackman (Lex Luthor), Christopher Reeve (Clark Kent/Superman), Margot Kidder (Lois Lane), Ned Beatty (Otis), Jackie Cooper (Perry White), Valerie Perrine (Eve), Terence Stamp (General Zod), Susannah York (Lara), Jack O'Halloran (Non), Clifton James (Sheriff), E.G. Marshall (The President), Sarah Douglas (Ursa), Marc McClure (Jimmy Olsen).

WHAT IT'S ABOUT:

Caped wonder Superman successfully thwarts a terrorist attack in France, but inadvertently unleashes three Phantom Zone arch enemies in the process. As they head for Earth, the romantic relationship between Lois Lane and Clark Kent continues, with a frustrated Lois looking for opportunities to expose Clark as the Man of Steel. Grim General Zod and his two confederates begin their invasion even as Superman makes the fateful decision to relinquish his immortality for the love of Lois. Ultimately, a bruised and humbled Clark must find his way back to the Fortress of Solitude and regain his powers in order to take on the ruthless super-villains and save the human race from enslavement.

WHY IT'S IMPORTANT:

Director Richard Lester (*A Hard Day's Night*, *The Four Musketeers*) brought something of his trademark verve to *Superman II*, the first sequel to the 1978 blockbuster helmed by a different Richard, Donner. This second movie pits Christopher Reeve's Man of Steel against three black-clad supervillains from home world Krypton, briefly glimpsed at the beginning of Donner's film. But Earth-threatening antics aside, the true power of the tale stems from Superman's heartfelt decision to give up his fantastic powers and live life as a mortal, all for the love of a thankful but bewildered Lois Lane (Margot Kidder). Not since Steve Reeves gave up his immortality for similar reasons in 1959's *Labors of Hercules* has the screen witnessed such a costly sacrifice. Fortunately, the retirement doesn't take and Big S is back saving our necks in no time, much to the delight of the U.S. President (E.G. Marshall wearing a very bad wig), and the movie-going population in general.

On the down side, *Superman II* looks cheap and decidedly uncinematic in comparison to its more elaborate predecessor, in spite of the fact that much footage had already been shot by Donner. The Phantom Zone villains are far more enigmatic and frightening in their brief Movie One appearance than in all their scenes here. And while much of the romantic comedy has bite, it can't make up for Lester's thinly-disguised contempt for the *Superman* mythology in general. It would take one additional film in the series to prove, without question, that this skillful director was better suited to other subjects.

As Clark and Lois, Reeve and Kidder effortlessly repeat their winning romantic chemistry, this time with an interesting whiff of melancholy added. And while the alien villains never reach their full potential, Gene Hackman seems to be having a great deal of fun playing opportunistic baddie Lex Luthor, with oafish sidekick Otis (Ned Beatty) wisely removed from most of the story.

In recent years, director Donner's alternate cut of this sequel has also been made available to interested fans. Some proclaim it superior, although *Superman II* seemed destined to be an uneven entertainment no matter who was calling the shots.

The Man of Steel (Christopher Reeve) gives up his super-powers for the love of Lois Lane (Margot Kidder), a decision he soon regrets after three black-clad Kryptonian villains (Jack O'Halloran, Terence Stamp, Sarah Douglas) escape from the Phantom Zone and threaten Earth.

Lex Luthor (Gene Hackman) adds to Superman's problems.

Bowing before General Zod, a clever Superman manages to outwit and defeat his vainglorious opponent.

Technicians and artisans create an entire American town in miniature. Ultimately the Phantom Zone baddies will descend upon this heartland environment.

35 ANT-MAN 2015

117   1.85

FROM THE STUDIO THAT BROUGHT YOU *GUARDIANS OF THE GALAXY*

PAUL RUDD   EVANGELINE LILLY   COREY STOLL   BOBBY CANNAVALE   MICHAEL PENA   AND MICHAEL DOUGLAS AS DR. HANK PYM

MARVEL

ANT-MAN

IN 3D, realD 3D AND IMAX 3D

HEROES DON'T GET ANY BIGGER JULY 17

WHO MADE IT:

Marvel Studios/Walt Disney Studios (U.S.). Director: Peyton Reed. Producers: Kevin Feige, Brad Winderbaum, David J. Grant, Stan Lee, Edgar Wright, Victoria Alonso, Michael Grillo, Alan Fine, Louis D'Esposito. Writers: Edgar Wright, Joe Cornish, Adam McKay, Paul Rudd, from the Marvel comic book by Stan Lee, Jack Kirby and Larry Lieber. Cinematography (color): Russell Carpenter. Music: Christopher Beck. Starring Paul Rudd (Scott Lang/Ant Man), Michael Douglas (Dr. Hank Pym), Evangeline Lilly (Hope van Dyne), Corey Stoll (Darren Cross/Yellowjacket), Bobby Cannavale (Paxton), Anthony Mackie (Sam Wilson/Falcon), Judy Greer (Maggie Lang), Abby Ryder Fortson (Cassie Lang), Michael Pena (Luis), David Dastmalchian (Kurt), T.I. (Dave), Hayley Atwell (Peggy Carter).

WHAT IT'S ABOUT:

The secrets of miniaturization have long been guarded by genius inventor Dr. Hank Pym, who functioned as the undetectable hero Ant-Man years ago, with his beloved wife adopting the guise of the equally-miniscule Wasp. Today, armed with the same astonishing ability to shrink in scale but increase in strength, con-man Scott Lang must embrace his inner-hero and help mentor Pym protect the secrets behind his spectacular Ant-Man suit from a new generation of towering threats. Against seemingly insurmountable obstacles, Pym and Lang plan and pull off a unique heist that will ultimately save the world.

WHY IT'S IMPORTANT:

Ant-Man was the MCU's first "stand alone" superhero adventure in a long time, although that term may now be meaningless, as viewers always get at least one Avenger character thrown in for needed support (Anthony Mackie's Falcon, in this case). Significantly, the film underwent a change of directors rather late in the game, with Marvel clearly having problems with artistic visions that threatened their carefully pre-planned conception. With the MCU, it's never about one work of art, but rather a series of efficient "episodes" in an overall collection that need to fit together seamlessly. One consistent vision, one tone, spread over Lord knows how many movies.

Hard to argue with success. Even a more conventional *Ant-Man* emerges as a reasonable entertainment with a legitimately fresh gimmick: the mini-thing. Instead of having to slog through the latest perfectly-filmed *Avengers* brawl, viewers are transported on the wings of a buzzing bug into a world with limitless possibilities. In terms of the human factor, Paul Rudd is endearing enough as con-man turned superhero Scott Lang, and Marvel gets its money's worth out of venerable scientist Michael Douglas, the original "ant guy" Henry Pym. On the negative side, Lang's streetwise pals/helpers are amusing for about two minutes, and then...

Insect world views notwithstanding, *Ant-Man*'s most inventive moments occur during its agreeably offbeat climax. Facing an obligatory monster-adversary known as Yellowjacket (Corey Stoll), Scott finds himself battling for life in his ex-wife's suburban home, literally upon his own daughter's toy train set-up. The mini-ideas are clever enough, but a reversal of the central concept tranforms the toy locomotive into a gigantic, happy-faced monster that smashes through the house and careens into the front lawn. Honestly, it's hard not to like a movie with a nutsy scene like this as its capper.

Not a super-smash for Marvel, but better than average and with some standout moments, *Ant-Man* is more enjoyable than its storyline might suggest. The titular hero was next seen in *Captain America: Civil War*, demonstrating his other major superhero trick, putting atoms in reverse and becoming a giant.

ABOVE: Scientist Darren Cross (Corey Stroll) attempts to smooth-talk colleague Hope van Dyne (Evangeline Lilly), but soon reveals his true villainous colors. RIGHT: Trying a stolen "motorcycle uniform" on for size, petty criminal Scott Lang (Paul Rudd) becomes the miniaturized superhero Ant-Man. He eventually faces a suited-up Cross in the fearsome guise of Yellowjacket (bottom right hand corner).

LEFT ABOVE, LEFT BELOW: Ant-Man has the power to communicate with actual ants during his adventures, soon getting close with one of them. BELOW: Fated to become the wonderful Wasp in the tradition of her superheroic mother, Hope confers with novice adventurer Lang and her estranged scientist father Hank Pym (Michael Douglas) as they embark on an especially risky mission.

Different species, kindred spirits. RIGHT: Imperfect dad Lang comforts his daughter Cassie (Abby Ryder Forston).

Actress Evangeline Lilly is prepped with some fighting lessons. Her character Hope van Dyne is the daughter of two tainted superheroes, a true double whammy.

AGAINST
ENORMOUS
ODDS

LEFT, ABOVE: The miniaturized Ant Man (Paul Rudd) hitches a ride in his 2015 debut adventure, which pitted him against nefarious opposite number Yellowjacket (Corey Stole, left bottom, facing a toy locomotive.) THIS PAGE: King Leonidas (Gerald Butler) of Sparta spits on the odds as he leads 300 men into battle against the massive Persian army in Zack Snyder's *300*, a 2006 film based on Frank Miller's graphic novel.

34

300 2006

(117) [2.35]

WHO MADE IT:

Warner Bros./Legendary Pictures (U.S.). Director: Zack Snyder. Producers: Gianni Nunnari, Mark Canton, Bernie Goldmann, Jeffrey Silver. Writers: Zack Snyder, Kurt Johnsted, Michael Gordon, based on the graphic novel by Frank Miller and Lynn Varley (Dark Horse). Cinematography (color): Larry Fong. Music: Tyler Bates. Starring Gerald Butler (King Leonidas), Lena Headey (Queen Gorgo), Giovanni Cimmino (Pleistarchus), Dominic West (Theron), David Wenham (Dillios), Vincent Regan (Captain Artemis), Tom Wisdom (Astinos), Andrew Pleavin (Daxos), Andrew Tiernan (Ephialtes), Rodrigo Santoro (King Xerxes), Stephen McHattie (The Loyalist), Michael Fassbender (Stellos).

WHAT IT'S ABOUT:

In 480 B.C. a state of war exists between Persia, led by King Xerxes, and Greece. At the Battle of Thermopylae, Leonidas, king of the Greek city state of Sparta, leads his badly outnumbered warriors against the massive Persian army. The 300 are accompanied by about 700 Thespians who protect the flanks of a narrow passage, and when combined, these forces manage to slay tens of thousands of Persians and prevent their entry into Hellas for several days. Betrayal in the form of a bitter shepherd named Ephialtes turns the tide against Leonidas and his valiant soldiers. Outflanked and awaiting certain death, the Spartans fight to the finish, their great sacrifice inspiring all of Greece to unite against their common enemy.

WHY IT'S IMPORTANT:

The inspiring story of the 300 Spartans has been told many times, in various creative venues. Zack Snyder's adaptation of Frank Miller's graphic novel is arguably the most striking cinematic interpretation, a winning blend of history, pseudo-Tolkein fantasy, and action movie values. To capture the unique look of the comic, Snyder films the entire experience in a stylized technique known as super-imposition chroma key, last fiddled with in *Sin City*, another Miller adaptation. Color washes and extreme contrast characterize this look of heightened unreality, imbuing an otherwise dusty period piece with timeless, fantastical flavoring.

But all the style in the world can't help a movie with unconvincing characters. *300* is brilliantly cast, starting with the all-important lead role of King Leonidas (Gerard Butler), who reflexively defies all odds and takes on an army he cannot possibly defeat, simply because surrendering is abhorrent to a true Spartan. Shouting orders with passion and unyielding pride, Butler, with his black beard and fixed yet sensitive gaze, is a revelation... a leader's leader. Almost as good is Lena Headey as Queen Gorgo, fighting political battles at home to secure her husband more aid even as he and his minions fight a bloody, historically significant battle against Persian oppression. As with *Spartacus*, the important thing is that brave warriors stood up to authority, inspiring others in the future to follow their example. Snyder smartly uses the voice-over narration of a single Spartan soldier (David Wenham) to track this spectacular confrontation and its aftermath.

Although not a fantasy film, *300* flirts with *Lord of the Rings*-style monsters and magic. There is a tormented, Gollum-like hunchback who turns traitor, bribed Oracles, an aggressive giant, and inbred races that take on the look of wretched non-humans. No fire-breathing dragons or orcs, thankfully.

Well-received by critics and audiences alike, *300* inspired a less-successful sequel (*Rise of an Empire*), and put Zack Snyder on the map as a comic book movie auteur of sorts (*Watchmen* would be next). Never was his talent on better display than in this movie.

ABOVE: King Leonidas (Gerard Butler) listens patiently to a Persian messenger before disposing of him. LEFT: The Persian army is an immense, seemingly unstoppable force. BELOW: Leonidas and his men meet up with their sometimes useful allies, the Arcadians.

ABOVE: Farewell to the King and his 300, from Queen Gorgo (Lena Headey) and child. BELOW: Sparta's wall of the slain.

RIGHT, TOP: Art concept of the wolf vs. young Leonaidas. RIGHT, BOTTOM: Art concept of the beautiful young oracle.

33

SUPERMAN AND THE MOLE MEN 1951 (58) [1.37] (

The All-Time ACE OF ACTION! in his **FIRST Full-Length Feature Adventure!**

SUPERMAN AND the Mole Men

Copyright MCMLI by National Comics Publications, Inc.

starring

George REEVES · Phyllis COATES

with

Jeff Corey · Walter Reed · J. Farrell MacDonald
Stanley Andrews

Produced by BARNEY SARECKY · Directed by LEE SHOLEM
Original Screenplay by RICHARD FIELDING
Released by LIPPERT PICTURES, Inc.

WHO MADE IT:

Lippert Pictures (U.S.). Director: Lee Sholem. Producer: Barney A. Sarecky. Writer: Richard Fielding (aka Robert Maxwell), based on the comic book by Jerry Siegel and Joe Shuster. Cinematography (b/w): Clark Ramsey. Music: Darrell Calker. Starring George Reeves (Clark Kent/Superman), Phyllis Coates (Lois Lane), Jeff Corey (Luke Benson), Walter Reed (Bill Corrigan), J. Farrell MacDonald (Pop Shannon), Stanley Andrews (The Sheriff), Ray Walker (John Craig), Frank Reicher (Hospital Superintendent), Hal K. Dawson (Chuck Weber), Phil Warren (Deputy Jim), Beverly Washburn (Child), Billy Curtis (Mole Man), Jerry Maren (Mole Man).

WHAT IT'S ABOUT:

Daily Planet reporters Clark Kent and Lois Lane travel to the small community of Silsby, where work on the world's deepest oil well has mysteriously shut down. It isn't long before strange, mole-like creatures from the center of the earth emerge from the abandoned well and terrify unsuspecting locals. Kent transforms into caped wonder Superman and attempts to aid the frightened alien visitors when the townspeople, led by hate-crazed Luke Benson, form a lynch mob and try to destroy them.

WHY IT'S IMPORTANT:

George Reeves' famous TV incarnation of the Man of Steel first greeted viewers in this modest theatrical film, which was something of a sideways launch of the series that followed. Ditching super-villains and far-out gimmicks, *Superman and the Mole Men* has more in common with the sci-fi thrillers that would soon dominate the post-atomic decade, with its relatively sophisticated "we are the monsters" subtext elevating the comic book genre to a smarter, more progressive and humanist level. Superman angrily comparing the lynch-minded townspeople of Silsby, USA, to "Nazi stormtroopers" is a good example of this film's uncompromisingly adult approach.

As befits a film made for theatrical showings, *SATMM* is better produced than the TV show it was designed to spawn. Real attention is paid to mood lighting and frame composition, particularly in the early suspense scenes. An original music score by Darrell (*From Hell It Came*) Calker was later replaced with stock cues when *SATMM* was re-edited into a small screen two-part episode of *Adventures of Superman* (Calker's eerie music would be heard in countless *Alfred Hitchcock Presents* shows during the '50s, including the master's own "Lamb to the Slaughter.").

Without Jimmy Olsen around for comedy relief, the Clark-Lois banter is allowed full reign, and to good effect. Rational (but getting impatient) Reeves and surly Coates are a couple Howard Hawks could've created, and it's fun to see the Clark Kent "masquerade" realized with both genuine urgency and a whiff of romantic comedy. Meanwhile, the titular Mole Men are cheaply conceived but well-played alien visitors, fearful little creatures at first but ultimately sympathetic victims of humanity's prejudice. An alien himself with little patience for bigotry, Superman instantly empathizes with these strangers and helps them return home. "You live your lives, and we'll live ours" seems a fair-enough coda to what amounted to a very different kind of comic book superhero movie... one with an unexpected adult conscience.

Superman (George Reeves) strikes an iconic pose. This movie offered a brief overview of the Man of Steel's extraterrestrial origin, later re-worked for the TV series. RIGHT: The armed and potentially dangerous Mole Men, actors Billy Curtis and Jerry Maren among them. Make-up by Harry Thomas.

Lois Lane (Phyllis Coates) and Kent with Bill Corrigan (Walter Reed) and rabble-rouser Luke Benson (Jeff Corey, soon to be blacklisted).

The producers resorted to cheapjack animation and a problematic dummy to convey this important flying/catching scene.

Offbeat, odd and ingratiating yarn about secretly-empowered alien busters...

MEN IN BLACK 1997

98 1.85

Poster/photos: © 1997 Columbia Pictures

MR. JONES MR. SMITH

PROTECTING
THE EARTH
FROM THE
SCUM OF
THE UNIVERSE.

MIB
MEN IN BLACK

WHO MADE IT:

Columbia Pictures Corporation/Amblin Entertainment (U.S.). Director: Barry Sonnenfeld. Producers: Walter F. Parkes, Laurie MacDonald, Steven Spielberg. Writers: Ed Solomon, based on the comic book created by Lowell Cunningham (Marvel/Malibu). Cinematography (Technicolor): Donald Peterman. Music: Danny Elfman. Starring Will Smith (James Darrell Edwards III/Agent J), Tommy Lee Jones (Kevin Brown/Agent K), Linda Fiorentino (Laurel Weaver), Vincent D'Onofrio (Edgar the Bug), Rip Torn (Agent Zed), Tony Shalhoub (Jack Jeebs), Siobhan Fallon Hogan (Beatrice), Mike Nussbaum (Gentle Rosenberg), Jon Gries (Van Driver).

WHAT IT'S ABOUT:

After chasing down a mysterious perpetrator who turns out to be an alien, flippant New York City cop James Darrel Edwards is recruited by K, a seasoned operative in a clandestine government agency that secretly polices the comings and goings of extraterrestrials on planet Earth. These "men in black" agents are assigned to recover an object that's been stolen by an intergalactic terrorist. Unless K and his new wisecracking partner, now renamed J, can stop the criminal and thwart his evil plans, an interstellar war will promptly ensue. Aiding and abetting the agents for a final showdown is a pretty, unflappable city medical examiner named Laurel who often finds herself zapped by K's ingenious memory-sapping device.

WHY IT'S IMPORTANT:

In the mid-1990s, TV's *The X-Files* seemed to dominate American culture, with tales about mysterious government conspiracies involving UFO cover-ups replacing starship journeys as the sci-fi flavor of the day. Out of this atmosphere came a minor comic book and a major movie adaptation: *Men In Black*, those Blues Brothers-like figures of dark mystery, saving the world from alien threats while looking totally cool doing it. Half-parody, half wackified adventure thriller, this large-scale production from the house of Spielberg was destined to be a crowd-pleaser.

Speaking of cool, star Will Smith was at the peak of his star power when this film went into production. His streetwise Agent J is perfectly complemented by Tommy Lee Jones' dour Agent K, and both gentlemen belong to a secret organization that knows damn well alien life forms are real, and is doing what it can to protect unsuspecting Earthlings from them. This guarantees a plethora of other-worldly creatures on continual display, a sci-fi application of the *Ghostbusters* concept, with exotic aliens replacing ectoplasmic entities. Also like *Ghostbusters*, events build to a major battle sequence with the fate of planet Earth at stake, our stalwart heroes taking their shots in the former location of the New York World's Fair for an appropriate retro wink.

Enjoyable and sure of itself under Barry Sonnenfeld's direction, *Men In Black* was a major box office hit, inspiring two sequels and a fervent cult following. Critics were quite enthusiastic, impressed by the bizarre wit of Ed Solomon's screenplay and Smith's winning performance. The movie snagged a well-deserved Academy Award for Best Makeup, and was also nominated for Best Art Direction and Best Original Score.

Although mainstreamers may have eventually outgrown the chilly '90s social atmosphere that led to *Men In Black*'s creation, the film still resonates as a humorous take-off of an era obsessed with government cover-ups, conspiracies, and all things Roswell.

LEFT: Agent J (Will Smith) and Agent K (Tommy Lee Jones) are super-armed and ready for anything as the intrepid Men in Black. ABOVE: Frightening, bombastic extraterrestrial threats are par for the course as stalwart J and K gear up for a fateful encounter at the site of the 1964 World's Fair in Flushing, New York.

Seasoned Agent K (Jones, left) doesn't bat an eye in the fearsome face of the cosmic unknown. Seeing through alien disguises becomes second nature.

Not all aliens are out to eat your face, as Agent J soon learns after a little field work.

Dr. Laurel Weaver (Linda Fiorentino) aids the Men in Black on a mission, and eventually joins this secret team of government-sponsored watchdogs.

LEFT: Make-up wiz Rick Baker and his aliens. INSERT: Director Barry Sonnenfield instructs Tommy Lee Jones.

31 V FOR VENDETTA 2005

WHO MADE IT:

Warner Bros./Virtual Studios/Silver Pictures (U.S./U.K./Germany). Director: James McTeigue. Producers: Joel Silver, Larry Wachowski, Andy Wachowski, Grant Hill. Writers: The Wachowski Brothers, based on the graphic novel by Alan Moore and David Lloyd (Vertigo). Cinematography (color): Adrian Biddle. Music: Dario Marianelli. Starring Hugo Weaving (V), Natalie Portman (Evey Hammond), Stephen Rea (Eric Finch), John Hurt (High Chancellor Adam Sutler), Stephen Fry (Gordon Deitrich), Tim Pigott-Smith (Peter Creedy), Rupert Graves (Dominic Stone).

WHAT IT'S ABOUT:

Setting: the futuristic landscape of totalitarian Britain. A mild-mannered young woman named Evey is rescued from a life-threatening situation by a masked vigilante known only as "V." Incomparably charismatic and ferociously skilled in the art of combat and deception, V ignites a revolution when he detonates two London landmarks and takes over

the government-controlled airwaves, urging his fellow citizens to rise up against tyranny and oppression. As Evey uncovers the truth about V's mysterious background, she also discovers the truth about herself – and emerges as his unlikely ally in the culmination of his plot to bring freedom and justice back to a society fraught with cruelty and corruption.

WHY IT'S IMPORTANT:

DC's Vertigo imprint, like its title implies, specializes in adult and edgy graphic novels that often indulge in subversive, anarchistic themes. An excellent example is 1988's *V for Vendetta*, the brainchild of popular comics writer Alan Moore (*Watchmen*, *From Hell*), which resurrects the iconic Guy Fawkes persona (co-creator David Lloyd's idea) in the form of V, a masked bringer of truth. Real life Fawkes was part of the legendary Gunpowder Plot of 1605, an unsuccessful attempt to blow up the House of Lords and assassinate King James I. Vigilante V has similar violent ambitions, but in this case it's to wake up the abused population and overthrow a totalitarian England.

Larry and Andy Wachowski, barely recovered from the high of their unexpected mega-success with *The Matrix*, chose to write but not direct *V for Vendetta*. The film feels like one of their creations; it's verbose, paranoid, and awash in violence. But V happens to be a stylized, poetic figure who is expected to enlighten us with his colorful words, so that approach works here. Natalie Portman does a wonderful job maturing from indifferent civilian to deep-feeling revolutionary, and Stephen Rea is even more compelling as the relentless detective who not only loses faith in his own bosses, but actually takes the torch from deceased V to complete his mission of justice.

Beyond the boldness of the storyline and a plethora of well-acted characters, *V for Vendetta* is cinematically alive. The climax is a triumph of cross-cutting, with director James McTeigue teasing his audience visually and morally: Will V's plan actually succeed? Will the Houses of Parliament blow up? Is doing something this terrible a good and necessary thing if it's in the cause of freedom? Provocative questions, stylishly addressed in a "masked avenger" movie with a lot on its sharp mind.

COLIN FIRTH   SAMUEL L. JACKSON   and MICHAEL CAINE

FROM THE DIRECTOR OF X-MEN: FIRST CLASS

Kingsman
THE SECRET SERVICE

FEBRUARY 13   #KINGSMAN   KINGSMANMOVIE.COM

MARV   IN PREMIUM LARGE FORMAT THEATRES

WHO MADE IT:

Twentieth Century Fox Film Corporation/Marv Films/TSG Entertainment (U.S.). Director: Matthew Vaughn. Producers: Adam Bohling, David Reid, Matthew Vaughn. Writers: Jane Gildman, Matthew Vaughn, based on the comic book *The Secret Service* by Dave Gibbons and Mark Millar. Cinematography (color): George Richmond. Music: Henry Jackman, Matthew Margeson. Starring Colin Firth (Harry Hart/Galahad), Samuel L. Jackson (Richmond Valentine), Taron Egerton (Gary "Eggsy" Unwin), Mark Strong (Merlin), Michael Caine (Chester King/Arthur), Sophie Cookson (Roxy Morton), Sophia Boutella (Gazelle), Mark Hamill (Professor James Arnold).

WHAT IT'S ABOUT:

A super-secret spy organization recruits an unrefined but promising street kid named Gary "Eggsy" Unwin into the agency's ultra-competitive training program. Unwin is the son of a man once known to recruiter Harry Hart, who takes a personal interest in his latest protege. At first reluctant, Eggsy is inspired by Hart's expertise with high-tech weapons in a battle with thugs, and soon launches himself into his mentor's rigorous training program, hoping to

secure a position as an agent. Meanwhile, an unexpected global threat emerges from a twisted tech genius, forcing the enthusiastic Unwin into harm's way a bit sooner than he expected.

WHY IT'S IMPORTANT:

More than just a take-off on 007 movies, *Kingsman The Secret Service* is an expansive, free-wheeling adventure fantasy tinged with self-aware satire and bursting with stylized, badass action. It's all based on a semi-obscure British comic book published in 2012 by Icon. Actor Mark Hamill, featured as himself in the comic's storyline along with other celebrities, cannily shows up in the movie version as Professor James Arnold, originally the tale's villain. That role is now filled by a character created specifically for the film, Richmond Valentine, played with beaming megalomania by comic book movie crown prince Samuel L. Jackson.

Director Matthew Vaughn dispenses with a good deal of the comic's plot, but retains the general idea of a mad scheme that forces unsuspecting, brainwashed human beings to slaughter each other around the globe as a result of a corrupted satellite. The movie makes this absurd idea slightly more palatable with microchip technology and cell phones worked into the plan. Also changed are names of characters and their relationships to each other, with young streetwise hero Gary (Taron Egerton) now being guided into Kingsman service by gentleman agent Harry Hart/Galahad (Colin Firth), profoundly guilt-ridden over the death of Gary's spy father, who sacrificed his life for Hart's team. The movie slips into "spy kids" mode for a bit, with Gary and other Kingsman recruits tested and trained by senior operative Merlin (Mark Strong), under the watchful eye of Chester King/Arthur (Michael Caine). But Vaughn and writer Jane Gildman have some fresh, unexpected twists up their sleeve, slyly playing on audience familiarity with the spy movie genre (referenced more than once by the characters). Of special note are some deliberately protracted fight sequences, enhanced by special effects and slow/fast-motion, that show us the remarkable Hart and eventually protégé Gary taking out scores of adversaries with seasoned grace and bloody panache. Wholesale slaughter never looked so cool.

29 KICK-ASS 2010

(117) 2.35

Poster/photos: © 2010 KA Films LP

KICK ASS

AARON JOHNSON · CHRISTOPHER MINTZ-PLASSE · MARK STRONG · CHLOE GRACE MORETZ · AND NICOLAS CAGE

SHUT UP. KICK-ASS.

IN THEATERS APRIL 16
KICK-ASS-THEMOVIE.COM

WHO MADE IT:

Lionsgate/Universal Pictures/Marv Films (U.S./U.K.). Director: Matthew Vaughn. Producers: Matthew Vaughn, Brad Pitt, Kris Thykier, Adam Bohling, Tarquin Pack, David Reid. Writers: Jane Goldman, Matthew Vaughn, based on the comic book created by Mark Millar and Johnny Romita Jr. Cinematography (color):Ben Davis. Music: John Murphy, Henry Jackman, Marius de Vries, Ilan Eshkeri. Starring Nicolas Cage (Damon Macready/Big Daddy), Aaron Johnson (David "Dave" Lizewski/Kick-Ass), Chloe Grace Moretz (Mindy Macready/Hit-Girl), Mark Strong (Frank D'Amico), Christopher Mintz-Plasse (Chris D'Amico/Red Mist), Stu Riley (Huge Goon), Lyndsy Fonseca (Katie), Omari Hardwick (Sgt. Marcus Williams), Corey Johnson (Sporty Goon), Elizabeth McGovern (Alice Lizewski), Michael Rispoli (Big Joe).

WHAT IT'S ABOUT:

Geeky teenager Dave Lizewski has few friends and lives a mostly unnoticed life. One day on impulse, he decides to become a costumed superhero like the characters he admires in the comics he collects. After a disastrous first brush with actual crime, Dave refines his act and soon becomes famous as the local vigilante Kick-Ass. He eventually joins forces with other like-minded misfits, including the even younger Hit Girl, with all squaring off against New York's biggest and most ruthless crime-boss, Frank D'aminco.

WHY IT'S IMPORTANT:

"What if the average teenage loser became a super-hero?" posits Matthew Vaughn's *Kick Ass*, partially a send-up of its own genre, but mostly a spirited adaptation of an ironic new age comic book. Its semi-geek protagonist (Aaron Johnson) isn't far off from prototypical Peter Parker in many respects, and his nonchalant narration deliberately calls to mind Raimi's classic film. Meanwhile, a sub-plot involving Big Daddy and Hit Girl complicates matters: what if there are others of this super-adventurous ilk already out there, but further up the food chain?

Although it takes us further away from the quasi-reality of the *Kick-Ass* setup, the weird, tragic life of Mr. Damon Macready cannot help but command our attention. Played agreeably by Nicolas Cage, he's a costumed vigilante patterned after Batman, an ex-cop gone mad, raising his bright-eyed, highly skilled daughter as the ultimate tiny tyke sidekick. This dynamic duo is operating on a more melodramatic level than Kick-Ass is – they're closer to actual comic book heroes, while he still has one foot planted firmly (more or less) in reality. Ultimately, these worlds collide and merge, with Kick-Ass joining Hit-Girl for a spectacular, over-the-top assault on their criminal kingpin's stronghold.

Beyond Cage, Chloe Grace Moretz' Hit-Girl is the main attention grabber, a foul-mouthed and irresistible tomboy enforcer who skewers victims with consummate style and seemingly reckless abandon. Mark Strong is appropriately vile as D'Amico, the main bad guy, never more reprehensible than when he's pummel-punching a downed Hit-Girl (who has, admittedly, just killed a small army of his bodyguards). As for Kick-Ass himself, he matures from curious geek to steadfast hero rather convincingly, given the wild and crazy circumstances.

Unsuccessful on the big screen, *Kick-Ass* was profitable enough on video to earn a somewhat belated sequel. *2* was a mostly unnecessary experience enlivened by a few amusing Hit-Girl moments.

LEFT: Mindy Macready (Chloe Grace Moretz) revels in her new birthday gift. RIGHT: Kick-Ass (Aaron Johnson) is visited by Hit Girl (Moretz) and Big Daddy (Nicholas Cage). BELOW: The Red Mist (Christopher Mintz-Plasse), Kick-Ass, Hit-Girl, Big Daddy.

LEFT: Damon Macready is an ex-cop who leads a double life as the Batmanesque superhero Big Daddy. BELOW: Frank D'Amico's criminal empire is no match for Big Daddy's great fury and exotic weapons.

ABOVE, TOP: Hit-Girl takes out D'Amico (Mark Strong). ABOVE, BOTTOM: Kick-Ass begins mastering his skills.

Director Matthew Vaughn prepares actors Aaron Johnson (Kick-Ass) and Chloe Moretz (Hit-Girl) for the film's exciting climax.

28 THOR 2011

(115) 2.35

WHO MADE IT:

Marvel Entertainment/Paramount Pictures (U.S.). Director: Kenneth Branagh. Producers: Kevin Feige, Alan Fine, David J. Grant, Craig Kyle, David Maisel, Victoria Alonso, Patricia Whitcher. Writers: Ashley Miller, Zack Stentz, Don Payne, J. Michael Straczynski, Mark Protosevich, from the Marvel comic book by Stan Lee, Larry Lieber, Jack Kirby. Cinematography (color): Haris Zambarloukos. Music: Patrick Doyle. Starring Chris Hemsworth (Thor), Natalie Portman (Jane Foster), Tom Hiddleston (Loki), Anthony Hopkins (Odin), Stellan Skarsgard (Erik Selvig), Kat Dennings (Darcy Lewis), Clark Gregg (Agent Coulson), Colm Feore (King Laufey), Idris Elba (Heimdall), Ray Stevenson (Volstagg), Tadanobu Asano (Hogun), Josh Dallas (Fandral), Jaimie Alexander (Sif), Rene Russo (Frigga), Jeremy Renner (Hawkeye), Samuel L. Jackson (Nick Fury).

WHAT IT'S ABOUT:

Crown prince Thor from the distant realm of Asgard is a powerful but arrogant warrior whose reckless actions reignite an ancient war with a race called the Frost Giants. As punishment, he is cast down to planet Earth by his caring but furious father, Odin. Forced to live among humans, Thor's heart is reached by a beautiful, young investigative scientist named Jane Foster. Meanwhile, his half-brother Loki, always jealous of the Thunder God, conspires with receptive Frost Giants to take over Asgard and ultimately invade the Earth. Joined by three trusted Asgardian comrades, and backed up by new Earthly allies, Thor puts his personal feelings in perspective and confronts the icy rage of Loki.

WHY IT'S IMPORTANT:

After one significant hit (*Iron Man*) and what can now be classified as a rare miss (*The Incredible Hulk*), the MCU needed to establish two additional "stand alone" movies introducing fanciful heroes from its mythology before they could all appear together in *The Avengers*. The MCU production of *Thor* provided an interesting opportunity for a legitimate world-class director to make something out of the highly improbable Norse God superman, whose last live-action incarnation was in a TV movie that pitted him against Lou Ferrigno's Hulk.

Speaking of Hulk, Ang Lee's unsuccessful 2003 movie version was criticized for allowing its expressionistic director a little too much creative freedom. By significant contrast, *Thor* would test the new, centrally-controlled MCU method of filmmaking: directors are generally hired to fulfill a pre-arranged vision, part of an ongoing trajectory, with one movie affecting the next in ways the current helmer may not be privy to. Ultimately, Marvel hires directors for their expert craftsmanship; chance-taking and inspired artistic flourishes are rarely if ever tolerated. MCU's core audience would probably consider that pretentious.

Thor starts out in distant Asgard, establishing the dangerously impulsive, hammer-wielding hero (Chris Hemsworth), heir to the throne of mighty Odin (Anthony Hopkins). But Thor isn't allowed to be reckless for long, because once sentenced to time on planet Earth for serious misbehaving, he promptly makes some likeable/useful friends, and inevitably faces off against his jealous, ever-scheming half-brother Loki (Tom Hiddleston) and the anti-Asgardian forces allied with him. Surprisingly, the romantic relationship between Thor and perennially blushing scientist Jane Foster (Natalie Portman) has a loopy charm. In a typically pleasant scene, Odin's easy-talking heir explains to Jane that what we humans interpret as "magic" is merely science on a more advanced level. This jives with the concept of Asgardian culture being a combination of classic pageantry and *Flash Gordon*-style weird science... something akin to the cosmos according to George Lucas.

The end result of all this effort is a most enjoyable, if not exceptional, stand alone Marvel movie.

Odin (Anthony Hopkins) and his sons (Chris Hemsworth, Tom Hiddleston).

The great fury of Norse god Thor (Hemsworth) is quelled by Earth scientist Jane Foster (Natalie Portman), his eventual sweetheart.

After retrieving his hammer, Thor and three allies must take on the towering enemy Destroyer.

Director Kenneth Branagh instructs actor Chris Hemsworth on just how much anger Thor must display for this key moment (see above image).

WHO MADE IT:

Twentieth Century Fox Film Corporation/Marvel Enterprises/Donner's Company (U.S.). Director: Bryan Singer. Producers: Lauren Shuler Donner, Ralph Winter. Writers: David Hayter, Tom DeSanto, Bryan Singer, based on the comic book by Stan Lee and Jack Kirby (Marvel). Cinematography (color): Newton Thomas Sigel. Music: Michael Kamen. Starring Patrick Stewart (Charles Xavier/Professor X), Hugh Jackman (Logan/Wolverine), Ian McKellen (Erik Lehnsherr/Magneto), Halle Berry (Ororo Munroe/Storm), Famke Janssen (Dr. Jean Grey), James Marsden (Scott Summers/Cyclops), Bruce Davison (Senator Robert Kelly), Rebecca Romijn-Stamos (Raven Darkholme/Mystique), Ray Park (Mortimer Toynbee/Toad), Anna Paquin (Marie/Rogue), Shawn Ashmore (Bobby Drake/Iceman).

WHAT IT'S ABOUT:

Professor Charles Xavier leads a school of skilled mutants known as the X-Men, a peacekeeping force that safeguards the world against genetically mutated humans. Among these gifted beings are weather-controlling Storm, shape-shifting Mystique, and the metal-clawed powerhouse Wolverine. At the same time, Xavier's old friend Erik Lehnsherr, endowed with astonishing magnetic powers since boyhood, has also begun to organize a team of mutants, one that he intends to use as a fatal blow against humanity, which he perceives as a threat. Both sides must contend with the nefarious plans of Senator Kelly, a heartless political leader who is pushing for a final solution against mutants of every stripe.

WHY IT'S IMPORTANT:

Considered by many to be the first of a new generation of comic book adaptations that make no apology for their exaggerated content, Bryan Singer's *X-Men* is a solid, straightforward social debate told in fantasy terms. Already distinguished as a filmmaker (*The Usual Suspects*), Singer instantly recognized the Martin Luther King – Malcolm X underpinnings of lead antagonists Professor X and Magneto. Moreover, the "outsider" aspect of youthful mutants who must keep their offbeat qualities hidden from haters became an obvious parallel to gay discrimination. All of these provocative ideas helped to elevate what the public perceived as "a comic book movie." Not being a fanboy, for better or worse, Singer proceeded to make a good science fiction adventure film, one with some important things to say about how human beings deal with the concept of change.

Singer's cast couldn't be better: Patrick Stewart left his Starfleet commission far behind to become the enigmatic Dr. Xavier, benevolent teacher, social scientist, and occasional superhero. Matching him every step of the way is Ian McKellen's war-hungry Erik Lehnsherr, aka Magneto, an elegant villain with a just cause mostly but not entirely eclipsed by his tragic commitment to vengeance. One of Marvel's most popular characters, the metal-taloned Wolverine, is ably brought to screen life by Hugh Jackman, soon to be drawn into an awkward romantic triangle with geneticist Jean Grey (Famke Janssen) and human dynamo Scott Summers/Cyclops (James Marsden). Other recognizable mutant characters from the comics inhabit Xavier's school, or are allied with Magneto, anticipating the multi-hero crossover approach made indispensible by MCU more than a decade later.

X-Men isn't perfect – the mutant-making machine is a clunky idea, and the climactic raid on the Statue of Liberty never quite lives up to its promise. But as a smart, conceptually fearless movie pointing comic book adaptations in the right direction, Bryan Singer's 2000 groundbreaker is worthy of praise.

ABOVE: Professor Charles Xavier (Patrick Stewart) and nemesis Magneto (Ian McKellen). RIGHT: taloned Wolverine (Hugh Jackman). BELOW: Storm (Halle Berry) in conjuring mode.

Other notable mutants, both evil and benign: feral henchman Sabertooth (Tyler Mane), tangling with Wolverine; beam-firing Xavier protege Cyclops (James Marsden), and the grotesque, tongue-whipping Toad (Ray Park).

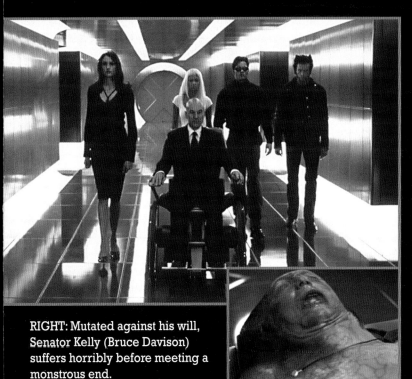

RIGHT: Mutated against his will, Senator Kelly (Bruce Davison) suffers horribly before meeting a monstrous end.

Bryan Singer contemplates Magneto's distinctive helmet. *X-Men* is often credited as the first modern comic book movie to eschew tongue-in-cheek humor for sci-fi seriousness.

26 THE INCREDIBLE HULK 1977 (95) [1.37] 6

Poster/photos: © Universal Studios/Marvel characters™

A scientist is exposed to a massive dose of gamma rays and becomes a superhuman beast...

WHO MADE IT:

Universal Studios (television; U.S.). Director: Kenneth Johnson. Producer: Kenneth Johnson. Writer: Kenneth Johnson, based on the comic book created by Stan Lee and Jack Kirby (Marvel). Cinematography (Technicolor): Howard Schwartz. Music: Joseph Harnell. Starring Bill Bixby (Dr. David Banner), Susan Sullivan (Dr. Elena Marks), Jack Colvin (Jack McGee), Lou Ferrigno (Creature), Susan Batson (Mrs. Maier), Mario Gallo (Mr. Bram), Charles Siebert (Ben), Eric Server (Policeman), William Larsen (Minister), June Whitley Taylor (Woman).

WHAT IT'S ABOUT:

Tormented by the death of his beloved wife in an auto accident, Dr. David Banner desperately searches for ways of tapping into the secret reserves of strength all human possess. An accidental overdose of gamma radiation contaminates Banner during the course of his research, transforming him into a green-skinned primitive creature whenever he becomes enraged. Working with colleague Dr. Elena Marks, Banner tries to reverse the effects of this gamma overdose, even as a dogged reporter named Jack McGee gets closer to his secret.

WHY IT'S IMPORTANT:

Arguably the first adult and "dark" comic book film adaptation, Kenneth Johnson's *The Incredible Hulk* came as a surprise in 1977. A two-hour made-for-tv movie, it was part of Marvel's brief arrangement with Universal to launch their characters as weekly TV properties (*Dr. Strange* and *Captain America* were also filmed, but never got beyond the pilot stage.) Followed promptly by a second TV feature, *Hulk* spawned a long running CBS series that is still fondly remembered.

By substituting a more grounded personal motivation for Dr. Banner (gone are the military sci-fi trappings of Stan Lee's original), this slow-moving, sensitive melodrama deliberately steered clear of anything remotely resembling a comic book experience, save for the green-skinned behemoth himself. Veteran TV star Bill Bixby proved an ideal choice for the driven but oh-so-civilized seeker of truth, just as bodybuilder Lou Ferrigno possessed an innocence that gave his terrifying pseudo-neanderthal a soul. Unfortunately, the Hulk's more fearsome make-up was modified for most of the TV episodes, so as not to frighten younger viewers.

Embracing intimacy while avoiding costly spectacle, this movie draws power from simple human interaction, eventually using the empathy between leads Bixby and Sullivan to convey a tragic plot point: "I love you, Elena. And I think you loved me too, although you never said it," Banner observes wistfully at Dr. Marks' grave in the film's final scene. Viewers realize that Elena did indeed confess her love for David before she died... but to the bewildered Hulk, proving just how submerged Banner's conscious mind is during his non-human interludes.

Both *The Incredible Hulk* pilot film and the two-hour episode "Married" (also directed by Ken Johnson) were released as theatrical features in various countries. Given their high level of production and performance, they easily passed for big screen fodder. Decades later, the same studio would produce a far more ambitious reboot of *Hulk* for the big screen, with CGI effects called into play and the military origins of Dr. Banner's dilemma restored. Directed by Ang Lee, it was truer to the comic in terms of story content, but less satisfying dramatically.

ABOVE: Dr. David Banner (Bill Bixby), guilt-ridden over the death of his wife, subjects himself to a dangerous experiment in order to tap into hidden reserves of strength. RIGHT: Banner and Dr. Elena Marks (Susan Sullivan).

ABOVE: Banner warns reporter Jack McGee (Jack Colvin) that he wouldn't like him when he's angry. RIGHT: Believed to be dead, David searches for a cure.

Body-builder Lou Ferrigno was the second choice to play Stan Lee's character; filming began with Richard ("Jaws") Kiel in the role.

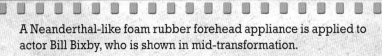

A Neanderthal-like foam rubber forehead appliance is applied to actor Bill Bixby, who is shown in mid-transformation.

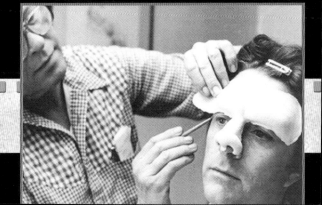

BEAST AND THE BEAUTY

Lou Ferrigno is just as much Universal Monster as he is Marvel Superhero in Universal's decidedly grown-up take on *The Incredible Hulk* (1977, written, produced, and directed by Kenneth Johnson). This TV pilot was released as a theatrical feature in many parts of the world and spawned a four-season CBS series.

RIGHT: One of the most stunning women in the world, curvaceous Jessica Alba made a lasting impression as dancer Nancy Callahan in *Sin City* (2005), a film scripted and co-directed by graphic novel writer/artist Frank Miller. Alba also played Invisible Woman Sue Storm in two *Fantastic Four* movies.

25 SIN CITY 2005

Poster/photos: © 2005 Dimension Films

WHO MADE IT:

Dimension Films/Troublemaker Studios (U.S.). Directors: Robert Rodriguez, Frank Miller, Quentin Tarantino. Producers: Bob Weinstein, Harvey Weinstein, Elizabeth Avellan, Bill Scott. Writer: Frank Miller, based on his graphic novels. Cinematography (color and b/w): Robert Rodriguez. Music: John Debney, Graeme Revell, Robert Rodriguez. Starring Bruce Willis, (John Hartigan), Mickey Rourke (Marv), Clive Owen (Dwight McCarthy), Benicio Del Toro (Det. Lt. Jack "Jackie Boy" Rafferty), Jessica Alba (Nany Callahan), Elijah Wood (Kevin), Rosario Dawson (Gail), Josh Harnett (The Salesman), Rutger Hauer (Cardinal Patrick Henry Roark), Michael Madsen (Bob).

WHAT IT'S ABOUT:

Four grim neo-noir tales that explore the tragic side of co-dependency. Imposing and volatile, a street thug vigilante named Marv tears his way through the criminal underworld of Sin City in search of his lost love Goldie, an apparently murdered prostitute. In another part of this sordid metropolis, Hartigan, an ex-cop with bad memories and a heart condition, foils the plans of a child-killer while protecting beautiful stripper Nancy from harm. Meanwhile, an ex-prostitute manages to evade her ex-pimp/corrupt cop Jackie Boy with the unexpected help of her new boyfriend, the ubiquitous photographer Dwight.

WHY IT'S IMPORTANT:

1980s comic book master Frank Miller became disillusioned by Hollywood after a decade of tepid screenwriting gigs and sub-par adaptations of his published work. This all changed with *Sin City*, which was produced and protected by a genuine fan who wanted the graphic novel translated to cinema as faithfully as possible. That fan was filmmaker Robert Rodriguez, who not only brought Miller directly into the project as co-director, but invited no less than Quentin Tarantino along for the ultra-stylish ride.

And the style of *Sin City* is what grabbed everyone's attention initially, a green-screen/digital combination that enabled an entire world to be constructed and flawlessly integrated with live-action elements. This approach was well-suited to the hyper, neo-noir unreality that characterized Miller's graphic novel, producing a high contrast black and white image punctuated by selected areas of color, often deep reds. Not content with just digital manipulation, the co-directors saw fit to employ startling makeups as well, reminding viewers of the exaggerated nature of comic art in general.

Underneath all these special effects are some fine actors, with Mickey Rourke mostly stealing the show as grotesque, quasi-superhuman avenger Marv searching for the killer of a hooker he fell in love with. Looking almost healthy by comparison, Bruce Willis is quite plausible as a noble ex-cop who lives long enough to see a child he once rescued grow up into a most appreciative sleaze bar dancer (Jessica Alba). Also throwing themselves into some juicy roles are Benicio Del Toro doing his spin on a corrupt cop and Rosario Dawson as the feisty leader of a prostitute-controlled part of town.

Effortlessly poetic, though sometimes a little too clever for its own good, *Sin City* is an offbeat creative experiment that pulls off its central conceit. Like Zach Snyder's *300*, which would follow a year later, it is a winning combination of stylized visuals and raw, volatile characters fighting like hell against considerable odds.

24

ADVENTURES OF CAPTAIN MARVEL 1941

WHO MADE IT:

Republic Pictures (U.S.). 12-chapter serial. Directors: John English, William Witney. Producer: Hiram S. Brown. Writers: Ronald Davidson, Norman S. Hall, Arch Heath, Joseph Poland, Sol Shor, based on the Fawcett comic book created by C.C. Beck and Bill Parker. Cinematography: William Nobles. Music: Cy Feuer. Starring Tom Tyler (Captain Marvel), Frank Coghlan Jr. (Billy Batson), William Benedict (Whitey Murphy), Louise Currie (Betty Wallace), Robert Strange (John Malcolm), Reed Hadley (Rahman Bar).

WHAT IT'S ABOUT:

While on a scientific expedition to Siam, a young boy named Billy Batson encounters Shazam, an ancient wizard, who entreats Billy to protect a magic talisman from being used for evil. This artifact, known as the Golden Scorpion, might be the most powerful weapon in the world, energized by lenses that have fallen into various hands. To thwart this potential threat, Batson is given the ability to transform himself into the adult hero Captain Marvel whenever he says the name Shazam. Returning to the United States, he battles a villainous hooded figure who hopes to accumulate all five lenses and gain world control.

WHY IT'S IMPORTANT:

In his day, Captain Marvel of Fawcett Comics was a serious rival for DC's Superman. Action specialists Republic Pictures did the iconic hero justice in this well-remembered serial, one with better photography and special effects than usual. The all-important flying sequences were truly groundbreaking in 1941, a deft mix of high-level acrobatics, rear projection photography, and large-size miniature models shot in bright daylight.

The gimmick of transforming from boy to adult crusader by shouting the godly word "SHAZAM!" is lifted directly from C.C. Beck's prose, and established early on. Billy Batson (Frank Coghlan Jr.) takes it all in stride, of course, putting his muscular genie back in its bottle for later use without thinking twice about the rather dramatic change his young body has just gone through. Batson and loyal pal Whitey (William Benedict) are almost like adolescent detectives, with pretty Louise (Betty Wallace) something of a Nancy Drew. But the real star of this serial slugfest is Captain Marvel himself, anything but the friendly fellow from the comics who so resembled actor Fred MacMurray. This Marvel (Tom Tyler) has more in common with the Incredible Hulk; he's a force of primal nature (Billy's unchecked youth showing through?) with a penchant for destruction and tossing crooks off high buildings. He's also mute for most of the story, which adds considerably to his aura of timeless power.

As with all serials from this era, the lack of characterization turns many peril scenes and their protracted set-ups into tedious affairs. But fortunately, creative camera moves/lighting and the unexpected ruthlessness of Captain Marvel's approach to combat make up for any lags – audiences still gasp when they see this clean-cut caped wonder gleefully turning a machinegun against fleeing opponents.

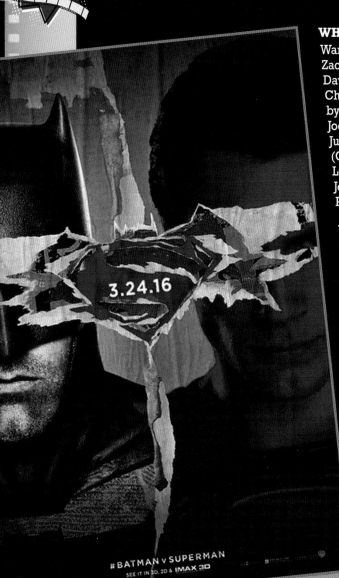

WHO MADE IT:

Warner Bros./Atlas Entertainment/DC Entertainment (U.S.). Director: Zack Snyder. Producers: Charles Roven, Deborah Snyder, Wesley Coller, David S. Goyer, Geoff Johns, Christopher Nolan, Michael Uslan. Writers: Chris Terrio & David S. Goyer, based on DC Comics' *Batman* created by Bob Kane and Bill Finger, and *Superman* created by Jerry Siegel and Joe Shuster. Cinematography (color): Larry Fong. Music: Hans Zimmer, Junkie XL. Starring Ben Affleck (Bruce Wayne/Batman), Henry Cavill (Clark Kent/Superman), Amy Adams (Lois Lane), Jesse Eisenberg (Lex Luthor), Diane Lane (Martha Kent), Laurence Fishburne (Perry White), Jeremy Irons (Alfred), Holly Hunter (Senator Finch), Gal Gadot (Diana Prince/Wonder Woman).

WHAT IT'S ABOUT:

Fearing the actions of a god-like super hero left unchecked, Gotham City's own formidable, forceful vigilante takes on Metropolis' most revered, modern-day savior, while the world wrestles with what sort of hero it really needs. And with Batman and Superman at war with one another, a new threat quickly arises, putting mankind in greater danger than it's ever known before.

WHY IT'S IMPORTANT:

Despised by many, appreciated by a growing number (especially after the extended edition was released), *Batman v Superman: Dawn of Justice* is a grim, grandiose battle royale between DC's most iconic superheroes, with special guest star Wonder Woman jumping into the fray for added spectacle. It's all a set-up for a new series of interconnected movie epics in the much-imitated tradition of Marvel's Cinematic Universe. *BvS* literally begins where previous entry *Man of Steel* left off, cleverly using the excessive collateral damage inflicted on Metropolis during that movie's climactic slugfest as motivation for out-of-towner Bruce Wayne's seething anger. Both superheroes have reason to suspect that the other is a public menace (Batman's harsh m.o. rubbing Clark Kent the wrong way), and before very long each is being manipulated by perverse, diabolical power-monger Lex Luthor, played with scene-stealing relish by a fearless Jesse Eisenberg.

Former Daredevil Ben Affleck serves well as stubble-faced Bruce Wayne, by turns haunted, staunchly committed, and ultimately hopeful. His Dark Knight is the closest yet to Frank Miller's edgy revisionist take, a brutal powerhouse made nearly unstoppable by advanced, pseudo-military technology. Cavill continues his sensitive, ever-patient, deep-thinker approach to Superman/Clark Kent, forever questioning the right path to take (if any) as defender of a possibly irredeemable species. In this cynical story, he is something of a pawn, the world's most powerful fall guy juggled politically by scheming terrorists and world leaders alike. "You don't owe (people) anything," Martha Kent wisely reminds him at a key moment. Still, true superheroes keep trying...

Steadily building to the title bout, director Zack Snyder skillfully addresses the extensive story and multi-character requirements of *BvS* without losing sight of personal drama, which reaches a crescendo in Act III. As for the much-criticized dark and serious tone, it is precisely this stylistic approach that lends the movie gravitas, elevating what might be described as a feud between two oddly costumed do-gooders with silly names into an intellectually astute, pseudo-operatic clash of modern, mythic titans.

Antagonizing viewers who demand a far cozier use of these comic book icons (for which Greg Berlanti's TV universe was invented), DC and Warner Bros. remain committed to their relentlessly realistic and unflinchingly adult big screen adaptations. Next out of the gate: *Wonder Woman* (2017), aggressively re-imagined for contemporary audiences in the striking form of Gal Gadot.

ABOVE: Bruce Wayne (Ben Affleck) is horrified by destruction caused by the battling Superman and General Zod. BELOW: Superman (Henry Cavill) and the press.

RIGHT: Clark Kent (Cavill) and Wayne are greeted by eccentric, power-addicted Lex Luthor (Jesse Eisenberg).

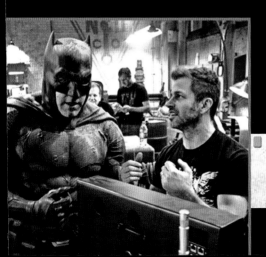

ABOVE: When titans collide. LEFT, ABOVE: Wonder Woman (Gal Gadot) joins the fight.

Director Zack Snyder discusses scenes with Batman (Affleck) and Superman (Cavill).

After introducing a less winky, more serious-minded take on the Superman legend with *Man of Steel* (2013, featuring Henry Cavill), director Zack Synder turned his attention to other DC demi-gods, adding the Dark Knight (Ben Affleck) and the Amazon princess Wonder Woman (Gal Gadot) to the heroic roster of *Batman v Superman: Dawn of Justice* (2016). RIGHT: Batman (Christian Bale) and a kick-ass Catwoman (Anne Hathaway) from *The Dark Knight Rises*.

22 THE DARK KNIGHT RISES 2012 (165) [2.35]

Poster/photos © 2012 Warner Bros./DC characters ™

WHO MADE IT:

Warner Bros./Legendary Pictures/Syncopy (U.S.). Director: Christopher Nolan. Producers: Christopher Nolan, Charles Roven, Emma Thomas, Kevin De La Noy, Benjamin Melniker, Michael Uslan, Jordan Goldberg, Thomas Tull. Writers: Christopher Nolan, Jonathan Nolan, David S. Goyer, based on the comic book created by Bob Kane (DC). Cinematography: Wally Pfister. Music: Hans Zimmer. Starring Christian Bale (Bruce Wayne/Batman), Gary Oldman (Commissioner Gordon), Tom Hardy (Bane), Joseph Gordon-Levitt (Blake), Anne Hathaway (Selina/Catwoman)

WHAT IT'S ABOUT:

It has been eight years since Batman vanished into the night, turning, in that instant, from hero to fugitive. Assuming the blame for the death of D.A. Harvey Dent, the Dark Knight sacrificed everything for what he and Commissioner Gordon both hoped was the greater good. For a time the lie worked, as criminal activity in Gotham City was crushed under the weight of the anti-crime Dent Act. But everything changes with the arrival of a cunning cat burglar with a mysterious agenda. Far more dangerous, however, is the emergence of Bane, a masked terrorist whose ruthless plans for Gotham drive Bruce out of his self-imposed exile. But even if he dons the cape and cowl again, Batman may be no match for Bane.

WHY IT'S IMPORTANT:

Christopher Nolan wrapped up his groundbreaking Dark Knight trilogy with this exciting, mostly satisfying conclusion. Nothing could top Heath Ledger's Oscar-worthy Joker from the previous film, of course, and *Rises* doesn't even try to: villainous front man Bane is more an imposing physical presence than a true personality, negating a nuanced performance of any kind. But, as things turn out, he's more a glorified henchman than the real deal: Bruce Wayne/Batman must come full circle and face the dark power that inspired his righteous crusade against crime to begin with. Despite some serious setbacks he rises to the occasion, risking all for the city he loves.

New to this final chapter is Anne Hathaway's Catwoman, a sharp professional thief who, criminal agenda aside, finds herself drawn to the targeted Mr. Wayne. This take reflects DC Comics' later interpretation of Selina Kyle, presented more as a victimized anti-hero than a villainess. Given Hathaway's youthful demeanor, she's as much Batgirl as she is Catwoman. Feline and unpredictable, Selina even becomes a legitimate Batman ally in the third act, permitting all to see and appreciate her finer instincts. Also new on the Gotham scene is a courageous young cop (Joseph Gordon-Levitt), destined to inherit the Dark Knight's vigilante mantle as protector-in-chief.

With tumultuous events leading to the breaking point, a resolved Batman must make the ultimate sacrifice in order to save his imperiled city. Nolan deliberately leaves the outcome of these final efforts ambiguous – did Wayne survive the bomb blast? Is he living a happy life anonymously with a beautiful woman who loves and understands him, far removed from those childhood demons that produced his fearsome alter-ego, as a hopeful Alfred imagines in his mind's eye? It's a wistful way to end this genre-busting trilogy, and a fitting conclusion to the most startling and provocative take on the Batman legend ever attempted on film.

Tidbit: Seriously committed to celluloid rather than digital photography, director Christopher Nolan utilized IMAX 70mm film cameras for a good deal of the shooting, including the all-important first six minutes (used for special promotions).

LEFT: Batman (Christian Bale) clashes with public menace Bane (Tom Hardy). ABOVE: Bruce Wayne (Bale) contemplates his next move. BELOW: Bane wreaks havoc in Gotham City following Batman's disappearance.

Matching Batman every step of the way is Catwoman (Anne Hathaway), a thief-turned-anti-heroine.

Resourceful young police officer Blake (Joseph Gordon-Levitt) chats with millionaire Wayne; Blake will eventually become Robin. Also aiding and abetting the Dark Knight is Commissioner James Gordon (once again played by Gary Oldman).

Actress Hathaway gets the feel of her stylized motorcycle (note the technician below) before shooting begins.

21 X-MEN 2 2003

 134 2.35

THE TIME HAS COME FOR THOSE WHO ARE DIFFERENT TO STAND UNITED.

5·2·03

MARVEL

WHO MADE IT:

Twentieth Century Fox Film Corporation/Marvel Enterprises/Donner's Company (U.S.). Director: Bryan Singer. Producers: Lauren Shuler Donner, Ralph Winter. Writers: Michael Doughtery, Dan Harris, David Hayter, Zak Penn, Bryan Singer, based on the comic book by Stan Lee and Jack Kirby (Marvel). Cinematography (color): Newton Thomas Sigel. Music: John Ottman. Starring Patrick Stewart (Charles Xavier/Professor X), Hugh Jackman (Logan/Wolverine), Ian McKellen (Erik Lehnsherr/Magneto), Halle Berry (Ororo Munroe/Storm), Famke Janssen (Dr. Jean Grey), James Marsden (Scott Summers/Cyclops), Brian Cox (Col. William Stryker), Rebecca Romijn-Stamos (Raven Darkholme/Mystique), Alan Cumming (Kurt Wagner/Nightcrawler), Bruce Davison (Sen. Robert Kelly), Anna Paquin (Marie/Rogue), Shawn Ashmore (Bobby Drake/Iceman), Aaron Stanford (John Allerdyce/Pyro), Kelly Hu (Yuriko Oyama/Lady Deathstrike).

WHAT IT'S ABOUT:

After a mutant named Nightcrawler infiltrates the White House and demonstrates how easy it would be to assassinate the president, a chain reaction of anti-mutant measures is promptly implemented by the shaken government. William Stryker, a military leader who has experimented on these gifted beings (Wolverine among them), tries to eradicate mutants through legislation and a bold, armed attack on Professor X's school and mansion. Having escaped from his plastic prison, hardliner Magneto forms an uneasy alliance with Xavier to protect their endangered species, even as metal-clawed Logan heads north to investigate his checkered past.

WHY IT'S IMPORTANT:

Impressed by the popularity of Sam Raimi's *Spider-Man*, 20th Century Fox green lit a sequel to their 2000 modest hit *X-Men*, gambling that interest in filmed superhero adventures was on the rise. The gamble paid off: *X-Men 2* did even better business than its predecessor, earning mostly rave reviews and establishing a legitimate franchise.

Everything is a bit smoother and more self-assured this time around, starting with one of the film's best sequences. The White House attack is a superb prologue, dramatizing the reality of this startling new minority group and humanity's understandable fear of it. The forces of tolerance are once again on a collision course with those that preach violence, but what mutants Professor X and Magneto have in common is at least as important as their obvious differences. Will humans always fear mutants because of their incomprehensible power? Is war between these species inevitable? With both races capable of terrible acts in the name of survival, the notion of peace seems more remote than ever.

Even as an escaped Magneto is planning his latest counterattack, tough-and-taloned Logan (Hugh Jackman) is off on his own personal journey of discovery, eventually learning some disturbing truths about his "birth" as presided over by nemesis Col. William Stryker (Brian Cox). Ultimately, Logan/Wolverine must defend himself against a female counterpart named Lady Deathstroke (Kelly Hu) in a colorful, no-nonsense battle, one of the film's more enjoyable third act set-pieces.

X-Men 2, like *Spider-Man 2*, was hailed as the best of its respective series, a smart entertainment with imagination and social commentary to spare. Director Singer would take a brief vacation from Marvel's mutants to tackle the Man of Steel over at Warner Bros. (*Superman Returns*), but would triumphantly return to the X-franchise a few years later with an even sharper re-invention.

ABOVE: The devil-like Nightcrawler (Alan Cumming) is cornered by Storm (Halle Berry) and Jean Grey (Famke Janssen) BELOW: Wolverine (Hugh Jackman) and Storm prepare for a landing.

ABOVE: Wolverine takes on military invaders within Xavier's school. BELOW, LEFT: Cyclops (James Marsden) and Grey in a tense standoff. BELOW: Leader of the mutant rebels, Magneto (Ian McKellan) is a figure of dignity and raw elemental power.

Yuriko Oyama, aka Lady Deathtrike (Kelly Hu) is a maid-to-order adversary for Wolverine, and the two taloned warriors tangle dramatically in act three.

Director Bryan Singer instructs his cast of young actors, Hugh Jackman as Wolverine conspicuously among them.

20 MAN OF STEEL 2013

(143) 2.35

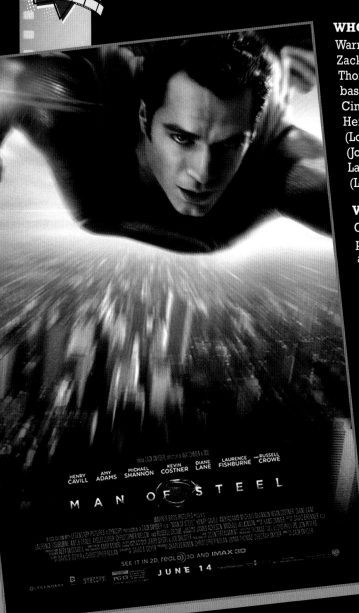

WHO MADE IT:

Warner Bros./Legendary Pictures/Syncopy (U.S./U.K./Canada). Director: Zack Snyder. Producers: Charles Roven, Christopher Nolan, Emma Thomas, Deborah Snyder. Writers: David S. Goyer, Christopher Nolan, based on the comic book created by Jerry Siegel and Joe Shuster (DC). Cinematography (color): Amir Mokri. Music: Hans Zimmer. Starring Henry Cavill (Clark Kent/Kal-El/Superman), Amy Adams (Lois Lane), Michael Shannon (General Dru-Zod), Kevin Costner (Jonathan Kent), Russell Crowe (Jor-El), Diane Lane (Martha Kent), Laurence Fishburne (Perry White), Antje Traue (Faora), Ayelet Zurer (Lara Lor-Van).

WHAT IT'S ABOUT:

Clark Kent/Kal-El is a journalist in his 20s who feels alienated by powers beyond anyone's imagination. Transported to Earth years ago from Krypton, an advanced alien planet, Clark struggles with the ultimate question – why am I here? Shaped by the values of his adoptive parents Martha and Jonathan Kent, the young man soon discovers that having super abilities means making very difficult decisions. But when the world needs stability the most, it comes under attack by General Zod and other surviving, genetically-bred aliens from long-gone Krypton. Clark must become the godlike hero known as "Superman," not only to provide Earth with its last beacon of hope, but to protect the imperiled people he loves.

WHY IT'S IMPORTANT:

More a solid science fiction drama than a traditional *Superman* adaptation, *Man of Steel* is refreshingly smart and provocative, embracing the adult tone established for Christopher Nolan's *Dark Knight* film series. But rather than simply imposing excessive darkness on this material (as *The Amazing Spider-Man* reboot did), the film simply mines the rich dramatic potential that was always inherent in Superman's Bible-inspired mythology: the tragic destruction of a mighty godlike civilization (shades of *Forbidden Planet*), and a possible repeat of this tragedy on Earth, are serious subjects that logically require no-nonsense creative treatment.

Star Henry Cavill is a revelation as Clark Kent/Superman, every bit as good as Christopher Reeve was in his light-hearted films for a less cynical era. Handsome and boy scoutish enough, he is also profoundly thoughtful, a pseudo-god trying to decide whether the angry, often irrationally hateful race he's pledged to protect is truly worthy of his considerable efforts. Cavill is ably supported by Amy Adams as hopeful but realistic Lois Lane, Diane Lane as his loving Earth mother, and a pair of wise dads who teach their son bravery (Russell Crowe on Krypton) and caution (Kevin Costner in *Smallville*), respectively.

Recognizing the familiarity of the main character's origin, David Goyer's screenplay smartly employs a flashback structure, focusing on key events that propel the drama forward. This and the movie's adult approach in general result in a number of affecting personal scenes, with young Clark's uncontrolled X-ray vision freaking him out in a schoolroom being perhaps the most memorable.

The Reeves/Kidder rom-coms, with Gene Hackman's campy Lex Luthor along for the ride, worked beautifully on their own late '70s feel-good terms. But this character and the dense mythology behind him are big enough to encompass a wide range of interpretations. Just as 1952's *Superman and the Mole Men* rejected frivolity and provided a strong, straightforward morality play about the dangers of human fear and prejudice, *Man of Steel* successfully takes on 21st Century angst with no apology. It is a good movie with more on its mind than merely a breezy, humorous escape from reality.

ABOVE, TOP: Kevin Costner as Jonathan Kent comforts his bewildered foster son. ABOVE: General Dru-Zod (Michael Shannon). BELOW: Superman is taken into custody and brought before Kryptonian adversaries.

ABOVE, INSERT: Jor-El (Russell Crowe). ABOVE: Superman (Henry Cavill) and Lois Lane (Amy Adams). BELOW: Friend or foe of the military?

Director Zack Snyder confers with star Cavill during the filming of a flashback, which traces Clark Kent's journey of self-discovery.

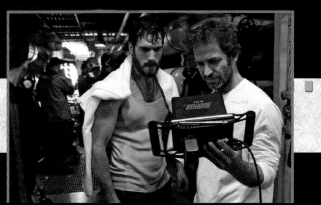

The merc with a mouth gets his own mad mad movie...

DEADPOOL 2016

106 2.35

WHO MADE IT:

Marvel Enterprises/TSG Entertainment/20th Century Fox Film Corporation (U.S.). Director: Tim Miller. Producers: Simon Kinberg, Lauren Shuler Donner, Ryan Reynolds, Jonathon Komack Martin, Rhett Reese, Paul Wernick. Writers: Rhett Reese, Paul Wernick, from the Marvel comic book by Rob Liefeld and Fabian Nicieza. Cinematography (color): Ken Seng. Music: Junkie XL. Starring Ryan Reynolds (Wade Wilson/Deadpool), Morena Baccarin (Vanessa Carlysle/Copycat), Gina Carano (Angel Dust), Ed Skrein (Ajax), T.J. Miller (Weasel), Stefan Kapicic (Colossus), Leslie Uggams (Blind Al), Brianna Hildebrand (Ellie Phimister/Negasonic Teenage Warhead).

WHAT IT'S ABOUT:

After former Special Forces operative turned mercenary Wade Wilson is subjected to a rogue experiment that leaves him with accelerated healing powers, he adopts the alter ego Deadpool. Armed with his new abilities and a dark, twisted sense of humor, newly-empowered Wilson hunts down the man who nearly destroyed his life.

WHY IT'S IMPORTANT:

The wild and crazy *Deadpool* seemed to come out of nowhere in 2016 to charm critics and smash box office records. This modestly budgeted extension of the *X-Men* franchise is a pseudo parody that happily manages to have it both ways: viewers tired of superhero movie clichés will appreciate its endless barrage of self-aware put-downs, while fans of the genre can revel in a new, major league wiseass titan whose rapid-fire witticisms rival those of Robert Downey Jr.'s Tony Snark (sorry, Stark). Everybody wins.

To say that Ryan Reynolds is the perfect choice for this role is an understatement, considering that the actor's likeness and persona inspired the comic book character to begin with. Former *Green Lantern* star Reynolds also played Deadpool/Wade Wilson in 20th Century Fox's *Secret Origins: Wolverine*, but the take wasn't quite right. By embracing an R-rating and all that goes with it, "merc with a mouth" Deadpool can, among other things, shout the f word at every frustrated opportunity. Turning the ubiquitous genre on its head with this kind of giddy irreverence seemed just about right in 2016, with traditional superheroes coming out of the woodwork in endless sequels and reboots.

Although Reynolds easily dominates these wacky proceedings, he is ably supported by a game cast, including thoroughly unexpected Leslie Uggams, who plays his blind hipster caretaker. Meanwhile, Morena Baccarin is actually believable as Wilson's sharp and loyal love interest, Vanessa. It should be remembered that *Deadpool* was released as a Valentine Day's offering, and this key relationship goes a long way in grounding a movie that is clearly obsessed with its own bizarre excesses. And while the inevitable villains are serviceable (Gina Carano is clearly enjoying herself as badass Angel Dust), it's fellow X-Men compatriots Colossus (a CGI'd Stefan Kapicic) and Negasonic Teenage Warhead (Brianna Hildebrand) who make a more lasting impression. No such thing as a true "stand alone" superhero movie anymore, of course... as the MCU discovered, audiences can never have enough costumed crusaders on screen. And if they fight with each other like petulant six year olds, so much the better.

With nonstop laughs – our hero not only breaks the fourth wall, he demolishes it (a carryover gimmick from the comics), and enough legitimate pathos to hold all the insanity together, *Deadpool* picks up where his equally subversive ancestor *The Mask* left off decades earlier, delighting audiences with anti-heroic heroism and in-your-face perversity. And those bogus opening titles are indeed a hoot.

LEFT: Deadpool (Ryan Reynolds) is pursued by X-Men Colossus (Stefan Kapicic) and Negasonic Teenage Warhead (Brianna Hildebrand). RIGHT, TOP: Wade Wilson (Reynolds), Vanessa Carlysle (Morena Baccarin). RIGHT: Fire-scarred Wilson.

Deadpool's eccentric friend Weasel (T.J. Miller) is imperiled by the villainous Angel Dust (Gina Carano).

A Weta Digital effects artist applies some touches to Deadpool's eye area. A variety of articulated masks were employed, depending on a scene's requirements.

18

THE CROW 1994

102 | 1.85

BRANDON LEE

BELIEVE

IN

ANGELS

THE CROW

MIRAMAX
DIMENSION

R

WHO MADE IT:

Miramax Films/Dimension Films (U.S.). Director: Alex Proyas. Producers: Jeff Most, Edward R. Pressman. Writers: David J. Schow, John Shirley, based on the comic book created by James O'Barr in 1989. Cinematography (color): Dariusz Wolski. Music: Graeme Revell. Starring Brandon Lee (Eric Draven/The Crow), Michael Wincott (Top Dollar), Ernie Hudson (Sgt. Albrecht), Rochelle Davis (Sarah), Bai Ling (Myca), David Patrick Kelly (T-Bird), Angel David (Skank), Jon Polito (Gideon), Tony Todd (Grange), Sofia Shinas (Shelly Webster), Michael Massee (Fun Boy), Laurence Mason (Tin-Tin), Anna Levine (Darla), Bill Raymond (Mickey), Marco Rodriguez (Torres).

WHAT IT'S ABOUT:

A year after poetic guitarist Eric Draven and his fiancée are brutally murdered, he is brought back to life by a mysterious, supernatural crow. Driven by vengeance, he methodically seeks out and imparts dark justice to his slayers: a knife thrower named Tin-tin, car fan T-Bird, drugged-out Funboy, and a simpleton called Skank. Their leader, a powerful crime lord named Top Dollar with a penchant for wiping out enemies with a Japanese sword, eventually learns about the legend of the crow and becomes a threat to Draven's agenda of bloody retribution.

WHY IT'S IMPORTANT:

The notion of an avenging spirit rising from the grave to punish those criminals responsible for his death is a familiar one in pulp fiction, horror movies, and most especially comic book melodramas. *The Crow* is a fine example of this serviceable premise, showcasing a standout performance by the late Brandon Lee and some stylish touches in direction by Alex Proyas.

The plot structure is more than a little familiar: the "ghost" returns; one-by-one his victims are expunged; the main villain finally figures out what's going on and fights the avenger on his own supernatural terms, briefly turning the tables; a loved one is taken hostage to up the ante. But despite almost unavoidable predictability, the film's streetwise ambiance and punkish, hyper visceral approach make the formula resonate with a curious credibility. Lee is a captivating lead, his mime makeup (inspired by a mask from his character's happier days) effectively conveying the ruthless persona of Death. His voice, while certainly threatening enough, is tinged with a seductive emotionalism that transcends the usual "make my day" deadened nastiness. This man and the woman he loved were brutally murdered in a shocking attack, and those raw emotions remain with his avenging spirit.

Other cast members do nice work. Ernie Hudson as world-weary Sgt. Albrecht grounds the madness, while youngster Rochelle Davis is both sad and feisty as the Crow's abandoned, spiritual surrogate child. The baddies have their moments to shine as well, with Michael Wincott as an incendiary urban terrorist named Top Dollar enjoying a brief advantage over the relentless protagonist (kill the crow, stop his agent) before good inevitably triumphs over evil.

Despite the tragic passing of Brandon Lee, *The Crow* spawned a series of equally bloodthirsty sequels, none of them up to this original's level of quality.

17 GHOST WORLD 2001

FORGETTABLE COMEDY FROM THE DIRECTOR OF "CRUMB"

Accentuate the negative.

a TERRY ZWIGOFF film

GHOST WORLD

UNITED ARTISTS FILMS and GRANADA FILM in association with JERSEY SHORE present a MR. MUDD production a TERRY ZWIGOFF film "GHOST WORLD" THORA BIRCH
SCARLETT JOHANSSON BRAD RENFRO with ILLEANA DOUGLAS and STEVE BUSCEMI casting by BARBARA A. HALL producers PIPPA CROSS JANETTE DAY GRAHAM MARK ZOPHRES
editor CAROLE KRAVETZ music by EDWARD T. McKOY director of photography ALFONSO BEATO produced by LIANNE HALFON JOHN MALKOVICH RUSSELL SMITH
based on the comic by DANIEL CLOWES written by DANIEL CLOWES & TERRY ZWIGOFF directed by TERRY ZWIGOFF distributed by MGM DISTRIBUTION CO.
www.mgm.com

WHO MADE IT:

United Artists/Granada Film Productions/Jersey Shore (U.S.). Director: Terry Zwigoff. Producers: Lianne Halfon, John Malkovitch, Russell Smith. Writers: Daniel Clowes, Terry Zwigoff, based on the comic book by Daniel Clowes. Cinematography (color): Alfonso Beato. Music: David Kitay. Starring Thora Birch (Enid), Scarlett Johansson (Rebecca), Steve Buscemi (Seymour), Brad Renfro (Josh), Pat Healy (John Ellis), Illeana Douglas (Roberta Allsworth), Bob Balaban (Enid's father), Stacey Travis (Dana), Teri Garr (Maxine).

WHAT IT'S ABOUT:

Just having graduated from high school, two close friends, cynical Enid and somewhat cheerier Rebecca, share mutual angst as they try to figure out what to do with their suddenly adult lives. Enid soon discovers that she'll have to take an additional class over the summer to earn her diploma, and winds up studying art with a teacher who seems determined to jump-start the
girl's creative impulses. Meanwhile, a geeky record collector nearly twice Enid's age takes an interest in her, as the two share a decidedly bleak view of the world around them.

WHY IT'S IMPORTANT:

There are no literal ghosts in *Ghost World*, a charming but ultimately semi-bleak coming-of-age story that focuses on two attractive teenage misfits (Birch, Johannson) embarking on the daunting adventure of life after high school. It's Birch's character, Enid, who becomes the movie's main focus, a sharp funkster who indulges in mischievous, borderline mean-spirited pranks, one of which leads her into a heartbreaking relationship with older geek/record and art collector Seymour (Steve Buscemi, convincing as always). Meanwhile, she and gal pal Rebecca grow farther apart as plans for getting an apartment together start to collapse, partially because anti-conformist Enid can't hold down a job. As a matter of fact, Enid gets herself into social trouble at the drop of a hat... but given the often superficial "ghost" world presented here, we understand this young woman's existential angst and want nothing more than to see her find happiness.

Director Terry Zwigoff embraced Daniel Clowes' equally unhappy comic book, inventing some necessary plot devices for something resembling a legitimate movie scenario, But he keeps his frames sparse, reminding us both of his characters' loneliness, and the corresponding confined feeling created by comic panels. It's a visual style and works both cinematically and emotionally.

Ghost World earned glowing reviews upon release, although it never really took off at the boxoffice. Given Scarlett Johansson's later importance to the comic book movie world – as Black Widow, she's the closest the MCU has to a poster girl – it's culturally fascinating to see her playing a droopy All-American teenager. Fans argue about the film's poignant, ambiguous ending, where Enid boards an out-of-service bus apparently on the road to nowhere. This critic prefers to think it's going somewhere, a place down the road where our frustrated but always enthusiastic heroine can hopefully breathe easy and maybe finally find some solace.

16 BATMAN BEGINS 2005

(140) 2.35

WHO MADE IT:

Warner Bros/Syncopy (U.S.). Director: Christopher Nolan. Producers: Larry Franco, Charles Roven, Emma Theomas, Benjamin Melniker, Michael Uslan, Cheryl A. Tkach, Writers: David S. Goyer, Christopher Nolan, based on the comic book created by Bob Kane (DC). Cinematography (color): Wally Pfister. Music: Hans Zimmer, James Newton Howard. Starring Christian Bale (Bruce Wayne/Batman), Michael Caine (Alfred), Liam Neeson (Ducard), Katie Holmes (Rachel Dawes), Gary Oldman (Jim Gordon), Cillian Murphy (Dr. Jonathan Crane/Scarecrow), Tom Wilkinson (Carmine Falcone), Rutger Hauer (Earle), Ken Watanabe (Ra's Al Ghul), Morgan Freeman (Lucius Fox), Linus Roache (Thomas Wayne).

WHAT IT'S ABOUT:

Young Bruce Wayne witnesses the death of his parents at the hands of a criminal, a traumatic experience that changes his life forever. He grows into a man and travels to the Far East, where he's trained martial arts combat techniques by Henri Ducard, a member of the mysterious League of Shadows. When Ducard reveals the League's true purpose – the complete destruction of Gotham City – Wayne returns to Gotham City, intent on cleaning up the crime-infested metropolis and thwarting his former mentor's vile plan. With the help of Alfred, his loyal butler, and Lucius Fox, a tech expert at Wayne Enterprises, the caped vigilante known as Batman is born.

WHY IT'S IMPORTANT:

Ever since Tim Burton's 1989 blockbuster proved Batman's enormous commercial potential (a strength the Caped Crusader demonstrated in 1966, as well), Warner Bros. has regularly re-visited Gotham City's most famous citizen in high-profile movies. After *Batman Returns* failed to live up to expectations, Tim Burton's inherent oddness was deemed something of a liability, and Joel Schumacher took over the series with the critically praised *Batman Forever*, followed by the critically-despised *Batman and Robin*. Next up at bat: Christopher Nolan, directing the first serious reboot of Tim Burton's very specific theatrical/serio-comic take, which had become slightly fractured during the Schumacher reign.

Right from the title, *Batman Begins* informs us that a new, ground-up interpretation has arrived, a clear shake-up of the status quo. More so than most comic book heroes, Batman happens to lend himself to the evocative shadows of urban film noir, where gritty reality and uncompromising brutality can somehow accommodate a bat-themed vigilante. The film also expands the scope of Bruce Wayne's territorial experience, providing him with life-changing travels to the Far East that turn what is essentially an urban story into a serious-minded global epic.

By embracing an enemy/mentor like Henri Ducard (Liam Neeson), and an equally vague supporting villain known as Scarecrow (Cillian Murphy), the producers succesfully gambled that less iconic adversaries would add to the movie's sense of stature. Christopher Bale's performance as Wayne/Batman fits smoothly into this dark and edgy emotional landscape; we get a sense of a seriously troubled man capable of amazing things, all as a result of childhood so tragically lost. Orbiting this unique individual are supporting characters played by first-tier actors. Only Katie Holmes as childhood sweetheart Rachel Dawes strikes a somewhat less-than-satisfying note (Dawes would be recast in the film's blockbuster sequel, *The Dark Knight*).

For better or worse, *Batman Begins* transformed comic book superhero movies into no-apology action thrillers with edge and emotional punch, removing tongue from cheek to explore the dark underpinnings of fantasy derring-do. Although *Dark Knight* would take this formula to even more impressive creative heights, this first attempt to place Batman in the context of adult drama works quite well on its own, less flamboyant terms.

ABOVE: Young Bruce Wayne (Gus Lewis) witnesses the murder of his parents. BELOW: Alfred Pennyworth (Michael Caine) takes a whack at assisting his employer.

ABOVE: Gotham City's Dark Knight (Christian Bale) watches over all. BELOW: Bruce Wayne must journey to the Far East in search of answers; mysterious mentor Ducard (Liam Nesson) is more than willing to enlighten him.

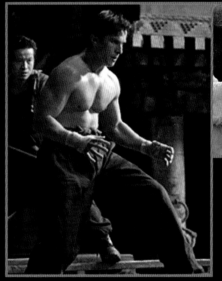

BELOW, LEFT: Lucius Fox (Morgan Freeman) instructs employer Wayne. BELOW, RIGHT: The fear-inducing Scarecrow (Cillian Murphy) threatens Gotham.

Christian Bale (left) and Michael Caine are given some pointers by director Christopher Nolan. Nolan would go on to direct two additional *Batman* movies.

15 SPIDER-MAN 2002

(121) | 1.85 |

Poster/photos: © 2002 Columbia Pictures/Marvel characters ™

WHO MADE IT:

Columbia Pictures Corporation/Marvel Enterprises (U.S.). Director: Sam Raimi. Producers: Avi Arad, Laura Ziskin, Ian Bryce. Writers: David Koepp, James Cameron, Scott Rosenberg, based on the comic book by Stan Lee and Steve Ditko (Marvel). Cinematography (color): Don Burgess. Music: Danny Elfman. Starring Tobey Maguire (Peter Parker/Spider-Man), Willem Dafoe (Norman Osborn/Green Goblin), Kirsten Dunst (Mary Jane Watson), James Franco (Harry Osborn), Cliff Robertson (Ben Parker), Rosemary Harris (May Parker), J.K. Simmons (J. Jonah Jameson), Joe Manganiello (Eugene "Flash" Thompson), Bill Nunn (Joseph "Robbie" Robertson), Michael Papajohn (Carjacker), Elizabeth Banks (Betty Brant).

WHAT IT'S ABOUT:

A shy, brainy teenager who lives with his loving Aunt May and Uncle Ben, Peter Parker pines away for the girl next door, Mary Jane Watson. While on a class trip, he is bitten by a radioactive spider, and soon develops the proportionate strength, speed and stamina of an arachnid. Peter keeps this condition secret, soon adopting the identity of Spider-Man for profit. Fed up with being a nice guy and finishing last, he looks the other way as a fleeing criminal eludes police. But when Uncle Ben is murdered by this volatile hood, guilt-ridden Peter vows to spend his life fighting crime. He finds a close-to-home challenge in the wicked form of the Green Goblin, in truth his best friend's deranged father. Airborne and armed with weird explosives, the devil-like Goblin invites Spider-man to become his partner in pillaging.

WHY IT'S IMPORTANT:

Marvel's flagship superhero, at least until the MCU shifted that perception, *Spider-Man* came to 2002 movie screens in an inspired adaptation by director Sam (*Evil Dead*) Raimi. Playing the shy teenager who becomes a web-swinging, crime-fighting hero in between dateless nights, Tobey Maguire – the "go to" nerd actor of his generation – is wonderful, and the scenario prepared here is an effective coming-of-age study. Much of this is reflected in Peter's puppy love relationship with girl-next-door Mary Jane Watson (Kirsten Dunst), who is very pretty, but just tarnished enough by family abuse to make her a sympathetic match for our lonely hero. On the threshold of adulthood, Parker/Spider-Man must ultimately choose between the opposing philosophies of two surrogate father figures: the path of decency, as embodied by Uncle Ben (Cliff Robertson), and the road to power without mercy, eventually offered to him by the seductive, devil-themed Green Goblin (Willem Dafoe).

But even before this clever choice of villain tries to lure Peter to the dark side, *Spider-Man*'s moral theme is traumatically established. The murder of Ben Parker as a result of Parker's momentary indifference to some wrong-doing teaches him that "with great power, comes great responsibility," forever establishing Spider-Man's motivation. While this statement is undeniably true, it's just as fair to say that young Mr. Parker rarely gets a break, and it's his luckless, behind-the-eight-ball melancholy that originally endeared readers to him. Raimi's sharp movie version taps right into that potent vein of pop melodrama.

Spider-Man earned two additional sequels from the same director and with the same cast, one hitting the creative bullseye, the other slipping off the target. But Sam Raimi's canny blend of teenage angst, satiric humor, and dark-edged adventure was a potent formula for a while, far more satisfying than *The Amazing Spider-Man* would be in a flawed, too-soon reboot.

ABOVE: Beloved Uncle Ben (Cliff Robertson) breathes his last as an anguished Peter Parker (Toby Maguire) looks on. FAR LEFT: Peter checks out his costume before embarking on a night of high-flying crime fighting. LEFT: Upside-down Spidey (Maguire) receives a sexy-as-hell kiss in the rain from Mary Jane Watson (Kirsten Dunst).

It's a case of double jeopardy as Spider-Man nimbly dodges attacks from the Green Goblin while navigating his way through the flames of a burning building.

The devilish Green Goblin, in truth his best friend's father Norman Osborne (Willem Dafoe) is a kind of twisted parental figure for Peter, the antithesis of Uncle Ben.

Veteran fantasy director Sam *Evil Dead* Raimi instructs his two leads (Toby Maguire in the Spidey-suit, Kirstin Dunst) during location shooting in New York City.

14

X-MEN: FIRST CLASS 2011 (132) 2.35 🎧

WITNESS THE MOMENT
THAT WILL CHANGE
OUR WORLD.

X-MEN
FIRST CLASS

MARVEL

Poster/photos: © 2011 Twentieth Century Fox/Dune/Marvel characters™

WHO MADE IT:

Twentieth Century Fox Film Corporation/Marvel Entertainment/ Donner's Company (U.S.). Director: Matthew Vaughn. Producers: Lauren Shuler Donner, Bryan Singer, Simon Kinberg, Gregory Goodman. Writers: Ashley Edward Miller, Zack Stentz, Jane Goldman, Matthew Vaughn, Sheldon Turner, based on the comic book by Stan Lee and Jack Kirby (Marvel). Cinematography (color): John Mathieson. Music: Henry Jackman. Starring James McAvoy (Charles Xavier/Professor X), Michael Fassbender (Erik Lehnsherr/Magneto), Rose Byrne (Moira MacTaggert), Jennifer Lawrence (Raven Darkholme/Mystique), January Jones (Emma Frost), Nicholas Hoult (Dr. Hank McCoy/Beast), Oliver Platt (Man in Black Suit), Jason Flemyng (Xavier Brown/Azazel), Lucas Till (Alex Summers/Havok), Edi Gathegi (Armando Munoz/Darwin), Kevin Bacon (Dr. Klaus Schmidt/Sebastian Shaw), Hugh Jackman (Logan/Wolverine).

WHAT IT'S ABOUT:

Before mutants had revealed themselves to the world, and before Charles Xavier and Erik Lensherr took the names Professor X and Magneto, they were two young men discovering their unique and unprecedented powers for the first time. Not archenemies, they were instead the closest of friends, scientists working together with other gifted beings to stop Armageddon. But in the process, a grave rift between these two opened, which began the eternal war between Magneto's ruthless Brotherhood and Professor X's more hopeful X-Men. The starting point for this split occurred in 1962, with ex-Nazi Sebastian Shaw's mad effort to plunge the United Stares and Russia into nuclear war.

WHY IT'S IMPORTANT:

After stumbling with *Superman Returns*, director Bryan Singer returned to the *X-Men* franchise as producer and guiding creative influence. A prequel exploring the early lives of Charles Xavier and Erik Lehnsherr had been in the works for some time (*X-Men Origins: Magneto* was intended to follow *X-Men Origins: Wolverine*). But with this exceptional effort, the result of five writers and a fresh young director, Fox's venerable Marvel property experienced a most welcome rebirth.

The film is set in 1962, and suggests that the Cuban missile crisis was instigated by former Nazi Sebastian Shaw (Kevin Bacon), currently leader of the nefarious Hellfire Club (as re-imagined by Marvel Comics). Power-hungry Shaw, who murdered Erik Lensherr's mother in a concentration camp to prove the existence of mutants, now surrounds himself with these superhuman beings, most notably diamond-skinned Emma Frost (January Jones). Meanwhile, young Xavier (James McAvoy) and Lensherr (Michael Fassbender) begin recruiting fledgling mutants of their own, extraordinary beings in need of guidance and training, even as Shaw closes in and the missile crisis escalates. Chief among these X-members is Xavier's childhood friend Raven (Jennifer Lawrence), a shape-shifter who struggles to accept her unique, grotesquely beautiful blue-skinned appearance.

Smart, self-assured, and briskly paced, *X-Men: First Class* won over most critics, but came up short at the boxoffice, possibly because the original iconic cast was absent. Bryan Singer corrected that misstep with the equally well-reviewed follow-up, *X-Men: Days of Future Past*, incorporating Patrick Stewart and his colleagues into the story while building on the solid creative foundation established here.

Personal and professional worlds collide in this darkly poetic odyssey...

13 ROAD TO PERDITION 2002

-117- 1.85

RAY FOR
MICHAEL SULLIVAN.

TOM HANKS
PAUL NEWMAN JUDE LAW

ROAD TO
PERDITION

FROM THE DIRECTOR OF AMERICAN BEAUTY

WHO MADE IT:

DreamWorks Pictures/The Zanuck Company (U.S.). Director: Sam Mendes. Producers: Richard D. Zanuck, Dean Zanuck, Sam Mendes. Writer: William Self, based on the graphic novel by Max Allan Collins and Richard Piers Rayner (DC/Paradox Press). Cinematography (Technicolor): Conrad L. Hall. Music: Thomas Newman. Starring Tom Hanks (Michael Sullivan, Sr.), Tyler Hoechlin (Michael Sullivan Jr.), Paul Newman (John Rooney), Jude Law (Harlen Maguire), Daniel Craig (Connor Rooney), Stanley Tucci (Frank Nitti), Jennifer Jason Leigh (Annie Sullivan), Liam Aiken (Peter Sullivan), Dylan Baker (Alexander Rance), Anthony LaPaglia (Al Capone).

WHAT IT'S ABOUT:

In Depression-era Chicago, hit man Michael Sullivan is known to friends and enemies as an extremely dangerous man. Uncompromising in his ongoing work, Sullivan is just as devoted to his private life as a husband and father of two young boys. But these two worlds inevitably collide, resulting in the tragic death of his wife and youngest son. Sullivan and his surviving son, Michael Jr., leave their peaceful home life behind and embark on a journey of revenge.

WHY IT'S IMPORTANT:

Road to Perdition is based on a 1998 graphic novel that took its inspiration from the Japanese manga series *Lone Wolf and Cub*. A powerful father-son relationship story with dark twists, it's set against the backdrop of organized crime during the Great Depression, providing significant star turns by Tom Hanks, Paul Newman (his final role), Jude Law and Daniel Craig.

Inevitable alterations were made for the movie incarnation, from simple name-changes (Looney to Rooney, etc.) to the invention of a totally new character (Law's ruthless hitman Harlen Maguire, something of an amoral doppelganger to family-man enforcer Michael Sullivan, played by Hanks). Director Sam Mendes, fresh off 1999's critical and financial hit *American Beauty*, was intrigued by the graphic novel's lean narrative, which explores themes of violence and family devotion mostly with poetic visuals. Armed with one of cinema's most accomplished directors of photography, *Beauty* colleague Conrad Hall, he fashions a compelling canvas of bleak landscapes and even bleaker weather, reflecting the emotional states of his mostly put-upon principals. Rain as a dramatic device is used to great effect, something of a Hall earmark. As with *Beauty*, the cinematographer won an Oscar for his exceptional work.

At the heart of the story is Sullivan's relationship with his son Michael Jr. (Tyler Hoechin), witness to his father's bloody business and catalyst for all that transpires. In one of the film's most interesting twists, Michael's love for his father actually increases during their nightmarish road trip, with the older Sullivan learning to appreciate his son's individuality after initially distancing himself from the boy. As with *The Godfather*, Sullivan wants a better, non-criminal life for Peter, but fears the aggressive teen may have too much of his old man in him. Will all this bloodshed and brutal violence lead him down the true road to Perdition, or will he somehow escape that tragic fate? There's no question where Mendes stands on this all-important issue, as he literally provides some voiceover narration that clarifies Michael's ultimate rejection of his father's criminal lifestyle... even while embracing the memory of his loving father in general.

Dreamlike, disturbing, but finally life-affirming, *Road to Perdition* remains true to its graphic novel roots by relying on a finely-realized visual style to complement the front-and-center emotions. The result is an exceptional "gangster" movie that eschews excessive brutality and gore for something much finer, and far more relatable.

12

CAPTAIN AMERICA: CIVIL WAR 2016

Poster/photos: © 2016 Marvel/Marvel characters™

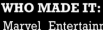

DIVIDED WE FALL

MARVEL

CIVIL WAR
CAPTAIN AMERICA

MAY 6

WHO MADE IT:

Marvel Entertainment/Walt Disney Entertainment (U.S.). Directors: Anthony Russo, Joe Russo. Producer: Kevin Feige. Writers: Christopher Marcus, Stephen McFeely, from Marvel comic book characters and stories by Mark Millar, Joe Simon and Jack Kirby. Cinematography (color): Trent Opaloch. Music: Henry Jackman. Starring Chris Evans (Steve Rogers/Captain America), Robert Downey Jr. (Tony Stark/Iron Man), Scarlett Johansson (Nastasha Romanoff/Black Widow), Sebastian Stan (Bucky Barnes/Winter Soldier), Anthony Mackle (Sam Wilson/Falcon), Emily VanCamp (Sharon Carter/Agent 13), Don Cheadle (Rhodes/War Machine), Jeremy Renner (Clint Barton/Hawkcye), Chadwick Boseman (T'Challa/Black Panther), Paul Bettany (Vision), Elizabeth Olsen (Wanda Maximoff/Scarlet Witch), Paul Rudd (Scott Lang/Ant-Man), William Hurt (Thaddeus "Thunderbolt" Ross), Tom Holland (Peter Parker/Spider-Man).

WHAT IT'S ABOUT:

Yet another international incident involving Steve Rogers and the Avengers results in collateral damage, prompting politicians to form a system of accountability and a governing body to determine when to call in the Avengers. This results in the fracturing of the team into two opposing factions – one led by Rogers who is anti-regulation, and one led by Tony Stark who supports government oversight.

WHY IT'S IMPORTANT:

Although a crowd-pleaser, *Captain America: Civil War* is a step down from the previous Cap opus, *The Winter Soldier*. Referencing the conspiracy thrillers of the '70s gave *Winter Soldier* a unique and unexpected adult perspective. *Civil War*, like the same year's *Batman v Superman*, places its heroes within a political context: can beings with godlike abilities be trusted as self-governing free agents outside the parameters of democracy? Is absolute power destined to corrupt absolutely? Heady social themes, which are mostly abandoned in favor of more familiar emotional catalysts (e.g., you killed someone I loved, so now I'm blind with rage and committed to revenge, until I finally recognize the wrongness of this).

In actuality, *Civil War* takes the personal revenge cliché and runs with it perhaps a little too robustly. When Iron Man (Robert Downey, Jr.) is forced to play out the inevitable hate-crazed response in order to justify a harsh, gut-wrenching final battle with Captain America (Chris Evans), it seems all too convenient and predictable. Meanwhile, *Civil War*'s most celebrated sequence has its own set of problems. Superheroes losing their cool and brawling with each other like children is a traditional Marvel motif; but here, the screen is so filled with costumed titans that a scorecard becomes necessary. Moreover, there is something fundamentally dishonest about the battle itself. In a real civil war, brother fights against brother and real blood is spilled; here, the super-combatants are so concerned about harming one another that legitimate conflict is absent. And when Stark recruits a novice kid hero named Peter Parker and places him directly in harm's way, credibility takes a back seat to convenience (Marvel was obliged to shoehorn Spidey into the *Civil War* proceedings via their deal with Columbia/Sony).

Unexpected negatives aside, *Captain America: Civil War* ultimately emerges as a commendably dark and serious overview of how differing opinions can turn friend into foe, ally into unrelenting enemy. One can expect additional dizzying battles with even more (probably unnecessary) Marvel superheroes on screen in *Avengers: Infinity War*, scheduled for a smack-down in 2018.

IN THIS CORNER: Black Panther (Chadwick Boseman), The Vision (Paul Bettany), Iron Man (Robert Downey Jr.), Black Widow (Scarlett Johansson), War Machine (Don Cheadle). BELOW: Newbie superhero Ant-Man (Paul Rudd) transforms himself into a giant for the big airport bash sequence.

Spider-Man (Tom Holland) nabs Cap's shield.

IN THIS CORNER: The Falcon (Sam Wilson), Ant-Man (Rudd), Hawkeye (Jeremy Renner), Captain America (Evans), The Scarlet Witch (Elizabeth Olsen), Bucky Barnes (Sebastian Stan). BELOW: A reflective Iron Man cradles his injured comrade War Machine following the big airport fight.

RIGHT: The Scarlet Witch (Olsen) powers up for super-action.

Director Russo monitors the fight between African superhero Black Panther (Chadwick Boseman) and his floored adversary. Vengeance and redemption are recurring themes in *Civil War*.

11 GUARDIANS OF THE GALAXY 2014 (121) 2.35

CHRIS PRATT ZOE SALDANA DAVE BAUTISTA VIN DIESEL AS GROOT BRADLEY COOPER AS ROCKET

MARVEL
GUARDIANS OF THE GALAXY
FROM THE STUDIO THAT BROUGHT YOU THE AVENGERS

IN 3D realD 3D 8.1.14 AND IMAX 3D

WHO MADE IT:

Marvel Enterprises/Walt Disney Studios Motion Pictures (U.S.). Director: James Gunn. Producers: Kevin Feige, Alan Fine, David J. Grant, Jonathan Schwartz. Writers: James Gunn, Nicole Perlman, based on the comic book by Dan Abnett and Andy Lanning (Marvel). Cinematography (color): Ben Davis. Music: Tyler Bates. Starring Chris Pratt (Peter Quill/Star-Lord), Zoe Saldana (Gamora), Dave Bautista (Drax the Destroyer), Vin Diesel (Groot), Bradley Cooper (Rocket), Lee Pace (Ronan the Accuser), Michael Rooker (Yondu Udonta), Karen Gillan (Nebula), Djimon Hounsou (Korath), John C. Reilly (Rhomann Day), Glenn Close (Nova Prime Irani Rael), Benicio del Toro (Taneleer Tivan/The Collector).

WHAT IT'S ABOUT:

Brash adventurer Peter Quill finds himself the object of an unrelenting bounty hunt after stealing a mysterious orb coveted by Ronan, a powerful villain with ambitions that threaten the entire universe. To evade the ever-persistent Ronan, Quill is forced into an uneasy truce with a quartet of disparate misfits – Rocket, a gun-toting raccoon; Groot, a tree-like humanoid; the deadly and enigmatic Gamora; and the revenge-driven Drax the Destroyer. But when Quill discovers the true power of the orb and the menace it poses to the cosmos, he must do his best to rally his ragtag rivals for a last, desperate stand – with the galaxy's fate in the balance.

WHY IT'S IMPORTANT:

Impressed viewers had just gotten used to what a Marvel-produced movie was all about (*Iron Man*, *The Avengers*, et al), when *Guardians of the Galaxy* appeared out of nowhere to expand the MCU's ever-widening genre possibilities. Considering that George Lucas' *Star Wars* owes an enormous debt to comic book-style heroics in general and Alex Raymond's *Flash Gordon* in particular, it was perfectly natural for Marvel to dazzle moviegoers with their contribution to the "space war epic" genre.

The premise of a motley crew of rejects-turned-heroes (a kind of anti-Avengers) was a sharp move that automatically guaranteed this tale Marvel's much-coveted "fun" flavoring. Leader Peter Quill/Star-Lord (Christ Pratt) had enough star quality to warrant his own comic book, while the rest of his crew of lovable losers were essentially supporting characters. Walking plant-man Groot (Vin Diesel) actually began life as one of Marvel's pre-superhero monsters, like Fin Fan Foom, the kind that used to threaten us puny humans with extinction at every turn. Here he's a lovable straight man for Bradley Cooper's wiseass but sensitive raccoon character, Rocket.

Interestingly, *Guardians of the Galaxy* gets better as it goes along. The garish-looking costumes and elaborate alien environments are somewhat off-putting at first, but they begin to take on their own peculiar charm about a third of the way through. By then our audaciously mismatched misfits are coming into their own as full-fledged characters, and there's more than enough chemistry between them to guarantee an amusing ride.

Surprising its own initiators, *Guardians of the Galaxy* wound up becoming one of the most popular of all Marvel-created movies. More Han Solo than Tony Stark, adventurer Peter Quill easily bridges the gap between superhero comics and space opera derring-do, in the process opening up fresh new territory for the always-expanding MCU to explore.

LEFT: The Guardians, clockwise: Star-Lord (Chris Pratt, also above), Groot (Vin Diesel's voice), Drax (Dave Bautista), Gamora (Zoe Saldana), Rocket (Bradley Cooper's voice).

ABOVE: Fearless Drax the Destroyer takes on all comers. ABOVE, RIGHT: Groot cradles his alarmed best pal Rocket. LEFT: All-powerful entity Thanos (voice of Josh Brolin) hovers about the galaxy, biding his time.

ABOVE: Self-reliant woman of action Gamora often has issues with space captain Peter Quill/Star-Lord, but romance blossoms anyway. LEFT: Baby Groot writhes to the beat of music, even as crewmate Drax looks on impassively.

Director James Gunn instructs his suited-up brother, Sean Gunn, who stood in for Rocket during motion-capture special effects sequences. Sean also appeared briefly as Kraglin, sidekick to Michael Rooker's Yondu.

They were comic book characters mainstreamers never heard of, but that didn't stop Marvel's *Guardians of the Galaxy* from becoming the most popular movie of 2014, even beating out Marvel's own *Captain America: The Winter Soldier* at the box office.

LEFT: Concept artist C. Wen's original take on the team. LEFT, BOTTOM: The misfit heroes as fleshed out by Zoe Saldana (Gamora), Chris Pratt (Peter Quill aka Starlord), Bradley Cooper (Rocket – voice), Dave Bautista (Drax), and Groot (Vin Diesel – voice). THIS PAGE: Marvel campaign art depicting Rocket and Groot.

Poster/photos: © 2005 New Line Cinema

VIGGO MORTENSEN   MARIA BELLO   ED HARRIS   WILLIAM HURT

Tom Stall had the perfect life...
until he became a hero.

HISTORY OF VIOLENCE

WWW.HISTORYOFVIOLENCE.COM
THIS SEPTEMBER

WHO MADE IT:

New Line Cinema/BenderSpink (U.S./Germany/Canada). Director: David Cronenberg. Producers: Chris Bender, J.C. Spink. Writers: Josh Olson, based on the graphic novel by John Wagner and Vince Locke. Cinematography (color): Peter Suschitzky. Music: Howard Shore. Starring Viggo Mortensen (Tom Stall/Joey Cusack), Maria Bello (Edie Stall), Ed Harris (Carl Fogarty), William Hurt (Richie Cusack), Ashton Holmes (Jack Stall), Peter MacNeill (Sheriff Sam Carney).

WHAT IT'S ABOUT:

A small town diner owner named Tom Stall is thrust into the spotlight after he deftly kills two robbers in self-defense. The sudden notoriety places a strain on his family, who have trouble adjusting. But things go from bad to worse when a mysterious stranger shows up at the diner and makes curious statements about Tom's personal past. It soon becomes clear that Stall is a gangster being pursued by former criminal associates from Philadelphia. In a scenario of escalating violence, he stalwartly faces ramifications from previous misdeeds that will change his life and the lives of his resilient loved ones forever.

WHY IT'S IMPORTANT:

A History of Violence is a powerful movie, one that wisely chooses character and irony over crime sequences... although it doesn't flinch in that latter department when the plot calls for uncompromising bloodshed. Director David Cronenberg made significant changes in adapting Jack Wagner's graphic novel, all of them improvements. Key characters Joey (Viggo Mortenson) and Richie (William Hurt) became brothers, not just best friends, and were deemed to be more convincing as Irish mobsters from Philadelphia, rather than Italians from Brooklyn. A lengthy flash-back detailing Joey's ultra-violence that led up to current events was removed entirely. Instead, the movie smartly focuses on Tom/Joey's post-crime family and how each member deals with the horrific realization that their beloved patriarch is a seasoned murderer who has placed them all in harm's way. And it is here where Cronenberg and screenwriter Josh Olson make their biggest and most important creative upgrade: in the graphic novel, Tom is forgiven by his loved ones; the movie ends with a profound question mark, as one demoralized wife and two rattled children wrestle with their moral dilemma and wordlessly wonder about the future.

All of this compelling material is brought to life by a marvelous cast: Mortenson has never been better, William Hurt provides another oh-so weird performance, and Maria Bello practically steals the show as Tom's suddenly besieged wife Edie, convincingly in love with her handsome husband but unable to equate his past actions with their current life together. Also showing up for memorable turns are Ed Harris as gangster Carl Fogarty and Peter MacNeil as dour, trustworthy Sheriff Sam Carney. Ashton Holmes keeps up with these heavy-hitters, playing Tom's bitter son Jack.

With cinematic ancestors as prestigious as *The Killers* and *Out of the Past*, *A History of Violence* stands on its own as a gut-wrenching modern tale of trust gone awry, the ongoing power of family love, and old sins that can never be forgiven. It is one of the finest movies based on a comic book/graphic novel ever made.

9 AMERICAN SPLENDOR 2003

101 1.85

WHO MADE IT:

HBO Films/Fine Line Features/Good Machine (U.S.). Directors/Writers: Shari Springer Berman, Robert Pulcini, based on the Dark Horse comic book series by Harvey Pekar and Joyce Brabner. Producers: Ted Hope, Declan Baldwin, Julia King, Christine K. Walker. Cinematography (color): Terry Stacey. Music: Mark Suozzo. Starring Paul Giamatti (Harvey Pekar), Hope Davis (Joyce Brabner), Judah Friedlander (Toby Radloff), James Urbaniak (Robert Crumb), Harvey Pekar (himself), Joyce Brabner (herself), Chris Ambrose (Superman), Joey Krajcar (Batman), Josh Hutcherson (Robin), Cameron Carter (Green Lantern), Daniel Tay (Young Harvey).

WHAT IT'S ABOUT:

Harvey Pekar is a file clerk at the local VA hospital. At home, he fills his days with reading, writing and listening to jazz. He regularly scours Cleveland's thrift stores and garage sales for old books and LPs, savoring the rare joy of a 25-cent find. It is at one of these junk sales that Harvey meets Robert Crumb. Years later, Crumb finds international success for his underground comics, the idea that comic books can be a valid art form for adults inspires 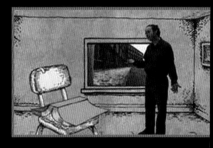 Harvey to write his own brand of comic book. Harvey makes his *American Splendor* a truthful, unsentimental record of his working-class life, a warts-and-all self portrait. The comic earns him cult fame and a new wife, the sardonic Joyce Barber, who end ups being Harvey's true soul mate as they experience the bizarre byproducts of his cult celebrity stature.

WHY IT'S IMPORTANT:

As offbeat and compelling as its subject matter, *American Splendor* re-defines the biopic as an inventive combination of reality and re-enactment. Dramatizing Harvey Pekar's bizarre life by adapting his autobiographical comic books would be enough to sustain a good movie, but the filmmakers could not separate the real Harvey from these proceedings – he was too powerful a presence. Cutting from the narrative to semi-surreal commentary from Peker (along with his equally odd soul mates Joyce Brabner and Toby Radloff) defines the wonky structure of *American Splendor,* very much the way Woody Allen's groundbreaking *Annie Hall* switched from time-hopping dramatization to Alvy Singer's pithy views on the subject.

Pekar has been described as America's "everyman," and certainly the power of his comics (always illustrated by someone else) stems from the bleak, semi-pointless existence of a gloomy guy with obscure interests and weirdo friends. The movie nails Harvey perfectly, with high-strung Paul Giamatti, often looking like a sweaty Edmond O'Brien from his noir period, delivering a remarkable performance that somehow escaped Oscar notice (the film's screenplay didn't – it was nominated for an Academy Award in 2004). Giamatti is matched by a plethora of fine supporting turns... Hope Davis as analytical third wife Joyce, Judah Friedlander as Toby the prideful nerd, and James Urbaniak as another celebrated underground comic creator with an oddball pedigree (and his own documentary), Robert Crumb.

Although comic book-style graphics, panels and captions are used to punctuate the drama, filmmakers Shari Springer Berman and Robert Pulcini carefully keep these animated conceits from becoming precious or distracting. It's like everything else in this aggressively unusual but inevitably affecting movie, which is just as "underground" in its storytelling as Pekar's original comics were. His whiny/raspy narration and the logical jazz score complete *American Splendor*, which wound up winning countless awards and even made Harvey a few bucks.

8 X-MEN: DAYS OF FUTURE PAST 2014 (132) [2.35] 🎧

WHO MADE IT:

Twentieth Century Fox Film Corporation/Marvel Enterprises/Donner's Company/TSG (U.S./U.K.). Director: Bryan Singer. Producers: Lauren Shuler Donner, Bryan Singer, Simon Kinberg, Hutch Parker. Writers: Simon Kinberg, Jane Goldman, Matthew Vaughn, based on the comic book by Stan Lee and Jack Kirby (Marvel). Cinematography (color): Newton Thomas Sigel. Music: John Ottman. Starring Hugh Jackman (Logan/Wolverine), James McAvoy (Charles Xavier/Prof. X), Michael Fassbender (Erik Lehnsherr/Magneto), Jennifer Lawrence (Raven Darkholme/Mystique), Patrick Stewart (Prof. X), Ian McKellan (Magneto), Halle Berry (Ororo Munroe/Storm), Nicholas Hoult/Kelsey Grammer (Hank McCoy/Beast), Anna Paquin (Marie/Rogue), Ellen Page (Kitty Pryde), Peter Dinklage (Bolivar Trask), Shawn Ashmore (Bobby Drake/Iceman), Omar Sy (Bishop), Evan Peters (Peter Maximoff/Quicksilver), Josh Helman (Major William Stryker), Famke Janssen (Dr. Jean Grey), James Marsden (Scott Summers/Cyclops).

WHAT IT'S ABOUT:

The entire world is threatened by powerful robots known as Sentinels, which were created in 1973 by Bolivar Trask to hunt down and destroy mutants. To save both species, Charles Xavier joins forces with Wolverine in a daring time travel gambit. With the help of Kitty Pride he sends the steel-clawed mutant to the pivotal era for an uneasy alliance with younger versions of both himself and opposite number Erik Lehnsherr. Shape-shifter Mystique is at the heart of this desperate effort on the part of various mutants to alter the past in order to save the future.

WHY IT'S IMPORTANT:

Bryan Singer's journey with Marvel mutants has been a curious one. Credited with jump-starting the modern comic book movie with *X-Men* back in 2000, he pushed the franchise to greater heights with the 2002 sequel, turned over *The Final Stand* to Brett Ratner, then came back with a smartly re-worked version of the premise as producer/prime mover of *First Class*. Finally, with *Days of Future Past*, Singer takes the best of everything he's been mining these past few years and synthesizes it into one extremely satisfying movie, a beguiling experience that works dramatically, visually, even poetically.

Somehow, familiar sci-fi concepts like machines taking over the world and time travel as a method of changing our destiny seem fresh in the context of this skillful thriller. There is genuine dread in the "let's go down fighting" battle scenes with the modern-era Sentinels, nicely designed as sleek dispensers of death. Just as effective in a completely different way is time traveler Logan/Wolverine (Hugh Jackman) responding in character to 1973 anachronisms, obviously ahead of Xavier and Erik Lehnsherr in their younger incarnations (James McAvoy, Michael Fassbender). It isn't long before future Professor X's plan to stop the Sentinels is seized as an opportunity for '73-era Erik, who hopes to use their introduction as a way to turn Nixon's tables and assume control of the world. Key to the outcome of this pivotal human-mutant conflict is young Xavier's childhood love, the conflicted but ultimately resolute shape-shifter Mystique (Jennifer Lawrence), chosen by fate to either wage civil war or strike a blow for peace.

Apart from cleverness in plotting and a few tangy revelations (JFK was a mutant – doesn't it figure?), *Days of Future Past* benefits from some beautifully directed sequences, most memorably the bullet-deflecting slow-motion run of Quicksilver (Evan Peters), all to the hypnotically joyous notes of Jim Croce's "Time in a Bottle." Almost always earning applause, this remarkable set-piece delivers a poetic charge that would never be allowed in the more straightforward narrative universe of Marvel-produced movies. Sadly for director Bryan Singer, the final entry in his proclaimed "First Class" trilogy, *Apocalypse*, was a step down from the elegant and flawless *Days of Future Past*. But its lesser status does not detract from the accomplishments of this second wave trilogy overall, which reinvigorated *X-Men* and gave the franchise some of its finest and most memorable moments.

ABOVE, BELOW: Kitty Pride (Ellen Page) sends Wolverine (Hugh Jackman) on a future-changing journey to 1970s America.

ABOVE: X-Men (Patrick Stewart, Fan Bingbing, Ian McKellan, Jackman) await the arrival of the dreaded Sentinels. LEFT: Sentinel creator Bolivar Trask (Peter Dinklage) confers with President Nixon (Mark Camacho). BELOW: Quicksilver (Evan Peters) suspends time for a standout sequence.

BELOW: Young Magneto (Michael Fassbender) levitates a sports arena.

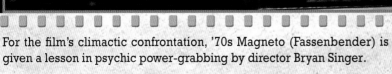

ABOVE, TOP: Young Mystique (Jennifer Lawrence) in action. ABOVE, BOTTOM: The Sentinels are poised for an American takeover.

For the film's climactic confrontation, '70s Magneto (Fassenbender) is given a lesson in psychic power-grabbing by director Bryan Singer.

173

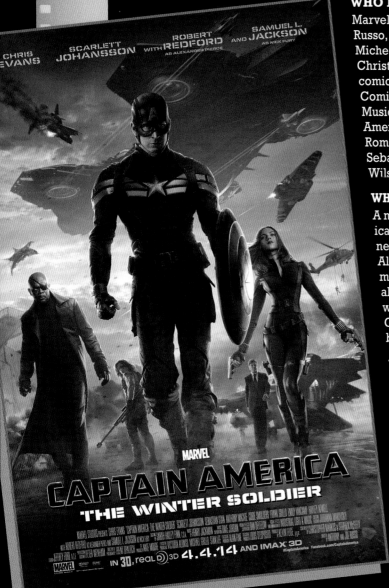

WHO MADE IT:

Marvel Entertainment/Walt Disney Studios (U.S.). Director: Anthony Russo, Joe Russo. Producers: Kevin Feige, Alan Fine, Louis D'Esposito, Micheal Grillo, Nate Moore, Mitch Bell, Lars P. Winther. Writers: Christopher Marcus, Stephen McFeely, Ed Brubaker, based on the comic book created by Joe Simon and Jack Kirby (Timely Comics/Marvel Comics). Cinematography (color): Trent Opaloch. Music: Henry Jackman. Starring Chris Evans (Steve Rogers/Captain America), Samuel L. Jackson (Nick Fury), Scarlett Johansson (Natasha Romanoff/Black Widow), Robert Redford (Alexander Pierce), Sebastian Stan (Bucky Barnes/Winter Soldier), Anthony Mackie (Sam Wilson/Falcon), Cobie Smulders (Maria Hill).

WHAT IT'S ABOUT:

A man born in an age of relative innocence and reborn into the cynical, bewildering modern world, Steve Rogers must focus on a bold new threat that takes the life of S.H.I.E.L.D. director Nick Fury. Although an assassin known as the Winter Soldier is to blame, he is merely the tool of corrupt forces in high places. With the invaluable aid of a flying operative named the Falcon and Black Widow, who clearly appreciate genuine valor when they work with it, Captain America battles his own organization, currently subverted by powerful enemies.

WHY IT'S IMPORTANT:

This sequel to *Captain America: The First Avenger* is as much a follow-up to *The Avengers* proper, putting the titular hero (Chris Evans) on a collision course with the government organization that employs his unique services. Has S.H.I.E.L.D been compromised? Violence directed at director Nick Fury (Samuel L. Jackson) certainly suggests an internal hijacking, and before long Steve Rogers is wondering who is friend and who is foe.

The evolution of MCU's Captain America is striking. Faced with the 21st Century's global conception of the U.S. as a bloated and potentially dangerous superpower, the studio knew its handling of a character bearing the country's name (and renown as a pillar of patriotism) would be a hard sell overseas. So it cleverly took an iconic hero from an age of innocence (fighting a legitimate war against the Nazis) and turned him into a modern skeptic... enabling him to emerge as a true, clear-thinking American hero brave enough to face off against corrupted U.S. officials in the highest of places. Representing the moral integrity we have lost, he has no patience with policies base on "fear," especially when they lead to lies, coercion and murder.

Coming to respect this position is Avengers ally Nastasha Romanoff/Black Widow (Scarlett Johansson), who can relate to the notion of loyalty evolving into skepticism based on her own experiences as a Russian super-agent. When others touched by Cap's shining example begin to trust him more than their government bosses, a new anti-hero is born, one more in keeping with today's regrettably jaded views.

Underneath all the political intrigue is a personal story about Rogers' 1940's sidekick Bucky Barnes (Sebastian Stan), resurrected and reprogrammed as a *Manchurian Candidate*-like assassin. Barnes' current state-of-mind and questionable relationship with his former best friend is set-up in *Winter Soldier*, with Marvel more fully exploring its tragic ramifications in the follow-up movie, *Civil War*. And although this sequel ultimately delivers a more ambitious conflict, *Winter Soldier* comes off as sharper, more sophisticated, less contrived. If it isn't the MCU's finest offering, it's certainly within the top three or four.

ABOVE: Casting Robert Redford as government biggie Alexander Pierce, the story's principal traitor (seen here with Chris Evans as Cap) was nothing less than inspired, since Redford became iconic as the face of moral and social integrity back in the 1970s. BELOW, LEFT: Although *Winter Soldier* ultimately leads to a prerequisite "big" fx climax, the conspiracy movie slant plays as refreshing and germane. RIGHT: Cap (Evans), Nick Fury (Samuel L. Jackson), Black Widow (Scarlett Johansson).

BELOW: Winter Soldier (Sebastian Stan) battles Cap; RIGHT, BELOW: Falcon (Anthony Mackie) flies into action.

BELOW: Captain America faces adversity on all sides.

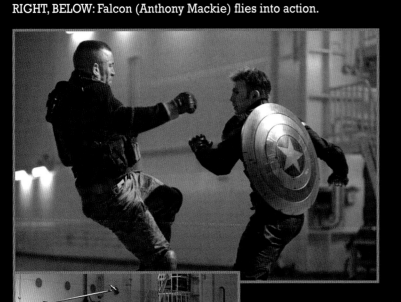

New to MCU, the Russo Brothers direct Captain America (Evans) in a significant fight sequence. Both would return to helm the film's 2016 sequel, *Civil War*.

WHO MADE IT:

Marvel Studios/Paramount Pictures (U.S.). Director: Jon Favreau. Producers: Kevin Feige, Avi Arad. Writers: Mark Fergus, Hawk Ostby, Art Marcum, Matt Holloway, based on the comic book created by Stan Lee, Larry Lieber, Don Heck, and Jack Kirby (Marvel). Cinematography (color): Matthew Libatique. Music: Ramin Djawadi. Starring Robert Downey Jr. (Tony Stark/Iron Man), Gwyneth Paltrow (Pepper Potts), Jeff Bridges (Obadiah Stane), Terrence Howard (Lt. Colonel James "Rhodey" Rhodes), Shaun Toub (Yinsen), Faran Tahir (Raza), Paul Bettany (J.A.R.V.I.S., voice), Clark Gregg (Phil Coulson, S.H.I.E.L.D.).

WHAT IT'S ABOUT:

Tony Stark, billionaire playboy and scientific genius, is kidnapped and badly wounded by enemy combatants in Iraq. He devises a miniature battery to keep himself alive, along with powerful metallic armor to escape from his captors. Partially for personal redemption, Stark soon becomes Iron Man, an instrument of high-tech justice. But betrayal lies right under Tony's nose, and soon he and loyal secretary Pepper Potts are imperiled by the monstrous new suit-based super weapons corrupted by Stark Industries' second-in-command, Obadiah Stane.

WHY IT'S IMPORTANT:

Frustrated by Hollywood's hit-and-miss approach to adapting comic books into film, Marvel got into the game big-time in 2008, forming their own movie-producing operation. Ironically, some of the company's famous and most popular properties had already been licensed out (*Spider-Man* to Columbia/Sony, *X-Men* to 20th Century Fox), but that still left hundreds of heroes, villains, and other assorted entities (how does one classify *Howard the Duck*?) to happily explore in state-of-the-art movies made without the baggage of a major film studio's obligations to other projects.

Out of the gate first was a relatively minor superhero, Iron Man, who just happened to lend himself to a superb CGI interpretation – he's an armored robot-like suit from head to toe, a good deal easier to nail than the semi-cartoonish Incredible Hulk. But the real revelation of this initial Marvel offering was the offbeat casting of "anything but a superhero" Robert Downey Jr. in the title role. A deadpan snarkster with a personality ideal for 21st Century cynicism, he single-handedly jump-started the MCU (Marvel Cinematic Universe) and turned what was essentially a boring Bruce Wayne clone into an engaging, always surprising and fully entertaining screen presence. The film's screenwriters seemed to have lifted a bit of Dr. Strange's origin – a self-absorbed wealthy guy who is forced by circumstance to grow up in a hurry and help his needy fellow humans, rather than simply profit by them. Billionaire industrialist Tony Stark literally needs a heart to go on living; he is helped into this new, suddenly altruistic mode by long-suffering girl Friday/romantic interest Pepper Potts (Gwyneth Paltrow, clearly having fun), even as best pal and surrogate older brother Obadiah Stane (Jeff Bridges) emerges as the Judas of the piece, a variation of Tony Stark without the benefit of an awakened conscience.

From beginning to end, Marvel's *Iron Man* soars, effectively conveying its humanist parable in direct and unpretentious terms. Although the third act degenerates slightly into rock 'em sock 'em robot territory – the obligatory CGI slugfest – Favreau's film never loses sight of its emotional core. Meanwhile, even in this early stage of their long-term game, the seeds of MCU's shared reality are efficiently planted with Samuel L. Jackson's cameo in the epilog, promising a full-fledged *Avengers* team-up movie in the near future.

Favreau's follow-up adventure, *Iron Man 2*, once again put Downey Jr.'s ironic scene stealer Tony Stark front and center, and even introduced a lithe female warrior codenamed Black Widow (Scarlett Johanssen) into the always-expanding MCU mix.

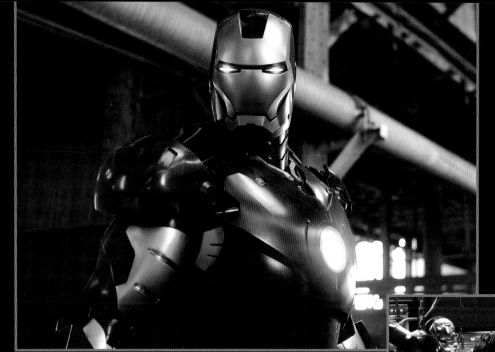

LEFT: the titular titanium hero (Robert Downey Jr.). ABOVE: Stark builds a primitive Iron Man suit to escape from captivity in Iraq. BELOW: Stark and trusted friend Lt. Colonel Rhodes (Terrence Howard).

LEFT: The unpredictable Tony Stark, complete with his manufactured heart, is helped through thick and thin by associate/love interest Pepper Potts (Gwyneth Paltrow).

BELOW: Iron Man takes on Obadiah Stane's new super-suit.

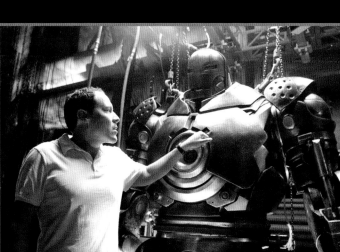

Launching Marvel's cinematic universe, director Jon Favreau makes a final check on the monstrous, robot-like suit created to do battle with Iron Man.

5 FLASH GORDON 1936

245 1.37

WHO MADE IT:

Universal Pictures (U.S.). A 13-chapter serial. Directors: Frederick Stephani, Ray Taylor. Producer: Henry MacRae. Writers: Frederick Stephani, George H. Plympton, Basil Dickey, Ella O'Neill, based on the comic strip created by Alex Raymond (King Features). Cinematography (b/w): Jerome Ash, Richard Fryer. Music: Stock. Starring Buster Crabbe (Flash Gordon), Jean Rogers (Dale Arden), Charles Middleton (Ming the Merciless), Priscilla Lawson (Princess Aura), Frank Shannon (Dr. Alexis Zarkov), Richard Alexander (Prince Barin), Jack 'Tiny' Lipson (King Vultan), Theodore Lorch (High Priest #2), Richard Tucker (Professor Gordon), James Pierce (Prince Thun), Duke York (King Kala), Earl Askam (Officer Torch), House Peters Jr. (Shark Man).

WHAT IT'S ABOUT:

Hoping to stop an outlaw planet from destroying the Earth, Dr. Alexis Zarkov journeys into space with last-minute passengers Flash Gordon and Dale Arden. Once on this threatening world, known as Mongo, they match wits with diabolical Ming the Merciless, who rules various local kingdoms with an iron fist. Flash must endure a succession of challenges to save Dale from Ming's matrimonial grasp, including fights with animalistic monkey men, a giant gocko, and the dreaded, tentacled octosac. Eventually an alliance forms between the Earth visitors and leaders of rebellious Mongo kingdoms, forcing Ming into a final showdown.

WHY IT'S IMPORTANT:

After bringing classic horror properties to the screen in the early '30s, Universal Pictures turned to Alex Raymond's flamboyant *Flash Gordon* newspaper strip for an ambitious, relatively lavish serial adaptation. Former Olympic swimmer/fledgling actor Buster Crabbe was given the title role, forever making it his own. Crabbe not only resembled the character drawn by Raymond, he turned out to be the perfect combination of athleticism, innocence, and inherent dignity. Just as impressive was Charles Middleton as his arch-nemesis Ming the Merciless, an interstellar Fu Manchu with eyes for blond and beautiful Dale Arden (Jean Rogers) and plans for Flash's impromptu mentor Dr. Alexis Zarkov (Frank Shannon), the brilliant scientist who sets this adventure in motion by flying himself, Flash and Dale to planet Mongo "in a rocketship of my own design" (in truth, a pre-existing prop borrowed by Universal from the recent 20th Century Fox sci-fi epic *Just Imagine*). Equally wonderful in their roles were Priscilla Lawson as Ming's amorous daughter Aura, overweight Richard Alexander as self-conscious freedom fighter Prince Barin, and various brave performers wearing the far-out costumes of Hawkmen, Lion Men, Shark Men, and the like.

Universal went out of its way to present the world of Mongo pretty much as Raymond had drawn it. Costumes were first-rate and elaborate for their day, although the studio had plenty of props left over from previous horror and adventure films to fill in the gaps. Their depiction of Raymond's gocko dragon was spot on, and the various spaceship miniatures (including those "revolving top" ships piloted by Thun and his warriors) were also true to the source material, providing unsophisticated viewers of the day with thrilling, if primitive, *Star Wars*-style space battles.

No serial ever came near the grandeur of this first *Flash Gordon* extravaganza. It was the studio's biggest success of 1936, more popular than Deanna Durbin's debut vehicle *Three Smart Girls*, according to Crabbe. Two additional *Flash Gordon* serials were produced in 1938 and 1940, respectively, with Crabbe, Middleton, and Shannon reprising their iconic roles. Although charming, they lacked the special, impossible-to-replicate quality of this funky yet spectacular original.

ABOVE: Dale Arden (Jean Rogers) and Flash Gordon (Buster Crabbe) are held at gunpoint by Dr. Zarkov (Frank Shannon). RIGHT: Princess Aura (Priscilla Lawson), Dale, Flash, Vultan (Jack 'Tiny' Lipson), Ming (Charles Middleton). BELOW: Flash in the furnace room.

LEFT, FIRST: a gocko. ABOVE: an orangupoid.

Flash Gordon is the only serial selected for preservation in the United States Film Registry by the Library of Congress as "culturally, historically, or aesthetically significant." Hear, hear!

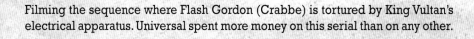

Filming the sequence where Flash Gordon (Crabbe) is tortured by King Vultan's electrical apparatus. Universal spent more money on this serial than on any other.

179

THE ACE OF SPACE

The incomparable Buster Crabbe as Flash Gordon, comforting the frequently imperiled Dale Arden, as played by Jean Rogers. RIGHT: Charles Middleton as Ming the Merciless, self-proclaimed Emperor of the Universe. It doesn't get much better than this, folks.

Diabolical Doc Ock makes for an exciting, heartfelt Spidey adventure...

4 SPIDER-MAN 2 2004

Poster/photos: © 2004 Columbia Pictures/DC characters™

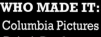

WHO MADE IT:

Columbia Pictures Corporation/Marvel Enterprises (U.S.). Director: Sam Raimi. Producers: Avi Arad, Laura Ziskin, Kevin Feige. Writers: Alvin Sargent, Alfred Gough, Miles Millar, Michael Chabon, based on the comic book by Stan Lee and Steve Ditko (Marvel). Cinematography (color): Bill Pope. Music: Danny Elfman. Starring Tobey Maguire (Peter Parker/Spider-Man), Kirsten Dunst (Mary Jane Watson), James Franco (Harry Osborn), Alfred Molina (Dr. Otto Octavius/Dr. Octopus), Rosemary Harris (May Parker), J.K. Simmons (J. Jonah Jameson), Donna Murphy (Rosalie Octavius), Daniel Gillies (John Jameson), Dylan Baker (Dr. Curt Connors).

WHAT IT'S ABOUT:

Frustrated with the inability to balance his everyday life with his career as a local superhero, Peter Parker is ready to ditch alter-ego Spider-Man. He contends with a growing romantic relationship with Mary Jane Watson and the dangerous anger of best friend Harry Osborn, who blames the web-spinner for the death of his father, Norman (Green Goblin) Osborn. Most daunting of all is the challenge of Dr. Octopus, a benign scientist father figure gone mad and transfigured by a fusion accident into a metal-tentacled menace.

WHY IT'S IMPORTANT:

The second *Spider-Man* movie from director Sam Raimi and star Tobey Maguire firmly establishes the "surrogate dad" theme as a key ingredient, once again offering up a scientist who is transformed into something evil by an experiment gone amok. Alfred Molina is equally convincing as charming, warm-hearted Dr. Otto Octavius and, later, as his multi-armed alter-ego Dr. Octopus, one of the most distinctive villains ever created for the Marvel Comics universe. Never before in the history of movies could special effects technology do justice to such an entity, but CGI and a smart use of on-set physical effects bring the illusion of Doc Ock to vivid life.

Along the way, Maguire and Dunst add dimension to their character's romantic relationship, and a sub-plot concerning frustrated Peter possibly abandoning his Spider-Man career (based on a classic '60s comic) resonates dramatically, even if it doesn't go anywhere beyond the obvious. Also on the down side are several lapses in logic – e.g., why does Octopus hurl a car at Peter Parker when he needs Parker alive to give him information? Still, all complaints pale with the arrival of *Spider-Man 2*'s standout sequence, the fight aboard an elevated train rushing toward a potentially devastating dead-end. Not only does Raimi wring every last parsec of suspense out of this speeding time-bomb scenario, he climaxes it with a heartfelt, intimate moment between hero and city that serves as the perfect emotional tonic.

Critics praised *Spider-Man 2* back in 2004 and audiences seemed equally pleased. Unfortunately, the next film in this series would take a downward turn, serving up too many villains and losing an all-important sense of freshness. But to many, *Spider-Man 2* remains the definitive movie realization of Stan Lee and Steve Ditko's human arachnid, the perfect blend of pathos, humor, and high-swinging adventure.

Tidbit: In addition to being a box office smash, the movie won an Academy Award for Best Visual Effects, and was nominated for Best Sound Mixing and Best Sound Editing.

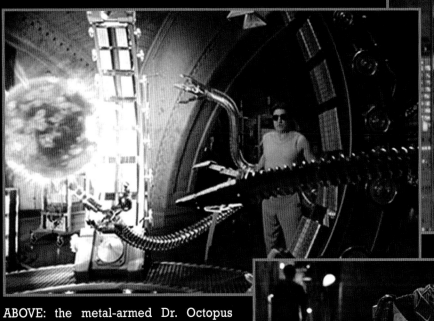

ABOVE: the metal-armed Dr. Octopus (Alfred Molina). RIGHT: Can this be the end of Spider-Man?

ABOVE: New York's arachnid super-hero (Tobey Maguire). BELOW: Spidey rescues Mary Jane Watson (Kirsten Dunst).

LEFT: Spider-Man is held fast by Dr. Octopus. BELOW, LEFT: Will Harry Osborn (James Marsden) exact his revenge? BELOW, RIGHT: Spider-Man gives his all to stop a train crash.

Tobey Maguire as Peter Parker is directed by Sam Raimi. Raimi would go on to helm the subpar *Spider-Man 3*, which prompted Columbia to reimagine the property.

SUPERMAN 1978

143 2.35

Poster/photos: © 1978 Warner Bros./DC characters™

WHO MADE IT:

Warner Bros./Dovemead Limited/Film Export A.G. (U.S./U.K.). Director: Richard Donner. Producers: Pierre Spengler, Ilya Salkind. Writers: Mario Puzo, David Newman, Leslie Newman, Robert Benton, based on the comic book by Jerry Siegal and Joe Shuster (DC). Cinematography (Technicolor): Geoffrey Unsworth. Music: John Williams. Starring Marlon Brando (Jor-El), Gene Hackman (Lex Luthor), Christopher Reeve (Clark Kent/Superman), Margot Kidder (Lois Lane), Ned Beatty (Otis), Jackie Cooper (Perry White), Glenn Ford (Jonathan Kent), Trevor Howard (First Elder), Valerie Perrine (Eve), Maria Schell (Vond-Ah), Terence Stamp (General Zod), Susannah York (Lara), Jack O'Halloran (Non), Phyllis Thaxter (Martha Kent), Sarah Douglas (Ursa), Marc McClure (Jimmy Olsen), Jeff East (Teenage Clark Kent).

WHAT IT'S ABOUT:

Jor-El of the doomed planet Krypton sends his only son, the infant Kal-El, to the far away world of Earth. The boy grows to young manhood as Clark Kent, guided by the values of his foster parents. He learns his true identity from crystals contained in the Fortress of Solitude, a remnant of Krypton that he creates deep in the Arctic. As the adult Clark, a reporter for the Daily Planet in Metropolis, he soon adopts the heroic identity of Superman, rescuing new girlfriend Lois Lane, the President of the United States, and a treed cat all in one fateful evening. But his greatest challenge comes in the form of master criminal Lex Luthor, who threatens to destroy all of California (and Hackensack, New Jersey) with a pair of stolen missiles.

WHY IT'S IMPORTANT:

A year after *Star Wars* hooked audiences on fanciful, *Flash Gordon*-style sci-fi adventure, *Superman* flew into theaters to provide a reasonable follow-up. The film had been in development for several years, generally designed as a campy joke. But the enormous success of Lucas' film pointed to a different and more satisfying direction, one that would combine mythic fantasy (the fate of planet Krypton) with disaster movie spectacle while still retaining a measure of silly, outlandish fun. It sealed the deal with a rom-com twinkle that was always inherent in the Clark Kent-Lois Lane relationship.

As many critics of the time pointed out, *Superman* never fully blends its various extreme flavors, the heavy *Greatest Story Ever Told* mysticism of the first act literally on a different planet from Lex Luthor and Otis campiness and a bumbling, caricatured take on mild-mannered Mr. Kent. As comic books were considered childish business back in the 1970s, producers Spengler and Salkind knew that *Superman* required superstar power to lend the project credibility. Marlon Brando and Gene Hackman provided that. But the film's real revelation was unknown, untested Christopher Reeve as the Man of Steel, who holds *Superman*'s seemingly at odds tonal components together by sheer force of charm.

Pleasures can be found in all stages of this epic story, from the simple confusion of youthful Kent in Smallville (Jeff East, voice-dubbed by Reeve), awed by his own unearthly powers, to the raucous snap of Daily Planet bullpen scenes, and eventually the unbearable, existential anguish of Superman as he must turn the world around and reverse time in order to save the woman he loves.

Well-received critically, *Superman* became an enormous hit, making Christopher Reeve a star and earning four sequels. The crowd-pleasing "Donnerverse" also informed not only TV's *Smallville*, but the 21st Century Berlanti DC TV series universe as well. It even inspired director Bryan Singer to re-embrace it for *Superman Returns*.

LEFT, TOP: Jor-El (Marlon Brando) on Krypton. LEFT, BOTTOM: Superbaby awes Martha and Jonathan Kent (Phyllis Thaxter, Glenn Ford). BELOW: Clark Kent (Christopher Reeve), Lois Lane (Margot Kidder), Perry White (Jackie Cooper).

LEFT: Eccentric, charmingly chatty, but completely out of his mind, power-craving Lex Luthor (Gene Hackman) presents his opposite number with a deadly chunk of Kryptonite. The Oscar-winning Hackman would play Luthor again in *Superman II* and *IV*, his comical take highly entertaining in limited doses.

RIGHT: Superman's helicopter rescue. BELOW: Facing the reality of Lois Lane' death.

Superman goes to creative extremes while trying to protect the population from a ravaging earthquake, becoming a literal Man of Steel to replace smashed rails.

Director Richard Donner, fresh from *The Omen*, discusses the early Krypton scenes with actors Marlon Brando and Susannah York.

WHO MADE IT:

Marvel Sudios/Paramount Pictures (U.S.). Director: Joss Whedon. Producers: Kevin Feige, Jon Favreau, Alan Fine, Jeremy Latcham. Writers: Joss Whedon, Zak Penn. Cinematography: Seamus McGarvey. Music: Alan Silvestri. Starring Robert Downey Jr. (Tony Stark/Iron Man), Chris Evans (Steve Rogers/Captain America), Scarlett Johansson (Nastasha Romanoff/Black Widow). Mark Ruffalo (Bruce Banner/The Hulk), Chris Hemsworth (Thor),Tom Hiddleston (Loki), Samuel L. Jackson (Nick Fury), Jeremy Renner (Clint Barton/Hawkeye),Clark Gregg (Agent Phil Coulson), Cobie Smulders (Agent Maria Hill), Gwyneth Paltrow (Pepper Potts).

WHAT IT'S ABOUT:

Loki, the wicked brother of Norse God Thor, gains access to the Tesseract, an energy cube of unlimited power. Facing this unprecedented threat to global security, S.H.I.E.L.D. director Nick Fury responds by initiating a unique superhero recruitment effort. Modern titans Captain America, Iron Man, the Hulk, Thor, Black Widow and Hawkeye must overcome personal differences and learn to work as a team in order to defeat Loki's plan.

WHY IT'S IMPORTANT:

With a handful of mostly successful superhero movies serving as lead-ins, Marvel unleashed *The Avengers* in 2012, helmed by acclaimed genre specialist Josh Whedon (*Buffy the Vampire Slayer*, *Firefly*). Audiences had seen these various evil-smashing titans in action before, but never together, functioning (more or less) as a state-of-the-art team. The result was a critical and box-office smash, validating Marvel's steady rollout approach of individual characters that began with Jon Favreau's *Iron Man* in 2008. Now film fans could watch Marvel's recently adapted demi-gods battling the forces of mayhem in a single powerhouse movie.

As always, it's personalities that rise above all the super-powered fisticuffs. Strongest of the group is Robert Downey Jr.'s Tony Stark/Iron Man, who immediately has issues with the team's designated leader, Steve Rogers/Captain America (Chris Evans). Fortunately, under Whedon's supervision, Rogers comes to life as a straight-arrow from a simpler time besieged by a modern world that perplexes him. The visceral rivalry between these two powerful heroes forms much of the film's dramatic conflict (Stark getting past his petulant ego is often the catalyst for Marvel movie plots). Also relatively new to the proceedings is Mark Ruffalo as the Hulk, the third actor to play Dr. Banner in less than a decade. But without an entire movie to support, he does his one-note transformation into a destruction-oriented mass of jade muscle without wearing out his welcome. Seeking an Earth-shattering event worthy of its mighty protagonists, the producers looked to Thor's perennial nemesis, his jealous brother Loki (Tom Hiddleson), who could tap into larger-than-life "godlike" forces of extraterrestrial evil to hurl at Earth. Even as it tracks the volatile relationship between these two mythological titans, the movie also explores the gamble Earthbound S.H.I.E.L.D. director Nick Fury (Samuel L. Jackson) has taken in assembling these powerhouses to begin with.

The Avengers inspired an ambitious sequel a few years later (*Age of Ultron*), also helmed by Whedon and featuring the same cast of heroes. While a serviceable tale, it failed to replicate the unique fun and freshness of the original. But given the MCU formula of combining characters even in supposedly "stand alone" storylines, this free-for-all vitality returned in the Russo brothers' *Captain America* sequels, which were, for all intent and purposes, *Avengers* movies.

The Avengers assembled: Iron Man (Robert Downey Jr.), The Hulk (Eric Bana), Captain America (Chris Evans), Hawkeye (Jeremy Renner), Thor (Chris Hemsworth), Black Widow (Scarlett Johansson).

Loki (David Hiddleston), Thor's bitter half-brother, is at the heart of this latest threat to humanity's security.

BOTTOM: Black Widow's heroic effort makes all the difference as mid-town Manhattan becomes a battlefield.

ABOVE: A peeved Thor and Captain America square off as Iron Man keeps score. LEFT: Tony Stark contemplates the ultimate power of Tesseract.

Director Joss Whedon and cast members indulge in some fun. Whedon remains a favorite of comic book and fantasy fans.

After giving each of their heroic titans his own introductory movie, Marvel brought everyone to the party with Joss Whedon's *The Avengers*, an energetic smackdown that earned high praise from critics, fans, and just about everyone else. LEFT: Loki (Tom Hiddleston). RIGHT, TOP: Each of the principals gets to shine in an exciting promotional graphic prepared by Marvel Studios. RIGHT, BOTTOM: The simian-browed Hulk as seen in *The Avengers* was an improvement over previous big screen attempts to realize the character through CGI.

THE DARK KNIGHT 2008

(152) 2.35

WHO MADE IT:

Warners Bros/Legendary Pictures/Syncopy (U.S.). Director: Christopher Nolan. Producers: Christopher Nolan, Charles Roven, Emma Thomas, Kevin De La Noy, Benjamin Melniker, Michael Uslan, Thomas Tull. Writers: Christopher Nolan, Jonathan Nolan, David S. Goyer, based on the comic book created by Bob Kane (DC). Cinematography (color): Wally Pfister. Music: Hans Zimmer, John Newton Howard. Starring Christian Bale (Bruce Wayne), Heath Ledger (Joker), Aaron Eckhart (Harvey Dent), Michael Caine (Alfred), Maggie Gyllenhaal (Rachel), Gary Oldman (Gordon), Morgan Freeman (Lucius Fox), Monique Gabriela Curnen (Ramirez), Ron Dean (Wuertz), Cillian Murphy (Scarecrow), Eric Roberts (Maroni), Nestor Carbonell (Mayor).

WHAT IT'S ABOUT:

Crime-fighting vigilante Batman allies himself with police lieutenant James Gordon and newly-elected attorney Harvey Dent to dismantle the remaining Mafia groups that plague Gotham City. These raised stakes lead to a terrible backlash in the form of the Joker, a vile, maniacal criminal who proceeds to plunge Gotham into anarchy. Dent becomes Bruce Wayne's rival in romance as well as heroics, with Wayne's childhood sweetheart Rachel caught in the middle. Sound advice from friends Lucius Fox and Alfred Pennyworth help a troubled Bruce maintain his emotional and moral balance as the Joker's horrific assaults on the city unfold.

WHY IT'S IMPORTANT:

What filmmaker Christopher Nolan started so impressively in *Batman Begins* reaches full potential in *The Dark Knight*, the centerpiece of a remarkable movie trilogy. Heath Ledger's unique turn as the Joker pretty much dominates this sequel, but the film itself is a groundbreaker, dispensing with tongue-in-cheek humor and embracing a gritty, adult tone that eclipses its predecessor. The Gotham City of *Batman Begins* is still a somewhat unreal conceit; here it is depicted as a gray, stone urban jungle, the perfect environment for this grim morality play to unfold. In terms of ambience, tough-as-hell Chicago doubling for Gotham (rather than New York) makes all the difference.

The Dark Knight continues to explore Batman's influence on those around him, from his beloved Rachel (now played by Maggie Gyllenhaal) to new hero on the block, courageous former DA Harvey Dent (Aaron Eckhart). The film quickly sets up the parallel between these two strong-willed men: one is a champion selected by the people, the other an unchecked vigilante whose very existence may be inspiring an unprecedented criminal retaliation. This comes in the deranged, jaunty form of a sadistic terrorist calling himself the Joker, who takes on his opposite number with mad abandon and plunges Gotham City into an almost unthinkable crisis. As always, Bruce Wayne/Batman is ably assisted by a trio of top-tier allies: Commissioner Gordon (Gary Oldman), butler Alfred (Michael Caine), and technology genius Lucius Fox (Morgan Freeman).

Nolan's spectacular movie surprises viewers at every turn. Taking a tip from superior action films like *The French Connection*, the big chase set-piece is delivered halfway through the film, clearing the decks and enabling *Dark Knight's* thesis to play out comfortably in Act III. The climax not only pits Batman against his nemesis in a tense physical confrontation, but allows the people of Gotham City to decide "who wins" their ideological debate, with imperiled civilians choosing an elemental faith in humanity over self-survival in response to the Joker's rigged death-traps.

ABOVE: Crusading D.A. Harvey Dent (Aaron Eckhart) has forged an uneasy alliance with Commissioner Gordon (Gary Oldman) and the Dark Knight (Christian Bale). RIGHT: Bruce Wayne (Bale) and his alter-ego. BELOW: The Joker (Heath Ledger) menaces Rachael (Maggie Gyllenhaal). BELOW: Gotham City is under siege, held hostage by criminal forces.

Only the ingenuity and courage of Batman can stand up to the Joker. Meanwhile, scarred, hideous Dent becomes a threat in his own right.

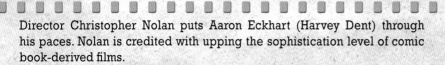

Director Christopher Nolan puts Aaron Eckhart (Harvey Dent) through his paces. Nolan is credited with upping the sophistication level of comic book-derived films.

Sadly, Heath Ledger passed away before *The Dark Knight* was released. But his posthumous Oscar win forever validates this impressive and unexpected take, soon to be imitated by others (most notably Javier Bardem's giddily deranged "Silva" from *Skyfall*). All things considered, director Chris Nolan pulled off the impossible: he not only rendered Batman as a fully adult character with dramatic resonance, but he actually transcended the source material by giving his Dark Knight a palpable, relatable soul, and his besieged city a voice in deciding its own destiny.

AFTERVIEW
OTHER NOTABLE ADAPTATIONS

2 GUNS (2013, Universal) is a violent, serviceable crime thriller about a pair of undercover agents working to ultimately take down the CIA's secret bank operations. It is based on the comic book series of the same name created by Steven Grant/Mateus Santolouco, and published in 2007 by Boom! Directed by Baltasar Kormàkur. Starring Denzel Washington, Mark Wahlberg, Paula Patton, Bill Paxton, James Marsden, Fred Ward, Edward James Olmos.

300: RISE OF AN EMPIRE (2014, Warner Bros./Legendary) is the satisfactory but less successful sequel/prequel to 2007's surprise hit *300*, both based on graphic novels created by Frank Miller. It continues its fanciful exploration of the legendary conflict between Sparta and all-powerful Greece; this time an otherworldly liquid transforms slain King Darius' revenge-seeking son into a godlike giant. Directed by Noam Murro. Starring Sullivan Stapleton, Eva Green, Lena Headey, Hans Matheson, David Wenham.

ACE DRUMMOND (1936, Universal) is a 13-chapter serial based on the comic strip by Captain Eddie Rickenbacker (writer) and Clayton Knight (artist). Set in Mongolia, it pits two-fisted airborne adventurer Ace against a villain known as the Dragon, who delights in obliterating airplane pilots with his death ray. Directed by Forde Bebe and Clifford Smith. Starring John King, Jean Rogers, Noah Berry Jr., Jackie Morrow, Lon Chaney Jr.

THE ADDAMS FAMILY (1991, Paramount/Orion) reboots the delightfully ghoulish suburban family created by cartoonist Charles Addams. The plot concerns long-lost Uncle Fester, and a nasty scheme to deceive Gomez and company with an imposter… who turns out to be memory-impaired Fester, after all. Cannily directed by Barry Sonnenfeld, the film inspired an equally well-received sequel, *Addams Family Values*. Starring Anjelica Huston, Raul Julia, Christopher Lloyd, Dan Hedaya, Christina Ricci.

THE ADVENTURES OF JANE ARDEN (1939, Warner Bros.) is a slight but tidy crime thriller based on the Jane Arden comic strip created by Monte Barrett and Russell E. Ross in 1927, a precursor to *Brenda Starr*. It follows the exploits of a daring female reporter who goes undercover to expose a gang of jewel thieves and smugglers. Directed by Terry O. Morse. Starring Rosella Towne, William Gargan, James Stephenson, Dennie Moore.

THE ADVENTURES OF SMILIN' JACK (1943, Universal) is a 13-chapter serial derived from the Chicago Tribune comic strip by Zack Mosley that began in 1933. Aviator hero 'Smilin' Jack' Martin battles both Japanese and German enemies in this World War II-era cliffhanger. Directed by Lewis D. Collins and Ray Taylor. Starring Tom Brown, Rose Hobart, Edgar Barrier, Majorie Lord, Keye Luke, Sidney Toler, Cyril Delevanti, Turhan Bey.

THE AMAZING SPIDER-MAN 2 (2014, Columbia) winds up Columbia's five-movie handling of the iconic Marvel webslinger with a sub-par interpretation of villain Electro and a confused, overstuffed scenario. Leads Andrew Garfield and Emma Stone continue to convey engaging chemistry, and Spider-Man's chatty interaction with the public seems fresh. Director: Marc Webb. Also starring Jamie Foxx, Dane DeHaan, Campbell Scott, Embeth Davidtz, Colm Feore, Paul Giamatti, Sally Field.

ANNIE (2014, Columbia) reimagines Little Orphan Annie has a Harlem youngster in this A-level movie musical, the third filmed incarnation of Broadway's 1977 hit (an impressive Disney TV version followed the disappointing John Huston take). This new *Annie* revolves around its race-change gimmick, charting pretty much the same ground as its predecessors. Director: Will Gluck. Starring Jamie Foxx, Quvenzhane Wallis, Rose Byrne, Bobby Cannavale, Cameron Diaz.

ART SCHOOL CONFIDENTIAL (2006, United Artists) mixes humor with pathos in a dark tale about artistic obsession, jealousy, and serial killing, based loosely on an obscure comic by Daniel Clowes. This second collaboration from the *Ghost World* writer-director team of Clowes and Terry Zwigoff is mostly derailed by muddled plotting and abstract ideas, although the ironic denouement has resonance. Starring Max Minghella, Sophia Myles, John Malkovich, Anjelica Huston, Jim Broadbent.

ATOM MAN VS. SUPERMAN (1950, Columbia) is a 15-chapter serial that pits the Man of Steel against formidable mad scientist Lex Luthor in the studio's follow-up to their 1948 *Superman*. Once again likeable lightweight Kirk Alyn dons the familiar cape and tights, transforming into an animated cartoon whenever flying sequences are required. Directed by Spencer Gordon Bennet for producer Sam Katzman. Starring Kirk Alyn, Lyle Talbot, Noel Neill, Tommy Bond, Pierre Watkin.

BATMAN AND ROBIN (1949, Columbia) is a 15-chapter serial that represents the studio's second crack at DC's Caped Crusader, this time in post-war mode. Menacing all with his electrical weapons is a mysterious villain known as the Wizard. Actor Lyle Talbot, who'd play Lex Luthor in an upcoming *Superman* serial, portrays Commissioner Gordon here. Directed by Spencer Gordon Bennet for producer Sam Katzman. Starring Robert Lowery, Johnny Duncan, Jane Adams, Ralph Adams.

BATMAN FOREVER (1995, Warner Bros.) provides an odd, colorful transition from WB's first two Tim Burton *Batman* movies to the more flamboyant Joel Schumacher follow-ups. Everything is neon green and glowing here, supporting Jim Carrey's hyper performance as the Riddler, while Tommy Lee Jones' Two-Face collapses into unbridled camp. On the plus side, a solid origin is dramatized for Boy Wonder Dick Grayson, and the "two brothers" flavoring of B & R is not without charm. Directed by Joel Schumacher. Starring Val Kilmer, Nicole Kidman, Chris O'Donnell, Michael Gough.

BLACKHAWK (1952, Columbia) is a 15-chapter serial based on a comic book that was published by Quality Comics in 1952 (DC has the rights today). The central character is an airman named Blackhawk who leads a squadron of WWII veteran flyers against criminals in the post-WWII world. It's a cheap and mostly bland chapter play, with former *Superman* star Kirk Alyn in the title role. Directed by Spencer Gordon Bennet and Fred Sears. Starring: Kirk Alyn, Carol Forman, John Crawford, Michael Fox, Don Harvey, Rick Vallin.

BLADE TRINITY (2004, New Line Cinema) is the third *Blade* movie based on the Marvel comics anti-hero created by Marv Wolfman and Gene Colan in the 1970s. It re-visits fanciful themes and ideas established in the previous films, but seems fresh whenever stylish action sequences take center stage. Written, produced, and directed by David S. Goyer. Starring Wesley Snipes, Kris Kristofferson, Jessica Biel, Ryan Reynolds, Parker Posey.

BLONDIE (1938, Columbia) is the first of 28 low-budget comedies produced over the course of five years. Based on the popular comic strip by Chic Young, this initial entry introduces film audiences to the always-colorful Bumstead clan, from frenetic hubby Dagwood and winsome wife Blondie to adorable Baby Dumpling. Directed by Frank Strayer. Starring Penny Singleton, Arthur Lake, Larry Simms, Gene Lockhart, Jonathan Hale, Jerome Cowan, Gordon Oliver, Ann Doran, Kathleen Lockhart.

BRENDA STARR (1989, Triumph Releasing) is an odd little campfest based on the long-running comic strip by Dale Messick. Feisty reporter Brenda jumps out of the comics and into the reality zone of her struggling illustrator, then plunges back again for more exotic adventures after feeling unappreciated. Desperate gimmick can't disguise the lack of an appropriate creative approach. Director: Robert Ellis Miller. Starring Brooke Shields, Tony Peck, Timothy Dalton, Nestor Serrano, Jeff Tambor.

BRICK BRADFORD (1947, Columbia) is a cheapjack 15-chapter serial based on the adventure/sci-fi comic strip created in 1933 by William Ritt and Clarence Gray. The far-fetched plot pairs fearless hero Brick with a brilliant scientist, and both combat criminals operating within the fifth dimension. As many have pointed out, BB owes much to the galactic derring-do of stalwart contemporaries Flash Gordon and Buck Rogers. Directed by Spencer Gordon Bennet and Thomas Carr. Starring Kane Richmond, Rick Vallin, Linda Leighton, Pierre Watkin, Charles Quigley.

BRINGING UP FATHER (1946, Monogram) is based on George McManus' comic strip about a long-suffering American husband named Jiggs and his ambitious-to-a-fault wife Maggie. This low-budget family comedy inspired four sequels, and the *Bringing Up Father* characters have enjoyed other screen incarnations as well, including a 1928 silent adaptation from MGM. Directed by Edward F. Klein. Starring Joe Yule, Renie Riano, Tim Ryan, June Harrison, Wallace Chadwell.

BULLETPROOF MONK (2003, MGM/Lakeshore Productions) combines laughs with flamboyant martial arts action, in this wildly fantastic and often fun film loosely based on the comic book by Michael Avon Oeming. It's mostly an opportunity to watch Chow Yun-fat command the screen with his unique, dynamic presence. Directed by Paul Hunter (debut). Starring Yun-fat, Seann William Scott, Jaime King, Karel Roden, Victoria Smurfit, Mako.

CAPTAIN AMERICA (1944, Republic) is a reasonably impressive 15-chapter serial adaptation of the Timely Marvel comic book, even though it has very little to do with the popular property that inspired it: there's no super-serum, no shield, no Bucky, no Nazis. It isn't even our friend Private Steve Rogers beneath the A-hood, but a crusty, crusading DA named Grant Gardner, squaring off against a mad scientist known as the Scarab. Directed by Elmer Clifton and John English. Starring Dick Purcell, Lorna Gray, Lionel Atwill, Charles Trowbridge.

CAPTAIN AMERICA (1979, Universal) is the feature-length second pilot for a never-launched series, released in the overseas markets as a theatrical movie. Pilot #2 is a bit more entertaining than its predecessor, with "guest star" Christopher Lee adding some class to the proceedings. Reb Brown is surprisingly convincing as a modern-day Cap, although his motorcycle/flying act is a bit cumbersome. Directed by Ivan Nagy. Starring Brown, Lee, Len Birman, Lana Wood, Connie Sellaca.

CATWOMAN (2004, Warner Bros.) is a high profile misfire based (more or less) on the popular DC villainess-turned-pseudo heroine. Made at a time when comic book movies were beginning to embrace their source material, this Halle Berre vehicle enthusiastically rejects it – Selina Kyle is now graphics designer Patience Phillips, recipient of cat-like powers bestowed by the Egyptian goddess Bast. Directed by Pitof. Starring Berry, Sharon Stone, Benjamin Bratt.

DENNIS THE MENACE (1993, Warner Bros.) is a spirited if somewhat familiar adaptation of the famous Hank Ketcham comic strip, leaning rather heavily on recent kid-hits *Home Alone* and *Back to the Future*. Mason Gamble is reasonably cute as precocious five year-old Dennis, but it's grumpy old Walter Matthau as Mr. Wilson who steals most of the scenes. Directed by Nick Castle. Starring Matthau, Gamble, Christopher Lloyd, Lea Thompson, Paul Winfield.

THE DIARY OF A TEENAGE GIRL (2015, Sony Pictures Classics) is a startlingly adult and honest personal portrait based on Phoebe Gloeckner's equally frank graphic novel. It's all about Minnie, a sexually active but profoundly insecure fifteen year-old in an often precarious journey of self-discovery. Written and directed by Marielle Heller. Starring Bel Powley, Kristen Wig, Alexander Skarsgard, Christopher Meloni, Auston Lyon, Madeline Waters.

DICK TRACY MEETS GRUESOME (1938, RKO Radio Pictures) is the fourth and final entry in this low-budget RKO movie series inspired by the famous Chester Gould comic strip. Dedicated sleuth Tracy has his hands full battling experimental nerve gas and a mysterious gangster who has apparently "returned from the dead." Starring Ralph Byrd, Boris Karloff, Anne Gwynne, Skelton Knaggs, Edward Ashley, June Clayworth, Lyle Latell.

DIXIE DUGAN (1943, 20th Century-Fox) is a modest but sprightly adaptation of J.P. McEvoy's comic strip. It is very much a WWII homefront confection, with heroine Dixie an indefatigable secretary to her long-suffering young boss, a Washington bureaucrat. Intended as the first in a series of low-budget comedies that never materialized. Directed by Otto Brower. Starring James Ellison, Lois Andrews, Charles Ruggles, Charlotte Greenwood.

DONDI (1961, Allied Artists) is a sub-par adaptation of the popular comic strip created by Gus Edson and Irwin Hasen, which ran from 1955 to 1986. The title character is a little orphaned Italian boy who stows away with the six American G.I.s he's befriended; this leads him to a fun, sometimes precarious adventure in New York City. Directed by Albert Zugsmith. Starring David Janssen, Patti Page, David Kory, Walter Winchell, Mickey Shaughnessy, Robert Strauss, Gale Gordon.

DON WINSLOW OF THE NAVY (1942, Universal) is a 12-chapter serial based on the comic strip created by Commander Frank V. Martinek. Very much a flag waver (it actually opened two months before Pearl Harbor was attacked), this generally effective cliffhanger pits stalwart naval hero Winslow against a ring of enemy agents out to destroy U.S. supply ships. Directed by Ray Taylor. Starring Don Terry, Walter Sande, Claire Dodd, Anne Nagel, John Litel, Ben Taggart, Kurt Katch.

ELEKTRA (2005, 20th Century Fox) is something of a sequel to 2003's *Daredevil*, with both properties based on Marvel's characters famously teamed by writer/artist Frank Miller. Back from the dead, Elektra masters remarkable martial arts techniques, uses them to become a contract killer, and winds up playing bodyguard to a young girl with special gifts. Workmanlike direction by Rob Bowman. Starring Jennifer Garner, Goran Visnjic, Terence Stamp, Will Yun Lee, Kirsten Prout, Cary-Hiroyuki Tagawa.

FANTASTIC FOUR (2005, 20th Century Fox) is an unremarkable but relatively entertaining adaptation of the classic Marvel comic book created by Stan Lee and Jack Kirby in 1962. It dutifully dramatizes a space mishap that transforms four exploratory scientists into super-powered beings. Also affected is their frequently unscrupulous boss, who intends using his fantastic new skills for personal gain. Directed by Tim Story. Starring Jessica Alba, Chris Evans, Michael Chiklis, Julian McMahon, Ion Gruffudd.

FRIDAY FOSTER (1975, American International) is a blaxploitation-era action flick based on the syndicated comic strip written by Jim Lawrence and illustrated by Jorge Longaron and Gray Morrow. Daring magazine photographer Friday Foster (Pam Grier) is targeted for death after she witnesses a political assassination. Like most films of this ilk, logic takes a back seat to cool defiance and kinetic fight scenes. Written and directed by Arthur Marks. Starring Grier, Carl Weathers, Eartha Kitt, Godfrey Cambridge, Ed Cambridge.

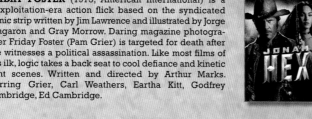

JONAH HEX (2010, Warner Bros./Legendary) is a limp and confusing adaptation of the DC Comics anti-hero created by John Albano and Tony DeZuniga in 1972. Star Josh Brolin does his best as the back-from-the-dead, scarred protagonist, revived by Native American mysticism. Vengeance and violence follow in his wake. Hex would be rebooted for the DC TV series *Legends of Tomorrow* (2016). Directed by Jimmy Haywood. Starring Brolin, Megan Fox, John Malkovitch, Michael Fassbender, Will Arnett.

FAUST: LOVE OF THE DAMNED (2000, Fantastic Factory) is a gory, independently-produced retelling of the *Faust* tale, based on a minor comic book by Tim Vigil and David Quinn. Vaguely similar to Marvel's *Ghost Rider*, it dramatizes how distraught artist John Jaspers sells his soul to Mephistopheles in order to avenge the killing of a loved one. Cursed to transform periodically into a horned demon, Jaspers eventually turns the tables on his evil master. Directed by Brian Yuzna. Starring Mark Frost, Isabel Brook, Jennifer Rope, Jeffrey Combs.

JUDGE DREDD (1995, Buena Vista) is the first screen adaptation of Britain's popular comic strip, which appeared for many years in 2000 AD comics. Although primarily a Sylvester Stallone action vehicle, *Judge Dredd* embraces many of the sci-fi strip's central ideas, and boasts an impressive cast. Directed by Danny Cannon. Starring Stallone, Armand Assante, Diane Lane, Rob Schneider, Joan Chen, Jurgen Prochnow, Max von Sydow.

GASOLINE ALLEY (1951, Columbia) is an energetic B-movie based on the exploits of characters from Frank King's long-running comic strip. The plot focuses on likable newlyweds Corky and Hope, who open up their own restaurant and get themselves into hot water at every opportunity. This film and a sequel, *Corky of Gasoline Alley*, were out of circulation for years because of copyright issues. Directed by Edward Bernds. Starring Scotty Beckett, Susan Morrow, Jimmy Lyndon, Gus Schilling, Charles Halton.

JUNGLE JIM (1948, Columbia) is the first of sixteen low-budget, studio-bound adventure films based on the comic strip character created by Alex (Flash Gordon) Raymond. Former Tarzan Johnny Weissmuller seemed a logical fit at this stage of his life and career, even using his own name instead of Jungle Jim in the last three movies. Directed by William Berke. Starring Weissmuller, Virginia Grey, George Reeves, Rick Vallin.

HAROLD TEEN (1934, Warner Bros.) is a flat, early musical comedy based on a mostly-forgotten comic strip by Carl Ed. The titular hero is a frustrated young cub reporter enduring a bout of bad luck; he finally gets his chance to shine at a school musical, where he dazzles all with his dancing prowess. Star Hal Le Roy is actually quite gifted, but the film makes minimal use of his talents. Directed by Murray Roth. Starring Le Roy, Rochelle Hudson, Patricia Ellis, Guy Kibbe, Hugh Herbert, Chick Chandler.

KICK-ASS 2 (2013, Universal) is an ill-advised sequel to the semi-fresh original, based on Icon/Marvel comics by Mark Millar and John Romita Jr. There's still some style on display, but an abundance of costumed characters ultimately divides viewer interest; not surprisingly, Hit-Girl's scenes are the most memorable. Directed by Jeff Wadlow. Starring Aaron Taylor-Johnson, Christopher Mintz-Plasse, Chloe Grace Moretz, Jim Carrey.

HELLBOY: THE GOLDEN ARMY (2008, Universal) is the second film based on Mike Mignola's cult classic comic book. It pits the horn-trimmed, red-skinned demon hero against formidable adversaries from another dimension. Directed with fanboyish glee by monster maven Guillermo del Toro, who also helmed the first *Hellboy* movie. Starring Ron Perlman, Selma Blair, Doug Jones, John Alexander, John Hurt, James Dodd, Seth MacFarlane, Luke Goss, Jeffrey Tambor.

KING OF THE ROYAL MOUNTED (1940, Republic) is a 12-chapter serial based on the popular "northern" comic strip created by Stephen Slesinger in 1935. He used Zane Grey's more commercial byline with art initially provided by Allen Dean. Courageous Sgt. Dave King battles enemy agents who are using a mysterious "compound x" to destroy Allied ships. Directed by John English and William Whitney. Starring Allan Lane (who would return in a sequel), Robert Strange, Robert Kellard, Lita Conway.

I, FRANKENSTEIN (2014, Lionsgate) is a disappointing fantasy-adventure-horror combo from Australia, based on the graphic novel by actor/writer Kevin Grevioux. It uses fundamental ideas from the *Frankenstein* story and extends them into the visually flamboyant worlds of sorcery and metaphysics. Written and directed by Stuart Beattie. Starring Aaron Eckhart, Bill Nighy, Yvonne Strahovski, Miranda Otto, Jai Courtney, Socratis Otto, Kevin Grevioux.

LI'L ABNER (1940, RKO Radio Pictures) is a cheap but engaging adaptation of Al Capp's famous comic strip, offering a script partially penned by Capp and a title song co-written by Milton Berle. Bumpkin hero Abner must choose between amorous girlfriends Daisy Mae and Wendy Wilecat, a decision that is finally settled at the Sadie Hawkins Day race. Directed by Albert S. Rogell. Starring Jeff York, Martha O'Driscoll, Mona Ray, Johnnie Morris, Billie Seward, Buster Keaton, Kay Sutton.

THE INCREDIBLE HULK (2008, Universal) represents the MCU's take on the green behemoth created for comics by Stan Lee and Jack Kirby in 1962. Less abstract than Ang Lee's approach, it fails for totally different reasons. A compromised-out-of-necessity origin story doesn't help, pretty much stranding star Norton, who is sympathetic without being especially compelling. MCU's Hulk would do better as a supporting character in *Avengers* movies. Directed by Louis Leterrier. Starring Norton, Liv Tyler, William Hurt, Tim Roth.

LITTLE ORPHAN ANNIE (1932, RKO Pictures) is an early, pre-Code adaptation of the popular King Features comic strip created by Harold Gray. It covers Annie's relationship with benefactor Daddy Warbucks (they live in a shack!), and charts her friendship with an orphaned boy named Mickey. Directed by John S. Robertson. Starring Mitzi Green, Buster Phelps, May Robson, Matt Moore, Edgar Kennedy (as Warbucks), Kate Drain Lawson, Sidney Bracey.

JOE PALOOKA, CHAMP (1946, Monogram) is the first of twelve low-budget boxing movies based on the well-known comic strip character. An early pre-code incarnation, simply called *Palooka*, was mostly a Jimmy Durante vehicle, but Monogram's little film series firmly established Joe Kirkwood Jr. as the definitive screen JP. Directed by Reginald LeBorg. Starring Kirkwood, Leon Errol, Elyse Knox, Eduardo Ciannelli, Joe Sawyer, Elisha Cook Jr.

THE LOSERS (2010, Warner Bros.) is a workmanlike action movie with comedy elements, based on the Vertigo/DC comic book series created by Andy Diggle and Jock. Very much reminisant of *The A-Team*, the plot concerns an eccentric band of government operatives who tackle a ruthless Bolivian drug lord, rescuing some enslaved children along the way. Directed by Sylvain White. Starring Jeffrey Dean Morgan, Zoe Saldana, Chris Evans, Idris Elba, Columbus Short, Jason Patric.

MISS ANNIE ROONEY (1942, United Artists) is ostensibly an adaptation of the 1927 King Features comic strip, which was a blatant imitation of *Little Orphan Annie*. This movie version, like Mary Pickford's 1925 film, provides an original story that has nothing to do with scrappy orphans and flea-bitten pets; instead, a tepid tale about a poor girl in love with a well-to-do boyfriend takes center stage. Directed by Edwin L. Marin. Starring Shirley Temple, Dickie Moore, William Gargan, Guy Kibbe.

RED BARRY (1938, Universal) is a better-than-average, 12-chapter serial based on the *Dick Tracy*-like comic strip created by Will Gould (no relation to Chester) in 1934. A San Francisco police detective stationed in Chinatown, Barry's on the trail of stolen bonds intended for Chinese War relief. Third of the five serials Buster Crabbe made for Universal. Directed by Ford Beebe and Alan James. Starring Crabbe, Frances Robinson, Edna Sedgewick, Cyril Delevanti, Frank Lackteen.

MODESTY BLAISE (1966, 20th Century-Fox) is an aggressively bizarre adaptation of Peter O'Donnell's comic strip, with O'Donnell himself providing the screen story. It concerns super spy Modesty Blaise, recruited by the British to protect a shipment of diamonds; relationships with both an international jewel thief and a former secret agent lover complicate matters. Directed by Joseph Losey. Starring Monica Vitti, Dirk Bogarde, Terence Stamp, Harry Andrews, Michael Craig, Clive Revill, Alexander Knox.

THE SAD SACK (1957, Paramount) is a major studio adaptation of the popular military-comedy strip created by George Baker. It was purchased by producer Hal Wallis as a vehicle for Martin and Lewis; when the team split up, it became a Jerry-only movie, with David Wayne in the Martin role. Nothing special, but watchable. Directed by George Marshall. Starring Lewis, Wayne, Phyllis Kirk, Peter Lorre, Joe Mantell, Liliane Montevecchi, Gene Evans, Shepperd Strudwick.

THE MOSTLY UNFABULOUS SOCIAL LIFE OF ETHAN GREEN (2006, Regent Releasing) is an obscure movie based on the edgy, sexually explicit syndicated comic strip by Eric Orner. It explores the emotionally volatile and unpredictable gay lifestyle of the title character, with off-beat events building to a chaotic commitment ceremony. The film received limited theatrical release. Directed by George Bamber. Starring Daniel Letterle, Meredith Baxter, David Monahan, Dean Shelton, Joel Brooks.

SIN CITY: A DAME TO KILL FOR (2014, Dimension Films) continues the neo-noir surrealistic thrills first on display in the 2005 groundbreaker, *Sin City*. Based on Frank Miller's graphic novels and partially written by Miller, the film offers violent, nihilistic mini-tales that serve as both sequels and prequels, all presented in the same visually-arresting combination of live-action and stylized graphics that characterized the first film. Directed by Robert Rodriguez. Starring a cast to kill for: Mickey Rourke. Josh Brolin, Bruce Willis, Ray Liotta, Jessica Alba, Eva Green.

MYSTERY PLANE (Monogram, 1939) is an extremely low-budget, hour-long feature movie based on the long-running comic strip illustrated by Hal Forrest. It capitalized on the public's fascination with aviation, as hero "Tailspin" Tommy battles enemy agents to rescue both his imperiled girlfriend and a new bomb-targeting system he's invented. Directed by George Waggner. Starring John Trent, Marjorie Reynolds, Milburn Stone, Jason Robards Sr., George Lynn, Betsy Gay.

SPAWN (1997, New Line Cinema) is a muddled adaptation of the popular occult-themed comic book created by Todd MacFarlane for Image Comics. Like many supernatural superheroes, Spawn, aka Al Simmons, is torn between good and evil, an assassinated special ops agent who refuses to lead Hell's army against Heaven after he is resurrected for that purpose. Directed by Mark A.Z. Dippe. Starring Michael Jai White, John Leguizamo, Martin Sheen, Nicol Williamson, Melinda Clarke.

THE PERILS OF GWENDOLYN IN THE LAND OF THE YIK-YAK (1984, Severin Films) is a mad, mad movie based on the fetish comics of John Willie, specifically *Sweet Gwendolyn*. The oft-imperiled heroine finds herself pursuing a rare butterfly in the exotic land of the Yik-Yak. An Indiana Jones-like character named Willard frequently comes to her rescue. Directed by Just Jaeckin. Starring Tawny Kitaen, Brent Huff, Zabou Breitman, Bernadette Lafront, Jean Rougerie, Stanley Kapoul.

SPIDER-MAN (1978, Columbia) is the 90-minute made-for-TV movie pilot that ran on CBS, and was released as a theatrical feature in the international market. This first live-action Spidey feature has a lighter touch than what followed, and Nicholas Hammond delivers a reasonably affable Peter Parker. Followed by *Spider-Man Strikes Back* and *Spider-Man and the Dragon's Challenge*, also culled from the TV series. Directed by E.W. Swackhamer. Starring Hammond, David White, Michael Pataki, Ellen Bry, Thayer David.

PRIVATE SNUFFY SMITH (1942, Monogram) is a mostly sub-par adaptation of Billy DeBeck's beloved comic strip. Hillbilly Snuffy Smith joins the Army to avoid revenuers, but winds up with old nemesis Ed Cooper as his First Sergeant, an invisible dog (!), a newfangled rangefinder, and a couple of larcenous Fifth columnists to tangle with. Big-nosed Bud Duncan returned in a sequel the same year. Director: Edward Klein. Starring Duncan, Edgar Kennedy, Sarah Padden.

SPIDER-MAN 3 (2007, Columbia) is the third and least satisfying Sam Raimi movie based on the seminal Marvel Comics hero created by Stan Lee and Steve Ditko. Too many fanciful plot elements sabotage the proceedings; did we really need the extraterrestrial Venom, Harry Osborne's Hobgoblin, and Sandman too? Directed by Raimi. Starring Tobey Maguire, Kirsten Dunst, James Franco, Thomas Haden Church, James Cromwell, Topher Grace, Rosemary Harris, J.K. Simmons.

R.I.P.D. (2013, Universal) is a disastrous movie incarnation of the comic book *Rest in Peace*, created by TV producer Peter M. Lenkov (*Hawaii Five-O*). Its funky, familiar concept combines buddy-buddy cop pleasures with urban supernatural thrills, fresher and better films like *Ghostbusters* and *Men in Black* being obvious inspirations. Directed by Robert Schwentke. Starring Jeff Bridges, Ryan Reynolds, Kevin Bacon, Mary-Louise Parker, Stephanie Szostak.

THE SPIRIT (2008, Lionsgate) is an undistinguished misfire based on the classic "avenging ghost" cop character created for comics by Will Eisner. Although director Frank Miller is a great admirer of Eisner's work, his ultra-dark, post-modern take seems wildly inappropriate. A 1987 TV movie starring Sam J Jones (*Flash Gordon*), unreleased theatrically, does a better job of catching *The Spirit*'s semi-satiric tone. Starring Gabriel Macht, Samuel L. Jackson, Scarlett Johansson, Eva Mendes.

RADIO PATROL (serial, 1937, Universal) is a 12-chapter serial based on the police-themed comic strip created by writer Eddie Sullivan and artist Charles Schmidt, which ran from 1933 to 1950. Radio cop hero Pat O'Hara has his hands full protecting a secret formula for bulletproof steel from ruthless international agents. Directed by Ford Beebe and Cliff Smith. Starring Grant Withers, Adrian Morris, Kay Hughes, Mickey Rentschler, Gordon Hart, C. Montague Shaw, Silver Wolf.

STEEL (1997, Warner Bros.) is a wrong move from director Kenneth Johnson, one of TV's most assured hands at humanist fantasy/adventure (*The Bionic Woman*, *The Incredible Hulk*, *V*). Although based on a DC Comics character, the film reinvents its own subject by creating new heroes and villains. Paralyzed weapons designer Steel wears an armored suit á la Iron Man to battle the nefarious plans of rival Nathaniel Burke. Starring Shaquille O'Neal, Judd Nelson, Annabeth Gish, Richard Roundtree.

SUPERMAN III (1983, Warner Bros.) is the third entry in the Salkind-produced movie series based on DC's comic book character, and the first "all Richard Lester-directed" entry (*II* was an odd hybrid of Lester/Richard Donner footage). The result is generally unsatisfying, with broad comedic requirements for second lead Richard Pryor setting the frivolous, cartoon-like tone. Starring Christopher Reeve, Margot Kidder, Pryor, Robert Vaughn, Annette O'Toole.

TIM TYLER'S LUCK (1937, Universal) is a 12-chapter serial based on the King Features Syndicate comic strip by Lyman Young that lasted from 1928 to 1996. Courageous and plucky Tim Tyler was something of a boy version of Indiana Jones, daring various perils. In this serial, he stows away on a ship to Africa to find his professor father. Directed by Ford Beebe and Wyndham Gittens. Starring Frankie Thomas, Francis Robinson, Jack Mulhall, Al Shean, Norman Willis.

SURROGATES (2009, Walt Disney/Touchstone) is a major studio adaptation of a mostly unknown, limited series Top Shelf comic book created by writer Robert Venditti and rendered by Brett Weldele in 2005/6. Set in the future, it follows the exploits of an FBI agent in a world where humans literally live their lives through remote-controlled androids known as surrogates. Equal parts *Blade Runner*, *Total Recall*, *Soylent Green*, *and Westworld*. Directed by Jonathan Mostow. Starring Bruce Willis, Radha Mitchell, James Cromwell, Ving Rhames.

TUCSON RAIDERS (1944, Republic) is the first of 23 low-budget feature films based on the popular *Red Ryder* comic strip by Fred Harman. The famous cowboy hero finds himself framed for murder in this inaugural installment, grappling with dishonest politicians and outlaws along the way. Directed by Spencer Gordon Bennett. Starring Wild Bill Elliot, Robert Blake, Alice Fleming, "Gabby" Hayes, Ruth Lee, Peggy Stewart, LeRoy Mason.

TAMARA DREWE (2010, Sony Pictures Classics) is an alternately charming/annoyingly chaotic indie adaptation of Posy Simmonds' graphic novel and newspaper strip. The heroine is an amorous young newspaper writer who returns to her sleepy hometown, where all manner of romantic madness ensues. Directed by Stephen Frears. Starring Gemma Arterton, Dominic Cooper, Luke Evans, Tasmin Greig, Jessica Barden, Charlotte Christie.

UP FRONT (1951, Universal) brings Bill Mauldin's likeable cartoon WWII G.I.s to life in this military comedy, which is enhanced by solid studio production values. A kind of *Odd Couple* escapade in the theater of war, the movie makes the most of its talented leads. Spawned a sequel: *Willie and Joe Back at the Front*. Directed by Alexander Hall. Starring David Wayne, Tom Ewell, Marina Berti, Jeffrey Lynn, Richard Egan, Vaughn Taylor, Maurice Cavell.

TANK GIRL (1995, United Artists) is an odd duck of a movie based on an equally far-out British comic book, created by Alan Martin and Jamie Hewlett for Deadline magazine in 1988. The film version of this post-apocalyptic action series plays like *Mad Maxx* on acid, with funky feministic flourishes thrown in (why not?). Directed by Rachel Talalay. Starring Lori Petty, Ice-T, Naomi Watts, Malcolm McDowell.

THE VIGILANTE (1947, Columbia) is a 15-chapter serial based on a cowboy hero from the DC universe, created in 1941 for Action Comics. This makes the Vigilante one of the first DC characters to appear on film. Although hero Greg Saunders still rides a motorcycle and wears a costume of sorts, this film incarnation took various liberties with its source material. Directed by Wallace Fox. Starring Ralph (Dick Tracy) Byrd, Ramsay Ames, Lyle Talbot, George Offerman Jr., Robert Barron.

TEENAGE MUTANT NINJA TURTLES: OUT OF THE SHADOWS (2016, Paramount) is the second and superior entry in this new, CG-era wave of *Turtles* flicks, based on the anthropomorphic characters created by Kevin Eastman and Peter Laird. It's another predictable slugfest between the half-shell heroes and their nemesis, Shredder. Directed by Jonathan Liebesman. Starring Megan Fox, Will Arnett, William Fichtner, Alan Ritchson, Noel Fisher.

VIRUS (1999, Universal) is a relatively ambitious adaptation of a Dark Horse comic book by Chuck Pfarrer. A suspense sci-fi/horror tale set in an isolated location, it has much in common with *Alien* and Carpenter's *The Thing*, which had also received the Dark Horse treatment. Directed by John Bruno. Starring Jamie Lee Curtis, William Baldwin, Donald Sutherland, Joanna Pacula, Marshall Bell, Cliff Curtis, Sherman Augustus.

THOR: THE DARK WORLD (2013, Walt Disney/Marvel) is the first sequel to Marvel's 2011 *Thor*, which introduced Marvel's resident god to a mainstream audience. This sequel is lively enough, with always-enjoyable Loki back for more mischief, but it demonstrates the downside of chapter-style movie adventures, a flatness Marvel swiftly remedied with their modern-era *Captain America* films. Directed by Alan Taylor. Starring Chris Hemsworth, Natalie Portman, Tom Hiddleston, Anthony Hopkins, Stellan Skarsgard, Idris Elba, Kat Dennings.

WHITEOUT (2009, Warner Bros./Dark Castle) is a tepid adaptation of a 1998 comic book by award-winning writer Greg Rucka and Steve Lieber. It revisits the familiar scenario of characters (including heroine Carrie Stetko, a U.S. Marshal) trapped in a storm-tossed location as an unknown killer plots their destruction. Directed by Dominic Sena. Starring Kate Beckinsale, Gabriel Macht, Tom Skeritt, Columbus Short, Alex O'Loughlin.

TILLIE THE TOILER (1927, Cosmopolitan Productions/MGM), a silent comedy released just as sound was transforming motion pictures, is based on Russ Westover's successful King Features comic strip (1921-1959). Lead character Tillie is a beautiful fashion model/secretary who somehow finds herself in a neverending series of highly improbable misadventures. Remade in 1941 by MGM. Directed by Hobart Henley. Starring Marion Davies, Matt Moore, Henry Crocker.

X-MEN 3: THE LAST STAND (2006, 20th Century Fox) is the ambitious conclusion of Bryan Singer's initial *X-Men* trilogy, except it wasn't directed by Singer, who was busy prepping the ill-fated *Superman Returns*. The storyline tries to tie-up plot points and problematic relationships introduced in the earlier films, while introducing a reasonably plausible Beast into the X-mutant pantheon. Directed by Bret Ratner. Starring Hugh Jackman, Halle Berry, Ian McKellen, Famke Janssen, Anna Paquin, Kelsey Grammar, Patrick Stewart.

TINTIN AND THE GOLDEN FLEECE (1961, Consortium Pathé) is an interesting French film adaptation of the comic "albums" created by Belgian cartoonist Herge (aka Georges Remi) in 1929. There have been various animated versions of *The Adventures of Tintin*, including a high-profile Steven Spielberg take, but this uneven but daring little movie represents the first live-action incarnation. It spawned an inferior sequel, *Tintin and the Blue Oranges*. Directed by Jean-Jacques Verne. Starring Jean-Pierre Talbot, Georges Wilson.

X-MEN ORIGINS: WOLVERINE (2009, 20th Century-Fox) is a decidedly uneven attempt to spin off Hugh Jackman's character from the *X-Men* pack, the first of a projected series of "origins," with villain Magneto scheduled next (an idea rolled into later *X-Men* films). This film does boast some interesting performances, and comic book historians may find Ryan Reynolds' first turn as Deadpool required viewing. Directed by Gavin Hood. Starring Jackman, Liev Schreiber, Danny Huston, Dominic Monaghan.

FROM
SCREEN
...

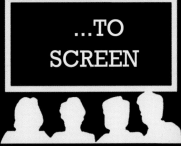

...TO
SCREEN

THEATRICAL FEATURES DERIVED FROM 1950s TELEVISION SERIES EPISODES

Stringing together episodes of TV series into feature-length "movies" for limited theatrical release was a profitable gimmick in the '50s and '60s (the same thing had been done with serials a short time earlier). In terms of comic book properties, the TV exploits of Superman starring George Reeves were reborn on the big screen in a series of hastily contrived compilations. All were briskly released by 20th Century-Fox in 1953 without the benefit of trailers, although some colorful one-sheet posters were produced. Cast members actually filmed bridging footage for these compilations, precious minutes that have been unseen by fans for more than half a century. Also making the journey from small screen to large was *Queen of the Jungle* (1955, right), derived from three related episodes of the *Sheena, Queen of the Jungle* TV series starring Irish McCalla and in this case, guest star Buddy Baer as "whip man" Bull Kendall.

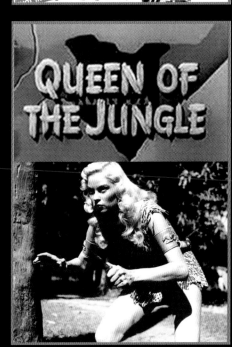

CHRISTOPHER NOLAN (1970 -?) Nolan is an acclaimed English-American movie director, screenwriter, cinematographer, editor, and producer. He raised the bar for comic book film adaptations with his adult re-invention of *Batman*, after the Tim Burton/Joel Schumacher movie series had degenerated into glossy camp. *Batman Begins*, *The Dark Knight*, and *The Dark Knight Rises* were all directed by Nolan, and all went on to become critical and financial hits. He also produced the equally adult-themed *Man of Steel* for Warner Bros.

KEVIN FEIGE (1973 -?) Boston-born Feige is one of the most successful film producers of the 21st Century. He is celebrated as the mastermind behind the Marvel Cinematic Universe, helming a series of interconnecting movies that were designed to mirror the comic book crossovers so popular with fans. Starting with *Iron Man* in 2008, the Marvel movies have made billions of dollars worldwide, earning fawning notices from critics in the bargain. Feige is also responsible for bringing top talent to this super-franchise.

BRYAN SINGER (1965 -?) dazzled audiences and critics alike with *The Usual Suspects* in 1995, a neo-noir with dramatic resonance. Hailed as an exceptional film director, Singer is often credited with starting the new century's avalanche of straightforward comic book adaptations with the original *X-Men* (2000). He has remained with that series even as it explored earlier incarnations of the principal superhero characters.

ZACK SNYDER (1966 -?) established himself as a comic book movie director with *300* in 2007 This aggressive and stylized adaptation of Frank Miller's graphic novel was an instant sensation at the boxoffice and earned enthusiastic reviews. Snyder directed *Watchman* two years later, and was chosen by producer Christopher Nolan to helm DC's Extended Universe on film (*Man of Steel, Batman v Superman, Justice League*).

JOSS WHEDON (1964 -?) was a comic book fan favorite even before he started directing big-budget Marvel movies. As a writer/producer, he created *Buffy the Vampire Slayer* and *Firefly* for television, earning a fervent cult following along the way. In 2011, Whedon was personally selected by Kevin Feige to direct the MCU's all-important *The Avengers*, which teamed several major Marvel superheroes in one film for the first time.

JON FAVREAU (1966 -?) is a successful American film director, actor and producer. He is best known for helming *Iron Man* in 2008, the very first movie produced directly by Marvel, which started the MCU on a high note (some consider it the best of all their films). Favreau received less praise for the inevitable sequel, and hit a low point with the ill-fated *Cowboys & Aliens* (2011), another comics-based feature.

THE RUSSO BROTHERS (1971 -?) are Anthony and Joseph "Joe" Russo, movie directors who started out as television talents (winning an Emmy for their work on *Arrested Development*) before graduating to the big screen. They upgraded Marvel's *Captain America* movie series with its first sequel, the critically-praised boxoffice hit *The Winter Soldier* (2014), and followed-up with the crowd pleasing *Civil War* in 2016.

WILLIAM WITNEY (1915 – 2002) started directing at age 21, the youngest man in Hollywood to do so in 1935. Often working with John English, he became famous for helming several popular serials for Republic Pictures, which specialized in the genre. His most praised comics-inspired efforts are *Adventures of Captain Marvel* in 1941 and *Spy Smasher* one year later. Other adaptations include three *Dick Tracy* serials, *Adventures of Red Ryder*, and *King of the Royal Mounted*.

SAM RAIMI (1959 - ?) is a celebrated Michigan-born movie director known for his offbeat subjects and idiosyncratic filmmaking approach. He helmed the popular *Spider-Man* series of films for Columbia starting in 2002. He also gave the world *Darkman* in 1990, a grim, ahead-of-its-time comic book-influenced adventure thriller hot on the heels of Tim Burton's *Batman* (1989). As a producer, Raimi's name can be found in the credits of *Timecop* (1994) and *30 Days of Night* (2007).

JAMES GUNN (1970 -?) is an American filmmaker who wears many caps: screenwriter, director, actor, producer, novelist and musician. Already an adaptor of cartoon properties into live-action features starting with 2002's *Scooby-Doo* and its sequel, he embraced the universe of comic book geeks specifically with his well-received *Super* in 2010. His most successful directorial gig so far has certainly been *Guardians of the Galaxy* (2014).

THE TOP TEN CBM PERFORMANCES

Robert Downey, Jr.	Heath Ledger
Paul Giamatti	Buster Crabbe
Morgan Freeman	Charles Middleton
Michelle Pfeiffer	Ryan Reynolds
Christopher Reeve	Brandon Lee

TOP FX CAPTURE ACTOR: **Bradley Cooper**

THE TOP TEN CBM MUSIC COMPOSERS

John Williams	Charles Fox
Danny Elfman	Alfred Newman
James Horner	Queen
Jerry Goldsmith	Dario Marianelli
Nelson Riddle	Thomas Newman

MOVIES WITH COMIC BOOK THEMES

There are countless worthwhile mainstream films that appear to be comic book-derived, but are in actuality comic book-inspired. Overtly fantastic characters like Tarzan, the Green Hornet, and Conan the Barbarian have sequential art written all over them, and did indeed wind up in comic books and strips; but their origin point was elsewhere. Other modern examples include Paul Verhoeven's *RoboCop* and Sam Raimi's *Darkman*, and to some degree all of the Bond and *Star Wars* films.

Comedies and parodies of the genre have been around for some time, from X-rated romps like *Flesh Gordon* to mainstream confections like *The Return of Captain Invincible* and *My Super-Ex Girlfriend*, among many others.

Then there are some curious examples of the movies imitating comics, the comics following suit, and then Hollywood bringing the whole crazy business full circle. Commando Cody, a shell-headed, rocket-packed hero, was created for screens big and small in the 1950s; years later,

he'd be re-invented by Dave Stevens as the comics hero Rocketeer, who was in turn adapted as summer movie fare by Disney. And then there are dramatic films that dovetail into cb sensibilities, some of them quite accomplished, like M. Night Shyamalan's *Unbreakable*, James Gunn's *Super*, and Alejandro G. Iñárritu's *Birdman: The Unexpected Virtue of Ignorance*.

COMIC BOOK MOVIES ON THE WAY...

With the comic book movie genre riding high after a spectacular 2016, new major offerings from Marvel and DC (and others) have fans panting with anticipation. Blasting at us in 2017: *Logan* (Jackman's last?), *Ghost in the Shell*, *Guardians of the Galaxy Vol. 2*, *Wonder Woman* (You go, Gal Gadot!), *Kingsman The Golden Circle*, *Spider-Man: Homecoming*, *Valerian and the City of a Thousand Planets*, *Thor: Ragnarok* (weird enough to work), *Justice League* (whether it's good, bad, or in-between, everyone will show up for this event), *Gambit*.

INDEX